RECOLLECTIONS AND REFLECTIONS

RECOLLECTIONS AND REFLECTIONS

RECOLLECTIONS AND REFLECTIONS

FROM MY LIFE IN NAZI GERMANY,
WARTIME ENGLAND, AND AMERICA

H. RICHARD LEVY

Epigraph Books
Rhinebeck, New York

ISBN 978-1-954744-64-6

Library of Congress Control Number 2022904138

Book design by Colin Rolfe
Cover photo: Leipzig Railway Station, courtesy H. Richard Levy, originally printed in *Syracuse University Magazine*

Epigraph Books
22 East Market Street, Suite 304
Rhinebeck, NY 12572
(845) 876-4861
epigraphps.com

Contents

Introduction

For some years, as I grew older and memories of the past faded, I occasionally thought about writing my autobiography. From time to time I wrote fragments for various occasions, and several individuals asked me to write more. Numerous projects occupied my attention and prevented me from spending the time to do so, but for the past few years I have written about several periods in my life and kept them for eventual inclusion in an autobiography.

I began assembling this memoir as my ninetieth birthday approached, hoping to bring back portions of my life that had faded in my memory, or had vanished completely. I was aided by numerous notes, letters and documents from several periods of my life that proved to be very helpful. Also, I enjoy writing.

It is not possible to write an autobiography that gives a true picture of the whole person. We are all so complex, shaped by our genes and by so many events in our lives, that no written document can give a complete picture of who we truly are. Our professional life does not exist in isolation but is shaped by, and interacts with, our family life, our social life, by unrecognized influences, and subconscious proclivities, desires and anxieties. A series of events occurred that interacted with my intellect and personality, and that led to my becoming an academic scientist. I believe I can trace some of those, but there are probably others that played an important role that I have not uncovered. At every point in our lives we make decisions that take us down a particular path and that lead to other decisions presenting further choices, but they are not predestined. My successes were propelled by the confidence that others had in me. This is especially true of my mother, whose love for and belief in me was unswerving even when I was at my lowest. She spurred me on as a child, and never accepted excuses from me that I was unable to do something. Like everyone else, I have fears and flaws that I try to hide from the rest of the world and that may have influenced my personal and career choices, some of which I am probably unaware of.

My principal difficulty in trying to piece together an autobiography is an extremely poor memory, with gaping lacunae in my life where I have no recollections at all. My mother believed that this was a common problem for those who, like I, experienced very disruptive events in their lives, but I have talked with some such individuals who do not have this problem. In a diary I kept in 1956-57, I wrote about a girlfriend with whom I was quite close. We shared many interests, we were both in the Glee Club, and I met her mother and brother, but I remember nothing about her, not even what she looked like.

Those individuals closest and most dear to me are my mother, my sister Liz, my wife Betty, and my daughter Karen. Also, very close are my Aunt Martha ("TaMa") and Win Schlesinger. It is worth noting that they are all women. There have been no men in my life to whom I have been as close, except my father, who died when I was only nine years old, so that our relationship was very brief. While I lived with the Schlesingers in England, Win's husband Bernard was away in the army for the duration of the war. (I did get to know him during my many visit to England after the war.) I was fond of TaMa's husband, my Uncle Ernest. He gave me good advice, but we were not particularly close. This lack of close relationships with men may have affected me, but I have not discovered how.

I have written this book primarily for myself, and have included many personal details about my life. Writing it has catalyzed the awakening of some long-forgotten memories. Some were painful, others embarrassing, most were revelatory. Reflecting about these has helped me to understand many events that shaped my life and has been a source of great personal satisfaction.

HRL, JANUARY 2022

CHAPTER 1

Childhood in Germany

One day, as a little boy, I wrote on a scrap of paper: "I don't believe you exist, God", and threw it out of the window, so he could find it. It didn't occur to me that God could have found the note inside our apartment, or, indeed, inside my head, but as a seven-year old I wasn't very sophisticated. In retrospect, I am astonished that I did this at such a young age, and I don't remember what caused me to do so. The effect, however, was swift. I quickly wrote another note to cancel the previous one. This little incident was a precocious precedent for my ambiguous relationship to religion throughout my life.

I was born in October, 1929 and given the name Hans Richard. My family were middleclass Jews living in Leipzig, Germany (my note to God was written in German) and religion was not an important part of our life. My father went to synagogue on some high holy days, and I accompanied him on a few occasions. My mother was an atheist. We sometimes had special family events in our apartment Friday nights, to mark the Sabbath, but none of them had any religious connotation. Like all Jewish children, I went to a Jewish school, until the Nazis closed it in 1938. But after Hitler came to power in 1933, being Jewish became increasingly important to all Jews, believers and nonbelievers.

Beginning in 1933, a series of harsh laws were enacted that made life increasingly intolerable for German Jews, which included anyone who had one Jewish parent or grandparent. At first, Jews were not allowed to own land, or to be newspaper editors, and they were excluded from participating in the arts or going to theaters or concerts. Later, they were barred from owning health insurance, prohibited from serving in the military or getting legal qualifications. In 1935, they were deprived of their German citizenship and subsequently barred from many professions such as accounting, dentistry and medicine. In 1938, Jewish businesses were taken over by the Nazis; Jews had to register their wealth and property; Jews over 15 years old had to carry identity cards and show them to any police officer on demand; Jewish men had to add the name Israel, and women the name Sarah, on all legal documents, and to have their passports stamped with a red "J".

My mother describes some of these events in her memoir: how our life began to crumble, how the noose got tighter. Friends and relatives left the country, often suddenly, without saying goodbye. We were shunned by former acquaintances. My school was closed, so several Jewish families made arrangements for their children to be home-schooled. When my sister was born in 1938, the only hospital where my mother could deliver was a small, private Jewish orthopedic clinic.

Despite all this, the few recollections I still have of the first nine years of my life are happy. We were a loving family, living in a beautiful flat in a modern apartment building at Brandvorwerkstrasse 80 in Leipzig, with a spacious living room and dining room, kitchen, my parents' bedroom, and mine. Behind the apartment building there was a lawn, and behind that a little forest. In the far corner of the lawn I had a sandbox. This is where my friend and second cousin Werner (later Pierre) Joske and I made mud pies we called "Beppermumpe". My mother was very fond of Werner, who was about a year and a half older than I, and his parents and mine were close friends. Like most middle-class, Jewish families, we had a maid, first Frieda, and later Änne. My father often ate a soft-boiled egg for breakfast, and when he cut it open he gave me the cap. My earliest childhood memory is one of being embarrassed. It was, I believe, my 2nd birthday and I was on top of a commode. I believe I was embarrassed because one or more of the children invited for my birthday party came in and saw me being dressed. It is extraordinary that I could experience embarrassment at such a young age.

Another memory is from an incident that occurred when I was about five years old. I was playing in the back with my friend (another second cousin) Frank Loewenheim (later Lionel). The door leading out to the lawn from the apartment building had a glass window pane. Frank locked me out and taunted me in some way. I got angry and banged on the window to get in, smashing it. My arm suffered a cut, but Frank got some glass into his eye, and he cried. My Uncle Ernst, who was a doctor, was called to fix Frank up. I felt proud that I hadn't cried, but that Frank had. Frank was the same age as I, and his parents were my parents' close friends.

My childhood friendships with Frank and Werner (Pierre) resumed in America, where Pierre and his family moved in 1949. Pierre and I went on a camping trip to Yosemite in the 1950s. Much later, when Pierre's prostate cancer had spread to his bones, he asked me and Frank to come to California a few months before his death in 2011. Frank was unable to come, but Pierre and I spent a very joyous weekend together. Pierre was a landscape architect, happily married to his sweetheart, Maryse, from France, with three children; a warm-hearted, generous man with strong convictions.

Frank and his family moved to England in 1939. We didn't see each other frequently, but he did visit with me at the Cripps home (see Chapter 2). Like I, Frank lost his father to cancer at an early age. We continued our friendship in America. Among the excursions that Pierre, Frank and I did together was a trip to a resort in the Catskills in 1949 or 1950. I introduced Frank to my friends David and Phyllis Ostrolenk, who invited him on several occasions when they lived in New Hope, PA. There, Frank fell in love with Lois, who was David's girlfriend, and whom David would marry, which led to much heartache. Frank was very bright, extremely industrious, did very well in college, and became an accountant. He always seemed to be buried in work, and not to enjoy life very much. Eventually, Frank married, but the marriage ended in divorce, and he then married again. He had two children with each of his wives. He died in 2012.

My third childhood friends were Walter Weg, a little older than I, and his sister, Renate, a little younger. Our parents were friends. Like Frank and I, they attended the Jewish school. I went on a holiday with the Weg family, to Friedrichroda, in 1937. Like I, Walter and Renate left for England on a Kindertransport, a few months before I did, where they remained for the rest of their lives. When my parents had to move from Brandvorwerkstrasse to Fregestrasse in early 1939, I stayed with the Wegs. By that time, Walter and Renate had already left for England. Mrs. Weg told my mother she was astonished at how adaptable I was. I don't recall seeing Walter and Renate while I lived in England during the war. Each of them subsequently married and had children, I visited them on several of my trips to England after the war, including while I was at Oxford University on sabbatical, and we have maintained contact through email. One especially meaningful visit occurred in 2009 (see Chapter 11).

One of my passions, as a child, was trains. I had a toy train set that I was allowed put up on my bedroom floor once a year, and the maid then kept out so as not to disturb it. My father sometimes played with the train with me. It was an electric train, but I preferred to move it manually. Some of the books I read included *Der Struwwelpeter*, consisting of illustrated rhymes, each citing the consequences of various forms of misbehavior; *Max und Moritz*, with illustrated rhymes describing the pranks of two mischievous boys; a book about birds of prey; books about astronomy; and many others. I was ill quite frequently, mostly with asthma. In an effort to alleviate that, I spent several weeks on at least two occasions in Celerina, Switzerland, in a children's home that was run by a Miss Zuppinger. My mother took me there, and I remember an incident related to our train ride. At one stage of the trip, in Switzerland, the train went over three successive high viaducts over a valley between two adjacent mountains, a thrilling vista. I told my mother that I couldn't feel the train making its U-turn after each crossing, so she brought a compass with her on our next trip so that I could see the needle turn as we went through the mountains. It was also at one of the Swiss train stations, Celerina, that my mother heard me spell out the name of the little town. I had not yet been to school, and had, apparently, taught myself to read. She didn't let on that this was special, but she did encourage me by reading with me.

Another trip I took with my mother, to try to alleviate my asthma, was to Wyk auf Föhr, a little island on the North Sea off the coast of Northern Germany. An extraordinary incident occurred there which I don't actually remember, but which my mother told me. We were at the seashore and apparently, I wandered off onto a pier, fell into the sea, and got my leg jammed between two pilings supporting the pier.

A little boy about my age (I must have been about 5) jumped in and dislodged my leg.

My parents took me to a performance of *Peterchens Mondfahrt* (Little Peter's Journey to the Moon) at a theater in Leipzig, which thrilled me. That must have been when I was very young, as Jews were no longer allowed to go to the theater sometime in the mid 1930s. At my Jewish school, I learned to read and speak Hebrew, but soon forgot it. I was in a school play that had to do with the Queen of Sheba visiting King David. I played the role of a servant who brought gifts, that I described as I pulled them out of a bag and presented them to the Queen (my first stage role!).

As a young boy in Leipzig, Germany, I had the normal child's curiosity in natural phenomena, but I was especially interested in birds of prey and in astronomy. I don't recall what it was that so fascinated me about birds of prey, but I do remember that my grandfather took me out into the garden at night told me about the stars and planets and how that really fascinated me. I still remember him telling me about how huge the star Betelgeuse is. I enjoyed collecting facts about astronomy, cutting out illustrated articles from magazines, and pasting them into a little book. I also wrote things into this book, like a table with the names of all the planets, how far they were from the sun, and other items that I found interesting. It was my earliest attempt to sort things out, to create order from facts. There were several books with scientific topics that I loved. One was called *Die Biene Maja*, about the adventures of a bee; another one I found especially fascinating was the story of a drop of water, how it rains down on earth, is absorbed by a plant, is eaten by an animal, and eventually flows into the ocean. My parents had a book called *Knaurs Konversations Lexikon*, an illustrated one-volume encyclopedia that I loved to read, especially when I was sick in bed.

At this point, I want to introduce members of my closest family into this narrative - my father, mother, sister, and grandfather.

My father, Berthold Levy, was born in Pössneck, 56 miles southwest of Leipzig, on March 21 in 1899. When he was very young, his parents moved to Leipzig, a much bigger town where business opportunities were better. His mother died of breast cancer when he was 6, his father died when he was 9. He was taken in and raised by his

Observing a glacier in Switzerland, 1934

uncle and aunt, Theodor and Alma Löwenheim (grandparents of my childhood friend and cousin, Frank). He attended a Jewish boarding school in Wolfenbüttel, about 100 miles north-west of Leipzig, until he was 16. He then became an apprentice in the firm *Gebrüder Frank*, one of whose owners was my maternal grandfather, Richard Frank, who took a personal interest in him, teaching him math in his office. In 1917, during World War I, he was called up into the army. Fortunately, he got a bad case of food poisoning, which prevented him from being sent to the front, and by the time he recovered, the war was over and he returned to *Gebrüder Frank* to complete his apprenticeship. He then took a job in a department store in Weissenfels owned by Emil Joske (grandfather of my other childhood friend and cousin, Werner Joske). After returning to Leipzig, he became manager of the toy department in a large department store, *Gebrüder Held* and, after a few weeks, was promoted to the manager of the whole store. My grandfather, who had been very impressed when Berthold was an apprentice at his firm, invited him to a party at his house, where he met my grandfather's two daughters, Charlotte (Lotte) and Martha. After some time, a friendship developed between Lotte and Berthold. They played tennis together, went on trips with a group of friends, and after a long courtship, became engaged in 1928. Lotte had been attending courses at the University of Munich, to study medicine, and was preparing to transfer to the University of Freiburg, when Berthold asked her to marry him. They were married on October 5, 1928, and my mother never completed her medical studies. After he and Lotte were engaged, Berthold left *Gebrüder Held* and joined *Gebrüder Frank*, where he was made co-owner with my grandfather in October 1929. He and my grandfather had a very close relationship, like father and son.

My father died at the age of 40 of stomach cancer. My mother became suspicious that something was seriously wrong six years earlier, but she could not convince him to see a doctor. In 1937, while my mother was expecting her second child, my father became very ill. My mother finally persuaded him to see a doctor. The excellent radiologist who was to see him that day was out of town, and the X-rays taken by his assistant were inconclusive. My father could not be persuaded to go back for another GI series. He was put on a strict diet but had another painful attack. He agreed to see a well-known internist. My mother voiced her fear that he had cancer, which had been prevalent in his family, at which the internist laughed dismissively and prescribed some medicine. My mother read up on cancer symptoms and was convinced that he had stomach cancer. She got him to see the foremost internist in Berlin, who diagnosed the symptoms as nervous, but asked him to return if the symptoms persisted. The next few months he was largely in remission, but then the pain returned worse than ever, and he went back to the internist in Berlin, who confirmed that my father had stomach cancer, which had already spread to the lungs. He was operated on his stomach, had X-ray treatments, and actually made a good recovery. My parents were still able to have a vacation together at a resort in October 1938, to celebrate their tenth wedding anniversary.

The morning after *Kristallnacht*, November 10, 1938, my father was badly beaten and sent to prison for 10 days, as I relate elsewhere. This trauma undoubtedly hastened his death, on April 23 1939, five weeks after I had left for England on a *Kindertransport*.

My father was a self-educated man with very high personal standards, who read widely, played the flute, and had an easy-going personality, a great sense of humor, a very positive outlook on life, and a gift of being able to get along with people. I only knew him as a young child, and my memories of him are intertwined with what my mother has told me. He was kind and loving, a good father whose life was cut short when he was still very young, never to experience his children growing up.

My mother, Charlotte (Lotte) née Frank was born in Leipzig, Germany, on July 3, 1900. She had a happy childhood, but during her adolescence, she had to assume many of the chores of managing the family household as her ailing mother was no longer capable of doing so. As a young adult, she took over this job completely, and it proved to be a formidable challenge during World War I and the food shortages and raging inflation in the 1920s.

As a young girl, Lotte was an excellent student who loved to learn, a love that remained with her during her long life. She had an active mind and was receptive to new ideas throughout her life. Her other interests included nature, and mountain climbing, which she and her sister Martha frequently did with their father. She was very musical, and for some time she sang with the Gewandhaus Choir in Leipzig, including performances under the conductor Wilhelm Furtwängler. She spoke English and French well, and read widely the German, French and English literature. When I was growing up in England, I no longer wanted to speak German. She read some of her favorite German poems to me, which impressed me so much that I began to converse and write with her in German again, and continued to read German poetry throughout my life.

In her late twenties, Lotte began studying medicine, but this was cut short when she met my father and married him. It was a truly happy marriage, but two ominous developments altered her life permanently: my father's long, and ultimately fatal illness, and the rapid rise of Nazism after Hitler became chancellor. The latter culminated in *Kristallnacht*, and my departure to England on a *Kindertransport*, that I describe below. Five weeks after my departure, my father died, and my mother had to begin the emigration process anew, and alone. With great courage, and while looking after her one-year-old daughter, and fending off the unimaginable obstacles posed by the Nazi regime, she escaped to England with my sister, leaving Holland on the last KLM plane before the outbreak of war.

She arrived in England with my sister virtually penniless, and had to find work in order to support herself. The only thing she could do was to cook and keep house - something she had learned while managing her father's house as a young adult. After several difficult situations, she found work with an extraordinary family named Cripps. I tell about how she connected with the Cripps family in Chapter 2. They lived in Filkins, a little village in the Cotswolds, and my mother worked for them for most of her stay in England. After her harrowing time in Germany, the peaceful life in this beautiful village greatly appealed to her; it was one of the happiest periods of her life. It was a very beneficial environment also for my sister, Liz, although she became very ill three times before her seventh birthday and had to be hospitalized - another trauma for my mother who was unable to visit her in the hospital.

My mother's move to the United States after the conclusion of the war, to join her sister Martha and her husband Ernest and daughter Lore, involved a very difficult decision. On the one hand, she had come to love England and its way of life, and sensed that America and the way of life there would be much less congenial for her. On the other hand, she recognized that the opportunities would be much better for both her children in the States, and that became the deciding factor. In May, 1946, she moved to Red Bank, NJ, into Ernest and Martha's apartment, and became their cook and housekeeper. She lived in Red Bank until she, and Martha, moved to a retirement home in Lakewood, NJ, in the late 1990s, where she lived out the rest of her years. She died aged 102, and Martha died five years later, also aged 102.

In her 50s, my mother decided to strike out on a business career while continuing to do the housekeeping and cooking for Martha. She sold flatware, and to do so she bought a car and learned to drive. She never became an outstanding driver, and driving with her was sometimes an adventure. Liz and I were very proud of the fact that our shy mother had made a success of this business, but we became increasingly concerned about her driving to visit strangers, and after some years, we persuaded her to stop. In 1954, while still working in her business, she used it as a pretext to attend the annual Leipzig Trade Fair. Her real purpose - which she achieved - was to set in motion the legal arrangements to bring her father to the United States.

While she lived in Red Bank, my mother spoke about her experiences in Germany at Brookdale Community College and at several schools. She did so as a tribute to her many relatives, including her mother, who were murdered by the Nazis, and because she believed that it was important for the pubic - and especially the young - to learn about the Holocaust. She took a keen interest in the world around her and read widely about current affairs. Unable, as a Jew, to vote in Germany, she relished this right when she became an American citizen. She was an active member of the League of Women Voters, serving as vice president of the local chapter.

After Liz and I were married, she often visited both of us and enjoyed her grandchildren. She also travelled frequently to Israel, Europe, and South America to visit relatives and friends, and enjoyed nature and the cultural offerings on all these trips. In 1987, she was struck by another tragedy when my sister died at age 49. There is nothing more terrible for a parent than to lose their child, but once again, her indomitable inner resources carried her through this calamity and it spurred her to become deeply involved in providing substitute maternal support for Liz's two sons.

My mother's love for her children was the central thread of her life, especially after she lost her husband and those dark days following *Kristallnacht* when she was trying to escape from Nazi Germany. Her relationship with me was always very close. She stated on several occasions that my birth was the single most joyful and fulfilling event in her life. This would have embarrassed me were it not meant so literally. Our closeness follows a pattern in several generations of my family. My mother was very close to her father; he was very close to his mother; my daughter, Karen, became very close to me after our life-changing trip together to Germany in 2009. This closeness, in each case, included the child looking after the parent in times of severe illness.

My mother's courage, resilience and determination were an inspiration for Liz and me. Despite her traumas and suffering, she was never, ever bitter. She learned from her ancestors, and taught me, that there is nothing in this world that is so terrible that some good does not come from it. She had the gift to find the good in people and circumstances. Shy by nature, she was intensely loyal and her friendships were deep and lasting. She was not involved in any formal religion, but was a member of Ethical Culture, and a deeply ethical and moral person.

My mother bestowed on me two gifts of vital importance. The first, which she gave me unwittingly, was her genetic constitution, which included longevity in good health. The second, which she strove throughout my childhood and adolescence to administer, was her absolute, unfailing confidence in me. There is probably nothing more important for a child than a parent's absolute confidence and support, because this will provide sustenance even in those bad times which will, inevitably occur, as it did for me (see Chapter 4).

My sister, Elisabeth (Liz), was born in Leipzig, Germany, on January

19, 1938. Born less than a
year before *Kristallnacht*,
her early life unfolded in the
context of a deepening crisis
for German Jews, the death
of her father when she was
15 months old, and escape
to England with our mother,
four months later, a few days
before the outbreak of World
War II. In England, before
her seventh birthday she
had three serious illnesses,
requiring hospitalization at
a time when English hospital
practice was to disallow parents to visit their children.
As a young child, she was
very loving and outgoing,

*With my father, mother, and sister Elisabeth,
Leipzig, 1938*

but later, as an adolescent her relationship with our mother became
very difficult. I think this was due to two factors. First, the separations
from her mother when she was hospitalized probably caused her to
feel abandoned, something she internalized. Second, as an adolescent, she became very attractive to boys, and our mother, who had
not experienced a real adolescence because she had to manage her
father's household, did not understand or know how to cope with this.
Liz engaged, for some years, in very destructive behavior, but she survived and flourished.

When she was young, Liz loved me as an older brother, and I loved
her as a little sister. Our age difference caused her to look up to me,
and perhaps I served a little bit in the role of a father figure. But my
mother turned to me during her difficulties with Liz later on, time
after time, with countless letters and conversations, which led me to
blame Liz for causing my mother's deep unhappiness and anxiety.
Fortunately, when I introduced Betty to Liz, Betty enabled me to see
Liz in a fresh light, and to understand the dynamic of her relationship with our mother. I am very indebted to Betty for this, and her
love for and deep friendship with Liz was very beneficial for Liz. She

often visited us while we lived in Chicago, even staying with us for a while after an operation, and continued to visit us after we moved to Syracuse.

Professionally, Liz was a social worker who worked extensively with eating disorders, compulsivity, and relationship issues, with families, groups or individuals. As an asthmatic, she drew from her own wide therapeutic background and personal experiences in her profession.

She earned her B.A. from Antioch College, majoring in philosophy, and an M.A. from the University of Chicago's Graduate School of Social Service Administration, specializing in psychiatric group work. Among her work experiences was assistant director of the press relations department at the Illinois Institute of Technology, where she also worked with small groups of perceptually handicapped children; as a psychiatric social worker at MacNeal Memorial Hospital, in Berwyn, IL; as a psychiatric group worker at Waller High School Satellite, Chicago, IL, where she led an experimental small group program for students who had dropped out of school, at an inner-city high school; and in a private practice in Chicago, primarily for group therapy. In her last years, she was Associate Director of the Lakeland (Edina, MN) Counseling Center.

In 1965, Liz married Ron Aronica, and with him she had two boys, David and Mark. While her children were still young, she and Ron got divorced, but they shared custody of the boys, who spent time with both their parents. The divorce was amicable, and Ron remained part of our family. Liz was an asthmatic ever since her childhood, and as a grown woman she suffered severe asthma attacks that required emergency hospitalization on several occasions. In November 1987, she died from one of these asthma attacks, not yet having reached her 50th birthday. The previous summer, I spent a long weekend with her at a camp in Northern Minnesota, just the two of us, a time when we were able to reminisce and reconnect, for which I am deeply thankful.

My maternal Grandfather, Richard Frank, was born May 9th, 1870, in Halle, Germany. He moved to Leipzig with his family in 1875 and lived there until he came to the United States in 1955, where he spent the last five years of his life.

My father's parents both died when he was very young, so I never knew my paternal grandparents. Nevertheless, I had two grandmothers - my mother's mother Elise, who had compulsions, phobias and anxieties that became so severe that she was moved to a private institution in Weimar in 1919. I occasionally visited her there. My grandfather and she were divorced in 1926, and subsequently he married Amanda Lawranz ("Muckchen") who was Christian, which would later save my grandfather's life. As she lived in Leipzig, I saw Muckchen frequently. I navigated the dilemma of apportioning my affection for my two grandmothers, one of whom was obviously closer to my mother, by confiding to my mother that I liked my grandmother in Weimar "just a little bit more".

My grandfather had wanted to become a physician, but was persuaded to enter his father's faltering business, a wholesale knitted goods firm, which my grandfather converted to a knitted goods factory. (It is ironic that both my grandfather and my mother wanted to become physicians, but neither did so, for different reasons). His business, Gebrüder Frank, thrived. Just as his father had run the business with his cousin, so, also my grandfather initially ran Gebrüder Frank with his cousin, Hermann Frank. After Hermann died, my father became co-owner. My grandfather was a very enlightened and principled man, deeply concerned for the welfare of his workers, who provided benefits for them, including showers, a kitchen, and lunch rooms, which was very unusual at that time. This, plus his mastery of all aspects of the factory, including all the machines, endeared him to his employees, and some of them repaid him during the war, when they secretly, and at great personal danger, brought him food that was difficult for him to obtain.

My grandfather was also a very cultured man with a deep knowledge of literature and music. He played the piano and flute, and he had an artistic flair, creating his own designs for the knitted goods produced in the factory. The Nazis confiscated the factory in 1939, and it was about 75% destroyed by allied bombing during the war, but it was restored to him after the war, and our family eventually received some compensation. I saw the ruins on my visit to Germany in 2009 (see Chapter 11). As I describe below, my grandfather survived the war in Leipzig, under harrowing conditions. He was brought to the United States by my mother and aunt in 1955, after Muckchen's death, and lived with them the rest of his life.

I sensed, early in my life, that my grandfather's marriage to Muckchen was a taboo subject in the family. My mother and aunt did not have great affection for her, and Muckchen was jealous of my grandfather's close relationship with my mother. As a child, I heard whispers that Muckchen had been a prostitute, and this was confirmed many years later by my cousin Marianne Wintgen, whom I met in Leipzig in 2009 (see Chapter 11). Some of my many revelatory reflections while writing this biography, led to my conclusion that during the years when my real grandmother's phobias caused her to become increasingly dysfunctional, resulting in her move to a private institution, my grandfather sought relief for his sexual urges with Muckchen. Being a highly principled man, he then married her at the first opportunity after my grandparents' divorce. This action, undoubtedly, saved his life. Being married to a Christian woman enabled him to survive the war in Leipzig.

Everything changed for us, and for all German Jews on *Kristallnacht* (the night of the broken glass), November 9-10, 1938, when Jewish shops and synagogues all over Germany were destroyed and thousands of Jewish men were arrested. This event, which occurred two weeks after my ninth birthday, is one of my few clear remembrances from that time, a vivid memory that still arouses deep, painful emotions in me more than 80 years later. Early in the morning of November 10, 1938, there was loud banging on our apartment door by some men who shouted vile epithets about Jews, and ordered us to assemble at a nearby location immediately. It was a raw day, so we dressed warmly. At the last minute, my mother decided not to take my sister Elisabeth, then only 10 months old, and left her with our trusted maid. The three of us walked together, I between my parents, holding their hands. I was very frightened. As we got closer, I heard loud banging, and I thought: they are killing Jews in there. But it turned out to be a shoe factory, and the whole thing was just a hoax to torment us.

As we walked back, a lady came toward us, very agitated, crying. She was the wife of the owner of a large, Jewish department store in Leipzig, Bamberger & Herz. It was the first time I saw an adult cry. She told us that the windows in their store were smashed, the store was looted, and that the nearby synagogue was set on fire. We met a man who described other, similar events, and said that he was going to board a train to Berlin, and travel back and forth between Leipzig and Berlin until, he thought, this thing would blow over. My father decided that he would do the same thing, but would first check on my grandfather and our knitted goods factory. He would call from there.

That call never came. Meanwhile, when we got back to our apartment building, my mother noticed an ominous sign: our nameplates had been removed. We were evicted a few weeks later. Germans no longer wanted to rent to Jews and so it became extremely difficult to find another apartment. Our friends Fritz and Senta Weg, whose children had already been sent to England on a *Kindertransport*, offered to take me while my mother looked for an apartment, with the help of her sister and sister-in-law. Finding an apartment under her conditions was very difficult. My father was mortally ill. My mother had to look after me and Elisabeth, who was less than a year old. She was preoccupied with trying to make arrangements to get the whole family out of Germany. Also, virtually no one would rent to Jews anymore. Finally, with the help of her sister and sister-in-law, she found a small apartment at Fregestrasse 7 to which we moved early in 1939.

For the next ten days after *Kristallnacht*, my mother tried desperately to find out what had happened to my father. She learned that he had been arrested at the factory and taken to a police station, but when she checked, he was not there. She eventually heard that he had been viciously beaten and then transferred to a prison, and that he would soon be sent to Buchenwald, a concentration camp that my mother had not heard of then. I cried every day he was away and asked my mother how God could let this happen. On the tenth day, my father was released. There were two reasons, apparently, why he was not shipped to Buchenwald, like most of the other men. First, demonstrating typical German legal fastidiousness, the Nazis needed him to sign some documents so that they could expropriate our factory. Second, my father had recently had a major operation for stomach cancer and had a large scar. The Nazis were afraid he might not survive the journey. Of course, later they had no such scruples.

Following *Kristallnacht*, it was abundantly clear that the Nazis' noose around the Jews' necks was tightening rapidly. My parents had already made plans to emigrate, but my safety now became their first priority. A hopeful way materialized when the British government agreed to grant refuge to a limited number of children, provided that they were under 17 years old, and came alone. (A similar plan was introduced in Congress in the United States but died in committee). These so-called *Kindertransports* were permitted by the Nazis, under strict conditions: the children had to come alone, and could only bring one suitcase, no toys. Between November 1938 and August 1939, some 10,000 mostly Jewish children from Nazi Germany and the occupied territories of Austria, Poland and Czechoslovakia, reached England, thus escaping almost certain extermination. How I was fortunate enough to be included among them is something I do not know to this day. My parents made the agonizing decision to send me to England, a little nine-year-old boy, alone, not knowing whether they would ever see me again. The children from the *Kindertransports* were billeted out to British families who volunteered to take them. The situations for many were very difficult, but they were alive! Unlike virtually all the other children, I was taken in by a family that my parents knew, though they had never met them: Bernard and Winifred (Win) Schlesinger.

Bernard Schlesinger was a well-known pediatrician and Win was the daughter of Anna Regensburg, my maternal grandfather Richard Frank's cousin and close friend. They lived in London. It was through Anna that Bernard and Win offered my parents to take me into their home. They had five children ranging in age from 6 to 13 at that time. The Schlesingers were a remarkable couple. They also rescued 12 other Jewish children from Nazi Germany and Austria, who came over on the same *Kindertransport* as I, and placed them into a hostel that they had established in London. They installed a staff that furnished all the children's financial, educational, social and religious needs. When the hostel had to close a few months later, due to the outbreak of war and the danger of remaining in London, all 12 children were sent to other homes or boarding schools and the Schlesingers remained in close touch with each of them, attending to their every personal and financial need. Bernard and Win remained in close contact with the 12 children until they died, and subsequently their children continued to maintain this friendship. Like I, all these children literally owe their lives to this extraordinary couple.

I left Leipzig by train on March 15, 1939. When I said goodbye to my father that morning, my mother knew that I would never see him again as he was already mortally ill with stomach cancer. He died six weeks later. My mother traveled with me and several other children to a town in Westphalia to meet the rest of the *Kindertransport* and to deliver us, and our documents to the authorities. From there on I was on my own, with a lot of other children, as we traveled through Holland and then by boat to Harwich in England, and by train to Liverpool Street Station in London. There, Win met me and took me to her home on Templewood Avenue in Hampstead, London. I spoke no English, but Win could speak some German. I can still see, in my mind, her two youngest children, Hilary and Susan, peering down the stairs when I arrived. The day I left Germany, Hitler marched into Czechoslovakia, and my mother was relieved to read the newspaper headline, when she got off the train, that Hitler had been received "with open arms", because, she realized, that this meant there would be no trouble for me to get out of the country.

My mother and sister fled, first to Holland, and then to England on August 27, 1939, on the last KLM plane before the outbreak of war. I was one of the very fortunate few *Kindertransport* children to be reunited with at least one parent. I lived with the Schlesingers, went to a boarding school, but I saw my mother and sister during the holidays, part of which I spent with them and part with the Schlesingers.

Regretfully, I have almost no memories of the voyage on the *Kindertransport*. Perhaps it was because of the onslaught of such dramatic changes in such a short time, changes that literally saved my life. Two incidents that I do recall have to do with food. When the train stopped in Rotterdam, some Jewish ladies came to the train to bring us children chocolates. And on board the ship crossing the very stormy English Channel, I threw up my dinner.

The *Kindertransport* is remembered in various ways, especially in Britain and the United States, where most of the *Kindertransport* participants live. The Kindertransport Association, of which I am a member, was founded in 1989 with a mission to locate and reunite *Kindertransport* participants and to educate the public about this event. It publishes a newsletter four times per year with news about *Kinder* and holds conferences, usually in London.

Many books have been written about the *Kindertransport*, most by former participants. A film, titled "Into the Arms of Strangers", released in 2000, won the 2001 Academy Award for best documentary. It recounts the stories of several of the children rescued through the *Kindertransport*, told by the children, their rescuers, their parents, and the foster parents who took them into their homes. The film's producer was Deborah Oppenheimer. Her mother was one of the children sent to England on a *Kindertransport*. She was one of the thousands of children rescued whose parents perished in a concentration camp. The fact that Deborah's mother never told her story motivated Deborah to create the film. Deborah contacted me to make arrangements to interview my mother, who was one of only three surviving parents whom she could locate, and who were interviewed for the film. She was living in a retirement home in Lakewood, NJ at the time. At Deborah's request, I came to help in conducting the interview. My mother was 99 years old at the time, and the interview was a bit shaky, so her story does not appear in the film, but it is included in the book, also titled "Into the Arms of Strangers", that was issued simultaneously.

Impact of the Holocaust on our family

First, a word about the word Holocaust, widely used to refer to the implementation of genocide, the systematic, state-sponsored murder of the Jews by the Nazi government between 1941 and 1945. As David Gordis points out in his book *God Was Not In the Fire* (p. 28), "Holocaust" comes from the Greek word *holokauston*, itself a translation of the Hebrew *olah*, meaning "completely burnt offering to God," implying that Jews and other "undesirables" murdered during World War II were a sacrifice to God, a totally abhorrent idea. They were not a sacrifice, they were murdered. Increasingly, Jews refer to this event as The Shoah, the Hebrew word for catastrophe or calamity, and while this is clearly preferable, the widespread use of the term Holocaust probably ensures that it will continue to be used.

I discuss some of the events that occurred after Hitler came to power above. My mother describes some of these events in her memoir: how our life began to crumble, how the noose got tighter. Friends and relatives left the country, often suddenly without saying goodbye. We were shunned by former acquaintances. My Jewish school was closed, so several Jewish families made arrangements for home schooling for their children. When my sister was born in 1938, the only hospital where my mother could deliver was a small, private Jewish orthopedic clinic.

Although I was too young to understand exactly what was happening, I was aware of the increasing anti-Semitism. When I was seven and eight years old I had to take the streetcar to my school and witnessed numerous anti-Semitic events which I noted in a little diary I called "Happenings on the Streetcar". These events made a big impression on me and I must have sensed that my parents would be upset if they knew, so I never showed it to them. The night before I left for England on the *Kindertransport*, my mother, who was packing my belongings found the diary. She asked my father whether she should pack it. He advised against doing so because he didn't think I should be burdened with these unhappy thoughts as I began my new life in England. How I regret that decision! I have no recollection about that diary and would be very interested to see it now.

The Shoah led to the demise of many individuals in our family. My mother assembled a partial list which includes 38 individuals, most of whom were murdered by the Nazis or committed suicide due to their intolerable circumstances. Those closest to me include my maternal grandmother, Elise Frank, who perished in the Theresienstadt concentration camp in 1942, my father's sister, my aunt Käthe Kanstein, who was murdered in 1942 in the Ravensbruck concentration camp, and her husband, my uncle Siegfried Kanstein, who was killed in the Sachsenhausen concentration camp in 1942. Numerous cousins and other relatives were also murdered. Seven members of the Salomon family, direct descendants of Mathilde Frank, sister of my great-grandfather Selmar Frank, committed suicide.

In 1993, the German artist Gunter Demnig began to create memorial stones to commemorate the victims of Nazi persecution and murder. The majority of these stones commemorate Jewish victims, but they also include Romanis, homosexuals, disabled individuals, Jehova's Witnesses, and numerous others persecuted by the Nazis. Each stone (*Stolpertstein*, plural *Stolpersteine*, literally "stumbling stone") is a 4-inch concrete cube, covered with a brass plaque containing the name of the victim and their date of birth and death, if known. They are placed into the pavement or street in front of the last known residence of the individual, so that people can, literally, stumble over them. Demnig personally installs them and by October 2018 there were 70,000 in Germany and nine countries formerly under Nazi occupation. Demnig has said: *Ein Mensch ist erst vergessen, wenn sein Name vergessen ist* (a person is first forgotten when his name is forgotten). *Stolpersteine* have been laid in memory of several of my relatives, including my father and grandmother.

The Nazi regime and subsequent World War led to the widespread scattering of the families recorded in my genealogical survey, almost all of whom originated in Germany. Members of the two Frank families now live in Australia, South Africa, Uruguay, Israel, England, Canada, the United States and elsewhere. A few remained in Germany under extraordinary circumstances, or returned after the Second World War. The stories of three who survived the Shoah are noted below.

My grandfather, Richard Frank, survived World War II in his hometown, Leipzig, one of the very few Jews to do so. It is estimated that about 16,000 Jews resided in Leipzig before the war. Sixteen of them survived. My grandfather survived because his second wife was not Jewish, although being married to a non-Jew did not guarantee survival of Jews in Nazi Germany. It depended, apparently, on how local officials dealt with the eradication of Jews by the Nazi regime. The conditions under which my grandfather lived during those years were horrendous, and there were several times when he narrowly escaped death during the heavy air raids. He and the other Jews lived together in a house, and they had to move several times. Due to the severe restrictions imposed on them by the regime, their food was very limited. They were only allowed to shop in certain stores at specified hours. There was very little heat or running water, and virtually no access to medical services. Because my grandfather was so revered by many of the employees of the factory he owned before the war, some of those individuals risked their lives by occasionally bringing him food.

My grandfather described his ordeal in several letters that he was able to get to his daughters, my mother and aunt, during the war. He was also very fortunate to be saved from almost certain death by a man who came to him just before the Russians liberated Leipzig, and warned him that he was about to be arrested, urging him to hide. He and his wife hid did among the rubble during the night. The next morning a Russian tank appeared before them. The Russian soldier could speak German and was able to reassure my grandfather that his ordeal was about to end.

My great-aunt, my grandfather's sister Hedwig Ems, survived two years in the concentration camp Theresienstadt (Terezin). She was 73 years old when she was deported to Thersienstadt, 75 when she returned to Berlin. At my mother's request, she described her ordeal in a remarkable memoir, which my mother gave to me, and which I donated to the U.S. Holocaust Memorial Museum in Washington, D.C.

The memoir describes the harrowing details of the cruelty of the Nazis and the horrendous living conditions at Theresienstadt. Despite this, and despite the fact that most of those incarcerated in Thersienstadt were eventually deported to Auschwitz to be murdered, the inmates enjoyed many cultural amenities, such as concerts, plays, lectures etc., because those sent to Theresienstadt included prominent Jewish intellectuals, musicians and artists, and because the Nazis attempted to make it a showcase camp in propaganda films. Especially powerful events at Theresinestadt were the several performances of Verdi's *Requiem* by the inmates, using only a single, smuggled score, including one performance before SS officials. The story of these remarkable events is told in a film titled *Defiant Requiem: Verdi at Terezin.*

Reinhard Frank, who was the grandson of Wilhelm Frank, co-founder with my great-grandfather Selmar Frank of the factory *Gebrüder Frank*, survived incarceration in two concentration camps. At age fifteen, he and his sister, Anita, were deported from Berlin to Thersienstadt. A year later, they were sent to Auschwitz. Anita was then sent to Bergen-Belsen, where she was murdered, but Reinhard survived. He participated in the brutal death march that began in January, 1944 when the Germans cleared out Auschwitz, hoping to erase evidence of their atrocities there. The march occurred during an especially severe winter, and the majority of the prisoners died, or were shot, before it reached Germany. Reinhard and six others escaped together during the march. After four months, they made their way to Bucharest, and Reinhard eventually wound up in the United States.

These three individuals are emblematic of what I have always considered to be Holocaust survivors, but the U.S. Holocaust Memorial Museum defines a Holocaust survivor as any person who was displaced, persecuted. and/or discriminated against by the racial, religious, ethnic, social, and/or political policies of the Nazis and their allies between 1933 and 1945. In addition to former inmates of concentration camps and ghettos, this also includes refugees and people in hiding. By this definition, my mother, sister and I are also Holocaust survivors.

Many Holocaust survivors, especially those who survived the brutal concentration camps, have never talked about their experiences. One reads about children of Holocaust survivors who knew nothing about their parents' ordeals. Others have spoken up because they believe that they have an obligation to keep the memory of the Holocaust alive in the hopes that nothing like it will ever happen again. My mother talked about her experiences on several occasions, prompted by the Holocaust Center at Brookdale College, near Red Bank, NJ, where she lived. I, too, have talked about my experiences on numerous occasions, including to a class of undergraduate students at Syracuse University, at several synagogues, to a class of elementary school students, and at the Jewish Community Center in Utica, NY. I also gave a class about Holocaust survivors, that included my experiences, at Oasis, a learning center for seniors in Syracuse.

CHAPTER 2

Adolescence in England

I arrived in England on March 16, 1939. I was without my family, but fortunately, I was reunited with my mother and sister six months later. I was, apparently, a very excitable little boy, and this disruption in my life must have caused me some trauma and must also have been difficult for the Schlesingers, although I have also been very resilient all my life and probably was able to deal with this change quite well eventually. I spoke no English, but this changed very quickly as I lived with an English family and went to an English school, and obviously had to learn very fast in order to survive. I don't recall anything about all this. The Schlesingers lived in a large house at 15 Templewood Avenue in Hampstead, London, They had five children, including twins, Roger and Hilary, who were 14 days older than I. They had a large dog, Tim, who accompanied some of the children as they walked to their bus in the morning to go to school. Bernard was a pediatrician. They were obviously well to do and had several maids, a cook, etc. and Bernard drove a Packard which had the license plate number HMK 15. It is extraordinary that I remember something so trivial while forgetting so much that was very important in my life.

There were occasional parties, to which the 12 Jewish children the Schlesingers had rescued from Germany and Austria, were invited. I went to school, but remember nothing about it, and remember virtually nothing else about those months except the day of my father's death, which occurred on April 23, just 10 days after my arrival. Win

In my school uniform, London, 1939

told me, and the only thing that I recall is that I was allowed to ride in the front seat of the car that day -- a privilege that rotated among us children – although it was not my turn.

Shortly after I arrived in England, I was enrolled at a nearby school in London called University College School. I have a photograph of myself, looking very proud, wearing the school uniform. I recall nothing about that school. It must have been an interesting experience, because at first I could speak no English. My attendance at this school was very brief because, prior to the outbreak of war in September 1939, the Schlesingers moved out of London to the country. They had purchased a small Queen Anne cottage called Mount Pleasant, between Kintbury and Inkpen, near Newbury in Berkshire, to which we all moved in August. The change from the spacious London house to tiny Mount Pleasant necessitated the loss of the large staff, consisting of a cook, at least one maid, a nanny, a chauffeur and some others I have forgotten. At Mount Pleasant, there was just a cook – Laura, who was a devoted character – and a nanny. A gardener helped out, but did not live there. In addition, Win's mother, "Granny", lived with us for much of the time. The quarters were quite cramped and the bedrooms very small, yet there were visitors much of the time. How they were accommodated I don't recall, and I don't even remember who slept in the same bed room as I, although I think it must have been Roger.

The grounds of Mount Pleasant included a vegetable garden and a small orchard. There was also a barn and three pigsties, which we children converted into "offices" that we decorated and furnished and where we went to play. I believe I shared my office with Hilary. There was also some sort of shed in which we sometimes slept during the summer, as Bernard insisted on hardening us in various ways.

The oldest of the Schlesinger children, John, would later become a notable film director whose films included the Oscar-winning "Midnight Cowboy". Wendy was the next oldest, then came Roger and Hilary, twins who were my age, and Susan, the youngest. John and Roger attended St. Edmund's Prep School and then a "public school" (what we, in the States, would call a private school) called Uppingham, which their father had also attended as a boy. Wendy went to a girls' public school called Badminton. Starting in the fall of 1939, Hilary, Susan and I (along with another girl named Bunty Rouse) received private schooling from a couple named Padel who lived about a half mile from Mount Pleasant. I presume that, because of our arrival so late in the year, we could not be placed in the local schools. The Padels had very left-wing political views. Mr. Padel was the retired headmaster of a school in western England or Wales; I don't recall whether Mrs. Padel had any teaching credentials. We went to the Padels' house every weekday for the entire school year. I have almost no recollections about this experience. I know that we children made fun of Mr. Padel among ourselves, and that Hilary wrote a poem, which included a line that went something like this: "He gets into terrible rages, and spits all over the pages." I have no idea what I learned there.

One year later, Hilary and Susan joined their sister Wendy at Badminton. Mrs. Schlesinger enrolled me in the nearby Newbury Grammar School, NGS. The complete name of the school was St. Bartholomew's Grammar School for Boys (in those days, schools in England were segregated by gender; since 1975 the school has been coeducational). It was founded in 1466! There were about 400 boys in the school, some 40 of them, including me, were boarders. Associated with the school there was also a "prep" school for younger children. (British Grammar schools are more or less the equivalent of middle school plus high school in the United States). Win told my mother that, she thought that as a highly excitable boy, I would be well served by being among the typically placid boys in Newbury. I think, in retrospect, that she also assumed, correctly, I'm sure, that as a Jewish refugee boy I would have fared rather badly at St. Edmund's or Uppingham, which enrolled many snobbish, upper class British boys. (John Schlesinger's recollections about Uppingham, as told in William J. Mann's biography "Edge of Midnight: The Life of John

Schlesinger", were devastating. He hated it because, unlike his father, he hated sports, a big thing at Uppingham, and he felt himself a complete outcast.)

At the end of every term, NGS sent a progress report to my mother (and probably also to Win). The report showed my rank in the class in each subject, and many of the teachers, particularly the headmaster and my form master (equivalent of home room teacher), wrote comments. These showed that, for some time my work was quite erratic, good in some subjects one term, then bad in another term. In my early years, many teachers noted my lack of effort or concentration. At the end of my second year there, the headmaster wrote: "A nice little boy. But his trouble is, I think, that he is just too silly & scatter-brained to concentrate on anything for any length of time. He must begin to grow up". The form master's comments were similar. I assume that much of my energy, during those years, was spent on fitting in. As a boy from Germany, a country with which Britain was at war, I was desperate to become "more English than the English". But the comments in my progress reports became more laudatory with time. In my final report before I left for the United States, the headmaster wrote "A versatile and cheerful character whose good influence is missed in many ways" and the form master wrote "He has had a busy term of great and good activity. Will do well". During my six years at the school, numerous comments indicated that I had ability; I owe it to my excellent teachers that they were able to draw out this ability. Looking back, I am very grateful to Win Schlesinger for enrolling me at NGS. Not only were my teachers excellent, the courses were rigorous, and the discipline was strict, something I needed badly at the time. Apart from the subject matter in my classes, I learned how to write well, the importance of discipline, the importance of fair play, and many other life lessons. I look back at my years at NGS very fondly.

We boys were assigned to one of four groups: Curnock, Davis, Evers and Patterson, named after school alumni who had fallen in World War I. I was assigned to Curnock. The boarders were housed in a wing of the school that contained a large dining room, a games room where there was a billiards table, several dormitory rooms, in which we slept about 8 to a room, arranged by age, a room for sick children known as the "san", a kitchen, and living quarters for a matron. Downstairs there were showers.

Win and Bernard Schlesinger, at their home, St. Mary Woodlands, England, 1973

Life for us boarders was highly regimented, which seemed to suit me well. When we got up, we had to go downstairs for our showers. Since the water was usually very cold, we mostly only pretended to take showers, moistening parts of our bodies in case the prefects inspected us. In retrospect that seems both unhygienic and silly; those prefects could not have been fooled as they did exactly the same thing when they were younger. Prefects were older boys, appointed by the staff to help keep order and discipline; like the rest of Britain in those days, our little group was hierarchical. Every morning we had to polish our shoes (the British set much more stock on clean, neat shoes than we do in the United States). Homework was done daily in enforced silence, sitting on the benches in the dining rooms, supervised by a prefect or teacher. Even on weekends we had to spend time sitting quietly in the dining room, writing letters or reading.

For our meals in the dining room we sat on the benches alongside two long tables, one for the boarders from the grammar school, and the other for those from the prep school. At the head of the former sat matron, at the head of the other the assistant matron. I recall the food as being pretty bad. Institutional food was, undoubtedly, bad in general, but in addition there was rationing during the war so that certain foods were rare, including meat, eggs and fruit. I remember being hungry on several occasions and buying a loaf of bread at the bakery across the street. The school also had a "tuck shop" where one could buy sweets (candy), but that was rationed, and one had to use coupons, which were limited every month. An incident relevant to this shows how much I prized the tuck shop sweets. One of the boarders was a boy named Snowman. Like several others, he was from London, sent down to our school, presumably, to escape the city, which was often the target of major bomb attacks. Snowman was a slick young man, who seemed to be much more sophisticated than the rest of us. I remember that he owned a car, but when I consider that now, I don't know how that would have been possible. Snowman collected stamps and knew that I did so also. My father had started my stamp collection. Snowman enticed me to exchange my stamp collection for his book of sweets coupons. My mother was, understandably, quite upset when she heard about this.

An important member of the boarder community was "matron". For most of my time at NGS matron was Miss Haynes. She was in charge of all the domestic affairs and also acted as a nurse. She was strict, but she cared very much for us boys and under a rather gruff exterior there was a heart of gold. She supervised our going to bed, made sure we ate properly, and in general acted as a substitute mother. Boys who were sick went to her for medication and, if necessary, confinement to the san. I was an asthmatic, and when I had bad asthma attacks I went to matron who had a vial of adrenaline, which she would inject into my arm. The san was also for those who came down with contagious diseases.

After about three years, Miss Haynes left. I don't recall whether she joined one of the women's auxiliary forces or just took another job, but her replacement was a total disaster. The new matron was a shy, insecure rotund woman who blushed easily and who seemed to lack all the skills necessary for her job. She told me she could not give me adrenaline injections when I had asthma (it seemed she was too squeamish), and gave me the vial of adrenaline and needle and told me to inject myself when necessary. Fortunately, I knew enough to wash the syringe and needle with soap and water, but of course could not sterilize it. Her nursing abilities were more or less limited to prescribing milk of magnesia for whatever problems we boys presented. One of the boarders, Peter Lovely, got hit on the finger by a cricket ball, and her remedy for that was milk of magnesia. It got to be a joke, but we took our sweet revenge. One morning we were able to exchange the milk on her breakfast tray for milk of magnesia. We all watched eagerly for her reaction when she drank her tea: her cheeks turned crimson, but she didn't say a word. Miss Haynes is on a photograph I have of the boarders, taken in 1945, my final year at NGS, so I presume that the replacement matron was only temporary, and that Miss Haynes returned to resume her usual role.

I remember many of my school teachers ("masters"), most of whom I liked, and one whom I loathed. Mr. Herbert, who taught physics and whose nickname was Johnny, had some sort of supervisory role with the boarders. He is included in that photograph of the boarders taken in 1945. He often came to our games room and played billiards with us. He had a perpetual cigarette in his mouth, from which he never took a puff, and from which ashes scattered about. He sometimes supervised "prep", i.e. the hours after class when we sat in the dining room doing our homework in enforced silence. He also walked through the dormitory rooms after "lights-out" to make sure we weren't talking or fooling around.

The headmaster was Mr. T. Rutherford Harley, known as "The Old Man", who lived at the school with his wife. He was a stern man whom you encountered mostly when your behavior warranted corporal punishment. This happened to me on a few occasions and my recollection is that the canings were painful but not too severe. In retrospect, I do not think they were sadistic. Mr. Harley also came to the boarders' premises occasionally, and he invited us all to his living quarters to hear a few of Winston Churchill's speeches during the war. I remember Mr. Harley as an enlightened man for the following reason. I was one of the very few Jewish boarders. All boarders had to go to church on Sundays, but Mr. Harley exempted Jewish boys. Nevertheless, I elected to attend church. I was a Jewish boy from Germany. Most of the boys only knew that I was "German" (my first name is Hans). Desperate to fit in, I didn't want attention drawn to anything that made me different so I joined the others at church on Sundays. That had unexpected rewards. There were several girls from the adjacent High School that also attended church, and we were able to exchange furtive glances and notes. More seriously, I became awe-struck by the beauty of the music, the readings from the bible, and the church itself. This prompted me to ask my mother whether I could convert to Christianity. Fortunately, her response was vague and evasive. The organist was a Mr. Sellick, and he had been hired by Mrs. Schlesinger to give me private piano lessons at the school. He would begin by asking me to play whatever he had prescribed for me to practice on the previous visit. I hardly ever practiced, but this failure rarely had the desired effect of chastisement from Mr. Sellick because I had learned to humor him. I would preempt his request for me to play by asking him instead, to play whatever he had played in church the previous Sunday. From there, a discussion ensued about other music, which he played for me. At the time, I thought I was very clever to use these distractions to avoid being discovered unprepared for my lesson. Later in my life I deeply regretted this foolishness in forfeiting my chance to learn the basics of piano playing.

Mr. Abell was the English teacher. His nickname was "Pud", for pudding-head. He was also in charge of the plays that the students put on every year. English was one of my best subjects and I became involved in the musical and drama productions, so I got along well with Mr. Abell. The highlight of my thespian activities was our production of Gilbert & Sullivan's "The Mikado", in which I played the role of KoKo. The production and my performance were judged to be very good. As I was of very small stature, I never achieved any successes in sports, so my successful theatrical roles, especially KoKo, were probably very good ego boosters for me. This also led to my first and only fan letter, from a girl named Madge Baily. That was a heady experience indeed. We met several times along the Canal (which was out of bounds for boarders, but as I was about to leave for the United States, I didn't let that bother me). Madge was my first "girlfriend". I was quite naïve, she was more mature and experienced than I, and I became quite smitten by her.

My favorite teacher was Mr. G.H. Keene, the music and art teacher. He was a very kind man who took an interest in me early on. I remember an event that occurred in one of his classes during my first year at the school. One of the boys made a nasty remark in class, something to do with my being German, and Mr. Keene immediately upbraided him. On my last day at the school, Mr. Keene played my favorite music before prayers. This incident is described in a broader context below.

Another favorite teacher was Mr. A.Q. Robinson (nicknamed "Beezam"), who taught French and some other subjects. He was a bachelor who lived with his mother in nearby Enbourne. He dressed rather unconventionally – scruffily in fact – but he, too, was exceedingly kind. He invited me to his house for a meal on at least one occasion, and he was one of the several teachers with whom I kept up a correspondence for several years after I came to the United States.

Mr. Charles Mathicson George, a Scotsman, was the senior Chemistry teacher. His enthusiasm for his subject had a great influence on me. I found learning organic chemistry from him to be fascinating and because of Mr. George, I chose chemistry as my major when I entered college in the United States.

Mr. Jessup taught Geography. He was younger than most of the other teachers and he made the subject interesting. Mr. Thomas taught History. When the headmaster learned that I would be moving to the United States in 1946, he asked Mr. Thomas to tutor me in American History. The Scripture teacher was Mr. Francis, nicknamed "Fanny". He was a very nervous man, reputed to have suffered from shellshock during World War I. My run-in with him is described below. Other teachers included Mr. Maggs. Mr. Ismay, Mr. Childs (the prep school headmaster) and a physical education teacher, whose name I have forgotten and who was killed in the only bombing attack on Newbury during the war and who also taught wood shop.

Finally, there was Mr. Mitchell, the only teacher whom I detested. He was the assistant headmaster. He also performed other duties, outside school: he was a scoutmaster with the boy scouts, and was also a Justice of the Peace. Mr. Mitchell was a very large man with a deep, booming voice and a menacing manner that engendered fear. I first encountered him as my Mathematics teacher during my first two years. He had what seemed like a peculiar habit to me (I was very naïve) of touching boys inappropriately (as I later understood) as they were sitting in class. Fortunately, he never did that to me. His nickname "Slime" presumably had its origin in this behavior. During my second or third year, our paths crossed as a result of an incident in my Scripture class, which was taught by Mr. Francis in a classroom with dark wood paneling that was marred by dozens of names, carved by students over many decades. Bored by the class, I was using my penknife to carve my name onto the wall by my desk when Mr. Francis caught me and sent me to

Mr. Mitchell's office to be assigned a punishment. Mr. Mitchell found a slab of wood approximately as long as I was tall, had two holes drilled into the ends and a piece of rope attached, and told me to wear it at all times until further notice, telling me that if I liked carving my name, I should do it in the wood hanging around my shoulders. It was a cruel, humiliating punishment. The wood was very heavy, and had the desired effect of eliciting much taunting by the other boys. I believe the headmaster heard about it and ordered it stopped. During the next years, I only had to endure Mr. Mitchell's occasional chastisements, which were always rendered in a tone of derision.

Then things changed. During my last year, the school put on a performance of Gilbert & Sullivan's "Mikado". I was selected to play the part of KoKo. There were many rehearsals, and after a while I noticed Mr. Mitchell's inimitable deep bellow, laughing whenever I was doing my part on stage. He seemed to really enjoy it. The actual performance was a great success, and it was not too long afterwards that I left school (in the middle of term) to go to the United States. On my last day, it happened that Mr. Mitchell officiated at morning prayers (he did so whenever the headmaster was unable to). The usual routine for the morning prayers was that Mr. Keene would play a piece of music on the piano, then there would be a reading from the bible, we would sing some hymns, and then the headmaster (or Mr. Mitchell) would ask the latecomers to come in and would make whatever announcements needed to be made that day. To my utter astonishment, Mr. Mitchell began the announcements that day by stating that the piece Mr. Keene had played before prayers (I forget what it was, but remember that it was by Tchaikovsky) he had especially selected because it was "Hans Levy's favorite", and that today was my last day, that I was going to America, and then he launched into effusive praise about what a remarkable boy I had been at the school, etc. etc. I was embarrassed and sickened that a man, whom I disliked and disrespected, who had punished me cruelly and had shown only derision, would talk about me in what seemed to me to be an utterly hypocritical manner.

Mrs. Schlesinger wrote to me, a year or two after I had moved to the United States, that Mr. Mitchell had been arrested and charged with, I believe molesting young boys. I believe he served time in prison.

Among many boys whom I remember there were several boarders, including my friends Tony Lynes and Roger Nix, with whom I took a one-week bicycle tour during the holidays one year; a boy named Hughes who had epileptic fits that frightened me, and Pitchford who was from India. There were two brothers named Stanley and D.H. Ryde whose former name was Gershcowit.

What consumed the interest of us boys the most, apart from school activities, was the war. Many of us followed the fighting on various fronts. After America entered the war, nearby Greenham Common airbase became headquarters for the U.S. Ninth Air Force and we sometimes saw U.S. airmen in town. During the early years of the war, we often heard German planes flying overhead on their way to bomb other towns, and occasionally the siren would go off as a warning, but I don't recall any shelters. The only time Newbury was directly attacked, was on our sports day in 1942 or 1943. We were all out on the field when suddenly, without warning, a German Junkers 88 flew overhead extremely low. The rear gunner could easily have fired into us, but it turned out that he was dead, as was discovered a bit later when the plane was shot down. That day, though, our gym and wood-shop teacher was killed, but I don't remember how.

As D-Day neared, there was a great increase in the number of planes flying overhead, many with gliders, presumably on practice runs. I kept a diary in 1944 and it is filled with counts of how many, and what kinds of planes I saw every day. Also, U.S. tanks and other army vehicles rumbled through town for hours on end. We all knew D-Day was coming, and I predicted that it would not occur until the Allies captured Rome. That occurred on June 4, 1944, and D-Day was the following day. In fact, the two events were totally unrelated, and it had just been a lucky guess on my part.

Another big event was V.E. Day, the day commemorating the end of the war in Europe. This elicited a huge national celebration, much bigger that V.J. Day, the day marking the end of the war with Japan, which was of greater significance in the United States. Win Schlesinger allowed Wendy, Roger and me to participate in the V.E. Day celebrations in London. We stayed with "Grandma", Bernard's mother, who lived in the Golders Green section of London. I described our adventure in a long letter I wrote to my mother. We took the tube to the West End, arriving about 7 p.m., and didn't get back until 1 a.m. the next morning. We were part of a huge, deliriously happy, singing, shouting crowd of about 100,000 people. We watched flares being set off from the bridge over the Thames next to Westminster Abbey. Outside Buckingham Palace we watched as the King, Queen, the Princesses and Winston Churchill appeared on the balcony to deafening roars from the crowd. We saw Admiralty Arch beautifully lit up, and crowds dancing in front of it, and Nelson's column at Trafalgar Square also beautifully illuminated. We surged past Picadilly, down Oxford Street and Baker Street, and tried to find a tube to take back, but none were running, so we had to walk all the way back to Grandma's. We had walked about 20 miles altogether, and though we were exhausted, we agreed that it was a thrilling once-in-a-lifetime experience.

Two things that happened while I was at school sharpened my interest in science. The first was reading Paul DeKruif's "Microbe Hunters", a book about the work of several microbiologists including van Leeuwenhoek, Koch, Pasteur, and Ehrlich. The scientists were portrayed as heroes whose work saved lives, and I was inspired by it. The second thing was a visit to one of the laboratories at Oxford University. My mother and sister were living in Oxford at the time, with my mother's cousin Eva Glees and her family. Eva's husband, Paul, was a neuroanatomist at Oxford University and one day he took me to see his lab, where he kept some monkeys on which he was experimenting. I found this fascinating, and I was especially intrigued by, and envious of a boy who worked for Paul. My recollection is that the boy was not much older than I, but this was probably not true.

I left Newbury Grammar School to come to the United States in June, 1946, a few weeks before completing my sixth year there. I am indebted to the school for an excellent education – the teachers were almost all excellent – and for instilling discipline into me, something I needed badly at the time. When I entered college in the United States a few months later, although I still had more than a year of schooling to complete, I was well prepared in mathematics and the sciences, often having already learned topics that were new to my classmates. This is a tribute to the rigorous British educational system in general, as well as to Newbury Grammar School.

My years in England were mostly happy. There were incidents in the Schlesinger household when we children would quarrel, or gang up against one another, which I suspect is not unusual.

Once, Hilary sought (and succeeded) to get me into trouble by writing my name, in large letters, on a freshly-painted wall in the house. Win assumed, of course, that I had written it. I don't recall what prompted Hilary to do this, but she eventually owned up to her prank after I was in America. One especially painful incident occurred when we were joined by some other children from nearby, in a field somewhere, when, for reasons I no longer remember, several of them ganged up on me and "debagged" me, i.e. took off my trousers and taunted me. It was probably not long after that, that I "ran away", with the goal of joining my mother who lived in Filkins, in the Cotswolds in Gloucestershire. My totally unrealistic plan was to sneak onto a train and, to get there, I would have had to change to another train at Didcot. I must have been about 12 at the time. I bicycled down to the railway station in Kintbury, about 4 miles away, and asked the station manager when the next train for Didcot would leave. As this was a small community, where everybody knew each other, he knew who I was and where I lived. He called Mrs. Schlesinger at once. Sensing this, I took off on my bicycle toward Didcot and not very long later Mrs. Schlesinger and "Nanny" overtook me in Mrs. Schlesinger's car and so my "freedom" was very short-lived. The worst part was that Nanny, who was very strict and whom I couldn't stand, berated me harshly.

This incident demonstrates that, although I was treated like the other Schlesinger children, and loved Win and Bernard enough to call them "Mummy" and "Daddy", the bond to my mother was still much stronger. This is in stark contrast to the experience of another *Kindertransport* child, Kurt Fuchel, one of the children who is featured in both the film and the book "Into the Arms of Strangers". Kurt, who was born in Vienna, lived, in England, with Mariam and Percy Cohen and their son John. He loved them, especially Percy, who was a warm-hearted man. His parents had made their way out of Austria to Southern France, where they were in hiding during the war. After the war was over, they contacted the Cohens, who told Kurt that he would sometime go back to live with them again. His reaction was that he was horrified. In 1947 Kurt went to France to be reunited with them, a very difficult transition for him, though ultimately successful. In a poignant scene in "Into the Arms of Strangers" he says: "Of course, I'm very lucky. I realize this: whereas most of the *Kinder* never saw their parents again, I not only had mine back, but another set of parents as well. What more could one ask for?" He speaks, not with joy, but with sadness and pain.

Some of my holiday time was spent with my mother and sister. At first, they lived in the north of England, where I could not visit them, but in 1940 they moved to Oxford (which is not far from Newbury) where they stayed with my mother's cousin Eva Glees and her husband, Paul, and their children, and where my mother worked as their housekeeper. I was able to visit them there but don't remember much about those visits. For various reasons, including the fact that my mother and Eva did not get along, so that she was very unhappy there, my mother found another job which she kept for the rest of her years in England, and where she and my sister were very happy. I visited her there often. The story of how she got there, and the deep friendships that developed there, is worth recounting here.

While she lived in Oxford, my mother became acquainted with a woman who was a Quaker, and who befriended her, and with whom my mother was able to share some of her concerns. This woman knew of my mother's difficulties and unhappiness at the Glees home and told her, that if ever the situation there became unbearable, she could just bring my sister and stay with her. It was through her, that my mother heard about an opening that became available with a family named Cripps, who lived in a little village called Filkins, in the Cotswolds, not far from Oxford. John Cripps was a Quaker, a conscientious objector, the son of Sir Stafford Cripps, a Labour member of parliament who was Britain's ambassador to the Soviet Union (1940-42) and subsequently a member of the War Cabinet. Stafford Cripps was a wealthy man who owned a large estate house in Filkins, called Goodfellows, which he bequeathed to John. John was the editor of the magazine "The Countryman". He also employed a number of individuals to help run Goodlfellows, which included a large garden, given over to growing vegetables during the war, and which housed a hostel for children, including its staff, that had been bombed out in Bristol. All his employees were Jewish refugees. The opening available in the Cripps home was for a cook and housekeeper, and my mother applied.

John's wife, Ursula, came to Oxford to interview my mother, who brought my sister, Elisabeth with her to the interview. Elisabeth was about four years old at the time and a very outgoing, charming little girl. It turned out that John and Ursula had a daughter, Judith, exactly the same age as Elisabeth, who was a difficult and withdrawn child. Ursula realized that Elisabeth might prove to be a very beneficial influence on Judith, and this was a major reason that she offered my mother the job, which she accepted. She and Ursula became good friends, as did Elisabeth and Judith. Ursula was a charming, petite outgoing woman (on whom I had a real crush), whereas John was a tall, shy, reserved man.

After a year or two, the British government took over Goodfellows as a home for women from the Women's Land Army. The Cripps family moved to another house in Filkins, and the only member of the staff that they took with them was my mother, who lived there, with my sister, until they came to the United States in 1946 -- a very difficult decision for my mother for whom the years with the Cripps family in beautiful, peaceful Filkins were among the happiest in her life, and an extraordinary contrast to the difficult, stressful years in Germany prior to her departure to England.

I visited my mother and sister during those periods of my holidays that I didn't spend with the Schlesingers. I had a bicycle there, and I was befriended by some of the Jewish refugees who were on the staff. One year, John Cripps kindly invited my cousin Frank to spend a week or two with me. An incident that occurred during that visit caused my mother embarrassment and made her very angry at me. John had a large barn, with a loft where he stored bags of lime. On the floor of the barn he had spread out a lot of vegetables that had been harvested and were there to dry. Frank and I climbed up to the loft and pretended to be bombers flying over Germany, unloading our "bombs" – handfuls of lime – onto the targets below – the vegetables. Needless to say, when John discovered this he was very angry, and told my mother, who was furious with me. John told her that Frank and I had to clean everything up the next day. The next day I came down with chickenpox, so Frank had to do all the cleaning. Somehow, this was emblematic of Frank's personality. He always seemed to have bad luck, as though a dark cloud hung over him, and his outlook on life was pessimistic.

CHAPTER 3

First Years in America

I arrived in the United States in June, 1946, having flown from London, where Win and Bernard saw me off, to New York with stops in Shannon, Ireland and Halifax, Nova Scotia. It marked a sort of initiation into adulthood, symbolized by two events: Bernard gave me a pack of cigarettes, and I flirted with some young women on the flight.

I was met in New York by my mother, who had arrived in America with my sister several weeks previously, and my cousin Frank, who had come with his family from England several years ago. We made our way to Red Bank, NJ, where my uncle Ernest, aunt Martha ("TaMa", i.e. Tante Martha) lived in an apartment with their daughter, Lore, and where my mother and sister had joined them. My uncle was a physician whose office was attached to the apartment, and my aunt was his receptionist/nurse. My mother earned her keep as their housekeeper and cook.

My first impressions of my new homeland were filled with astonishment. The abundance of food, the variety and size of cars, the colorful clothing, the perception of plentitude contrasted starkly with what I had become accustomed to in war-time England. Boys and girls my age, were physically and socially more mature than I, and their counterparts in England. Houses and roads were bigger and the landscape more expansive.

With Pierre, Frank, and my sister Elisabeth, Red Bank NJ, 1947

My taciturn uncle was clearly relieved to have another male member in the household, having resided for a decade with my aunt and their daughter, and more recently two more females, my mother and sister. My mother and aunt, although devoted to each other, were temperamentally very different: my mother was reserved, serious and intellectual, my aunt gregarious, vivacious and fun to be with. My mother, who had been so happy in England, had a difficult time becoming accustomed to America, the country that my aunt had come to love. The fact that my aunt was essentially my mother's employer, aggravated the situation. These differences sometimes resulted in tensions and exploded into unpleasant arguments, especially during dinner. For me, who loved both my mother and my aunt, this was painful, especially as I was often in the role of having to take sides. In retrospect, I realize that it provided an early lesson for me in learning how to arbitrate without offending either my mother or my aunt, a skill that proved to be useful throughout my life.

As soon as it became clear that I would emigrate to the United States, my aunt and uncle began sending out applications for me to various colleges. An entrance requirement was taking the SAT college entrance exams, and arrangements were made for me to take these in

London before my departure. This was an interesting, and somewhat unnerving experience, because I had never taken this type of exam – at my school I had only ever had essay exams. There were also some technical difficulties for me, such as the fact that American log tables are displayed differently than British ones, and I had to figure that out while taking the exam. But I did well enough that I was accepted at Brown University and Rutgers University. I chose to go to Rutgers, since it was close to Red Bank, where we lived with my uncle and aunt.

When I came to America as a sixteen-year old, I discovered that others of my age had summer jobs. I had never heard of anything like that in England, but I was eager to find a job. In the apartment building where we lived, there was a couple named Martin and Rose Wachtel with whom my aunt and uncle were friends. Martin was the owner of Albino Farms, where pure strains of laboratory rats and mice were raised for experimental purposes and shipped to research laboratories nation-wide. He offered me a job, helping to feed these animals, clean their cages, etc., which I accepted.

After a week or two working at Albino Farms, it turned out that I was allergic to these animals (later, as a postdoc, I had to work with rats again and by that time I was no longer allergic). Mr. Wachtel suggested that I could work outdoors instead, trimming hedges, etc., and I began doing that. Soon I was covered with a nasty, itchy rash from head to toe. It was poison ivy. No one had warned me about that plant, which does not exist in England and which I had never encountered before. So, that was the unpleasant end of my first job.

Very soon I found another job. My friend David Ostrolenk and I went to an orchard just outside Red Bank and offered to help them pick apples and peaches. The lady who owned the orchard agreed to hire us. Our job was not to pick the fruit, but to take it from the orchard, which was set back from a highway (Route 35) where we set up stands, one on each side of the road, and sold the apples and peaches to passers-by. We had an old Hudson at our disposal, which we used to transport the fruit to the stands, and we had a blast. It was my first chance to drive a car. The Hudson had running boards, and David and I would take turns driving the car, while the other person stood on the running board. The driver tried to maneuver the car so as to bring the passenger on the running board close to the hedges on the side of the dirt road from the orchard, to try to dislodge him. The dirt road from the orchard to the highway crossed a railway track, and one day the car got stuck on the track. I don't recall how we got it moving again. Also, when we weren't busy selling the apples and peaches, we threw them at each other across the highway. This was clearly not what the owner had in mind, but it was great fun and I don't think she ever found out.

Rutgers University

I began my freshman year at Rutgers in the Fall of 1946. That year, many veterans entered college under the G.I. Bill of Rights; they were somewhat older than the average student entering college and, at 16, I was somewhat younger. Because I had been turned on to Organic Chemistry by Mr. George, my teacher in England, I decided to major in Chemistry at Rutgers. When I came to the United States I still had more than a year left to complete my schooling in England (i.e. I never completed high school), but I soon found that in math and the sciences I was far ahead of most of my fellow freshmen at Rutgers, presumably because of the superior British education system. However, socially I was behind, and this immaturity probably accounted for some problems I had adapting. In my dormitory at Rutgers some men were much older than I, including my roommates who were veterans. I did quite well in my courses, but by the time I was a junior, my interest in Chemistry began to wane. My schedule that year included Organic Chemistry with lab, Physical Chemistry with lab, Quantitative Analysis with lab, and Psychology. The Chemistry courses were, mostly, quite boring and I began to question whether I would be interested in a career as a chemist. The subject matter did not seem to have much real-life relevance for me. The contrast with the Psychology course was stark – that subject seemed to be full of relevance, and I began to consider a career as a Psychiatrist. I spoke with my uncle about switching my major to Psychology, and he gave me some valuable advice: finish what you have begun, graduate with a degree in Chemistry, you can always go on with Psychology later if your interest remains strong.

Sadly, I remember very little about my academic work at Rutgers. As a Chemistry major, a large proportion of my courses were in the sciences and math. I enjoyed a very good psychology course (see above) and also a stimulating philosophy course taught by Mason Gross, then provost, and later president of Rutgers. Chemistry majors were required to take a Geology course titled Optical Crystallography, which I enjoyed and which was taught by James Prucha, whom I would encounter again many years later at Syracuse University, where he arrived and was appointed Chair of the Geology Department the same year I arrived, and where he later became dean of the college of Arts & Sciences and then Vice Chancellor of Academic Affairs. Prucha remembered me from the course at Rutgers in which, he said, I had done very well. Another transplant from Rutgers was Henry Schmitz, who had been my Physical Chemistry Lab instructor at Rutgers and who was employed at Bristol Laboratories. His wife, Edith, who was a refugee from Austria, later helped me in deciphering some of the genealogy notes from my grandfather that were written in the old German script.

Two seminal events occurred in my senior year that cemented my choice of a career. First, I was invited to participate in the senior special honors program, which involved performing independent research and writing a thesis. My research was on the conductometric determination of sulfates in urine, under the guidance of Prof. William Riemann III. The objective, to develop a method that was simpler and quicker than the standard method in use, was only partly successful, largely because of time constraints, but it was an excellent opportunity for me. It provided the heady experience of being creative, it taught me how to research the literature and how to write a scientific paper, and it led to my giving my first public lecture. This occurred at a joint conference of the North Jersey Section of the American Chemical Society with the Intercollegiate Student Affiliate Chapters of the A.C.S. I was one of the half dozen students who were invited to give presentations at this meeting, and I spoke about my senior honors research. A panel of judges chose my presentation as the best. For this I received acclaim and some prizes. Participation in undergraduate research at Rutgers made me a vigorous champion of undergraduate research later as a faculty member at Syracuse University, where I frequently had undergraduate students work in my laboratory.

Second, I took a course in Biochemistry. I was very fortunate, because, I believe, Rutgers was unusual at that time among colleges in offering an undergraduate course in biochemistry, which was given by Prof. Jay Roth, who was an outstanding teacher. I loved the course, which had all the relevance that I found missing in my Chemistry courses. These two experiences led to my decision to embark on a career in Biochemistry, presumably biochemical research, though I had no clear idea about how to achieve that yet.

I continued to earn money doing summer jobs while I was in college. The summer after my freshman year at Rutgers I was hired by the Psychiatric Hospital in Marlboro, about 12 miles from Red Bank, working in their laboratory doing routine tests of blood and urine. I don't recall how I got that job, nor how I got back and forth, perhaps there was a bus service. I enjoyed the work and learned about various medical testing procedures.

The following summer I got a job selling ice cream, working for a man named Jimmy Longo in Long Branch. Jimmy was of Italian heritage. He owned two or three little ice cream trucks, similar to those commonly seen driving up and down the streets in the summer, ringing their bells. Each of us got one of the trucks, and we created our own territories, trying not to impinge on each other's routes. Children came running out with their money to buy ice creams. Also, we had large insulated boxes, with dry ice in them, which we filled with ice cream and carried around to places where we couldn't drive the trucks. I went to some of the beaches along the shore with my box and sold ice cream to people there. I also tried to sneak into the Monmouth Race Track. This was a great job. The money was excellent – I made enough that summer to pay for all my incidental expenses at Rutgers the following year. It was fun driving the little trucks and to see all those happy kids.

I got the same job again the following summer, and again, I did very well financially and enjoyed my work. An incident occurred that summer, however, that was very unpleasant, but that taught me a lesson. Another of the people working for Jimmy that summer was a large man named Bruno – also with an Italian surname – who was quite a bit older than I. One day he and I showed up at the same street, along a route that had always been "mine". In front of a bunch of customers he made anti-Semitic remarks about me, threatened me physically, and accused me of taking his route. I reported this incident to Jimmy, who told me that Bruno had been in prison, was out on bail, and if I reported this incident, he could go back to jail. I spoke with my uncle about this that evening, and he advised me to report Bruno. But I thought about it and decided not to do so, thinking that if Bruno knew I could report him and I didn't, it might teach him a lesson. And, indeed, at the end of the season, Bruno apologized to me and thanked me for handling the situation the way I did and I felt good about that.

I also had a job for a while, working at Davidsons, a grocery store in Red Bank. My aunt and uncle knew the Davidson family, so perhaps I got the job through that connection. The one memorable thing about that job was that once a week an African American woman and her adolescent daughter came there to shop. There was something about their demeanor, which was very dignified, almost regal, that made a deep impression on me.

At Rutgers University, I had a number of jobs at various times, including a very dull office job, and one where I had to clean up cages of animals being used for research, including geese, which are very messy birds. A job I had for four years was working at one of the food stands at the football games. I enjoyed that, especially when, after the second year, I became manager and was able to take time to see more of the games than before.

On my ice cream truck, Long Branch, NJ 1947

My principal extracurricular activity at Rutgers was participation in Queens Players, which put on plays every year. I no longer remember in which plays I participated, but because of my size, the roles available to me were very limited. However, I must have done quite well because during my senior year, while I was beginning to apply to graduate programs in biochemistry, I received an offer from Columbia

My Aunt Martha (TaMa) and Uncle Ernest, Red Bank, NJ, 1954

University for financial support to their drama program. I was quite flattered but quickly realized that an acting career would be extremely limiting and difficult, so that choosing to pursue biochemistry rather than acting was not a difficult decision.

Prior to Queens Players, I was involved briefly in crew. Again, my size was the factor that played the crucial role in this activity. I was an excellent fit as coxswain, and for a few weeks I actually tried out this role, but soon gave it up in favor of acting in Queens Players.

I lived in a dormitory my entire four years. For my first year, I had three room-mates, all of whom were veterans and much older than I. They introduced me to various card games, and I spent much too much time playing cards. In my last year, one of my room mates was Fred van Aken who was born in Germany. He seemed to be slightly anti-Semitic, and I was surprised to learn that he was Jewish, that his original name was Fritz Goldstein, and that he and his family hailed from Aachen, and they changed their name to mark this fact. Later, I read an interview that an office at Rutgers conducted with him, as a Holocaust survivor, and from that formed a much more favorable opinion.

My social life at Rutgers was quite limited because I spent a lot of time with my then best friend David Ostrolenk and his family. I did attend a few Hillel events, but was never comfortable there (see Chapter 10). I participated in a few events at the NJ College for Women (subsequently named Douglas College).

With my grandfather, Richard Frank, Red Bank, NJ, 1956

David, who was a few months older than I, was the son of Sam and Mina Ostrolenk, who were good friends of my aunt Martha and Uncle Ernest. David also had a sister, Phyllis ("Phus") who was a year younger than I. The Ostrolenks lived in River Plaza, just outside Red Bank. Sam was a patent attorney in New York with a company called Ostrolenk & Faber. My friendship with David and Phyllis developed rapidly, and toward the end of the summer Sam and Mina asked me to accompany their family on a trip to Canada. For the next four years, while I attended Rutgers University, I spent at least as many weekends at the Ostrolenk home as I did at ours.

Among my first recollections about the Ostrolenks is the fact that they were comfortably well off, that Mina "wore the pants" in the family, that Sam was a kind, gentle man with an infectious sense of humor, and that the atmosphere in their house was relaxed. One of my earliest meals with them included steak and water melon. The steak on my plate was huge, the size of a couple of weeks' meat ration in wartime England. I had never had watermelon before and I loved the taste and the sport of spitting out the pits. David took me to one of his high school classes, and I was blown away by two facts: there were GIRLS in the class, and they looked so mature! During my boys' boarding school life in England girls were like forbidden fruit. The other extraordinary fact was that so many of the students drove to school in their own cars.

With my sister Elisabeth, Red Bank, NJ, 1956

That first summer David, Phus and I spent quite a lot of time together, on the beach or at their house. David and I got a job at a peach farm (see above). Our trip to Canada toward the end of the summer was a blast. Sam, Mina, David, Phus and I were in their old car, nicknamed "Asthma", and among its other problems was the fact that it kept having flats. David and I would change the tires, and Phus would clock us; our times improved with each flat. When we finally got to Montreal, Asthma died in the middle of a busy intersection; I don't remember how we got out of that one. But before we got there, a number of memorable things occurred. At a rest stop near Lake George, NY, David and I saw the following notice posted on a urinal: "We aim to please, you aim too, please!". At a little restaurant near there I noticed that one of the items on the menu was a typed correction, taped over the original. It read: "Southern Fried Chicken, $1.25". I asked why there was a correction, and the waitress replied that there had been a terrible typo on the original printed menu, which had read: "Southern fried children, $1.25". When we got to the Canadian border there was a major problem, namely my citizenship status. I did not know, or remember, that when we left Germany in 1939, our German citizenship was revoked. During the war in England, we were unable to become British citizens, so we were stateless. This was obviously a problem for the officers at the border crossing. I don't remember how it was resolved, but I know that Sam Ostrolenk had to call someone in Washington.

When I entered Rutgers University that fall, the Ostrolenks accompanied my aunt and mother on my first trip there, and Sam sat me down to explain about fraternities, and to advise me against joining one. This was one of the many kindnesses shown by the Ostrolenks, who realized that I knew nothing about American universities. Four years later, when I graduated, they were there to witness the event. Sam also made a loan available to me, for my college expenses, through a foundation he had set up called the Ostrolenk Foundation.

At the beginning of my freshman year at Rutgers, the Ostrolenks moved from River Plaza to New Hope, PA. David, who still had one year to finish high school, attended Peddie, a Prep School in Hightstown, NJ, and Phus went to Holmquist near New Hope. I spent many weekends with the Ostrolenks, which became the focus of my social life. Among the family members whom I met at their house was Mina's mother "Grandma Green"; cousin Bernie; one of Sam's nephews who later joined Sam's patent attorney firm; and another cousin, who was, reputedly, a communist. The Ostrolenks also had a dog, a German Shepherd they named "Trouvée" because they had found her in Red Bank. Those weekends were always very stimulating. There were long political and philosophical conversations between David and me, sometimes also involving other family members. David used to drink hard liquor, which seemed to have no effect on him. There were parties, which included some Jewish high school girls from nearby Trenton. David first dated a girl named Flossie Dietz, then, later, Lois Beilinson, whom he eventually married. I dated a girl named Carol Wertheimer. In Chapter 12, I relate an event involving Carol which taught me an important lesson.

David went to the University of Pennsylvania, and then to the Medical School there. He became a physician, specializing in radiology. David and Lois married and had a boy, Barry, whom I knew, and then two other children I never met. For a while, when I was at the University of Chicago, he and Lois were in Chicago where he did an internship or residency, but then we drifted apart. I heard that his marriage went sour. I was still in occasional touch with Phus, who married Marvin Soffen, a patent attorney who joined the Ostrolenk & Faber patent attorney firm. They had five children. Through her I learned about a very strange turn of events in David's life. For reasons I never understood, he turned against his parents and tried to sue them for "malpractice" in raising him. This was inconceivable to me, as he seemed to have had an idyllic childhood and seemed to be very happy while I knew him as a friend. He also wanted to have nothing more to do with any of his former friends and acquaintances. In 1987, upon hearing of my sister Liz's death, he wrote me a brief letter, explaining that he only rarely contacted friends and family from his earlier life, finding it extremely painful. By that time, he was in his third marriage, and third job. Another strange fact is that when Phus told me about David's death (in 2007), she mentioned that the police were at his house to investigate the death. I never learned why, whether he had committed suicide or what had occurred. All of these strange events followed what was, apparently, a bitter divorce from Lois, after which David was never the same again. It is very sad, because during those years in the 1940s and 1950s he was a really good friend, with whom I shared many good times.

After David's estrangement from me I continued to remain friends with Phus and occasionally visited with her and her family. Marvin died in his sleep in 2003 and I went to a memorial service for him in Princeton. Phus moved into a retirement community and she and I communicated sporadically via e-mail or telephone. After a while I noticed that she seemed to be becoming somewhat confused, and all communication ceased.

As I mention elsewhere (see Chapter 4), Sam Ostrolenk played an important role while I was at the University of Chicago. His help during that critical, difficult period was exceedingly important and an act of great kindness and friendship.

CHAPTER 4

Becoming an Academic Scientist

My excitement about Biochemistry and research was the beginning of my path toward becoming an academic biochemist, though I only had a vague concept of what that was. First, I will describe what an academic scientist is, and the steps that were necessary to attain my goal.

An academic scientist is employed by a college or university to teach and conduct research. The university's primary interest is in his function as a teacher, but it recognizes that the best way to entice him to join the faculty is to allow him to conduct research. Thus, academic institutions try to create a climate supportive of research endeavors, for example by reduced teaching loads. Teaching loads are usually very low in Medical Schools, higher in Research Universities, and highest at Liberal Arts Colleges.

The university provides the requisite facilities, which are usually expensive. The scientist has to apply to federal funding agencies, such as the National Institutes of Health or the National Science Foundation, to purchase the equipment and supplies that support his research, but the university benefits from such grants as the funding agencies provide overhead costs to help with the ancillary services that are needed to maintain the facilities. In addition, universities gain prestige from having research scientists on their faculties.

Academic scientists generally conduct basic research, i.e. research that is designed to gain an understanding of basic problems, not necessarily to achieve a practical goal, such as curing a disease. However, especially in the life sciences, the basic research is often formulated in such a way as to be applicable to a particular disease, because the National Institutes of Health are set up to study specific diseases and their grants reflect that interest.

Conducting my Ph.D. research, University of Chicago, 1954

The academic scientist is faced with a tension that results from the fact that he is a member of two distinct communities, his scientific profession, and his university. His success and renown in the scientific community is based on his research, whereas his success, and opportunity for promotion within the university is based primarily on his success as a teacher, although his research does play an important role. The time spent in teaching and service, impinge heavily on the time devoted to research. Evaluation by the broader scientific community occurs as a scientist's research becomes recognized by his peers through citation in their publications, invitations to present seminars, appointment to leadership positions in scientific societies, and appointment to "study sections" for peer reviews of grant applications at agencies such as the National Institutes of Health, the National Science Foundation and the American Cancer Society. One sign of having achieved professional acceptance is election to the scientific society representing one's discipline, in my case the American Society of Biochemistry and Molecular Biology, to which I was elected in the 1960s.

My decision to become an academic scientist necessitated that, after obtaining my bachelor's degree, I had to obtain a graduate degree. I applied to several graduate programs in Biochemistry and was accepted at two: one at the University of Illinois, in the Department of Animal Husbandry, or Agricultural Biochemistry, and one in the

Biochemistry Department at the University of Chicago. Both offered some support, and although this was better at the University of Illinois, I chose the University of Chicago because theirs was a regular Biochemistry Department.

The Biochemistry Department at the University of Chicago was a very fortunate choice because, although I didn't know it, it was one of the best in the country at that time, including among its faculty such luminaries as Konrad Bloch, Albert Lehninger, Eugene Kennedy, Paul Talalay, Birgit Vennesland and many others. I decided to do my research with Birgit Vennesland, an enzymologist working on several projects, including the stereospecificity of hydride transfer in pyridine nucleotide-linked dehydrogenases, a project that was, at that time, at the cutting edge of enzymology. The academic and intellectual atmosphere at Chicago was extremely stimulating, but I began to harbor doubts about whether I was sufficiently capable to succeed there. Self-doubt had plagued me previously from time to time. I was conscious of the fact that others invariably thought extremely highly of me, but I sometimes had the feeling that my accomplishments were a fraud. A stark manifestation of this paradox occurred after my talk about my undergraduate research at the ACS meeting, which was judged to be the best presentation (see Chapter 3). I had to take the train back to Red Bank and when I got home, instead of being elated I actually broke down and wept. I don't recall all the details, but I think it took a day or two before I was well again, and I don't think that either I, or my mother really understood why this nervous breakdown occurred, and it never occurred again. My Uncle Gerhard Ems was visiting us at the time, and I'm sure he must have been puzzled, or perhaps he was reminded about his sister, my mother's mother, who was highly neurotic and spent many years of her life in a private institution.

In order to be officially accepted into the Ph.D. program in the Biochemistry Department in Chicago, students had to take an oral preliminary exam, known as "the prelims". This usually took place after a year or so of study. I was scheduled to take mine in October 1951. That summer, in order to earn some money, I enlisted as a subject in a research program at one of the University hospitals. The project involved the effect of corticosteroid injections on renal function. The benefits, apart from "contributing to the advancement of medical knowledge", which appealed to my idealism, included a $200 cash stipend and 12 weeks of free meals at the hospital, alternating between a week of strictly regulated diet (everything was weighed to the nearest gram), at the conclusion of which came the steroid injections, and a week of food *ad libitum*. The intramuscular injections (in the buttocks) were very painful, making sitting difficult. My uncle did not approve of my doing this, noting that sometimes such experiments with unknown procedures can be very dangerous, and in those days, there were no federal regulations on experimenting with human subjects. It so happened (though I never told my uncle about this) that I learned subsequently that one of the student participants in this experiment died, though the cause was not fully explained and, perhaps, covered up. I also was working in the laboratory of Dr. Earl Evans (chair of the department) doing experiments involving bacteriophage. I doubt that either of these activities had any impact on my performance in the prelims, except that they took time from study.

I took the prelims and failed them.

I was exceedingly nervous, probably because I realized I had not studied enough. My failure came as a complete shock and surprise to the faculty and my fellow students in the Biochemistry Department. I was considered to be one of the best students, and everyone thought that I was certain to pass. Again, I seem to have fooled a lot of people about my abilities - I felt again like I did after winning prizes for my talk about my honors research at Rutgers. My mother and others in the family were also shocked, but everyone rallied around me. There were letters of great encouragement from my mother, from Win Schlesinger, from my grandfather and some of my fellow students, but some of these also warned me that I had to really work hard and intelligently to avoid a repeat of this mishap. My mother, who knew me better than anyone, told me that she thought I had not put enough effort into studying for this important exam, and that I seemed to be on a path of self-destruction.

This, now, was a crisis, the low point of my professional life. I went home to Red Bank, to lick my wounds and consult with my family. Again, I received strong support from everyone. One person who was especially helpful was Sam Ostrolenk, the father of my best friend David, a patent attorney, with an office in New York (see Chapter 3). He had talked to me before about a career in patent law, and now he offered me a job in his office, to get some hands-on experience.

I thought this was a good thing to do temporarily while I thought about my future, so for a couple of weeks I put on a suit and tie, took a commuter train to New York every morning and back to Red Bank in the evening, and learned something about how to review patent applications.

Meanwhile, I received a letter from my friend John Westley, a fellow biochemistry graduate student in Chicago, which was to have a crucial effect on my life. John wrote to tell me that he had made some inquiries in the Biochemistry Department about my situation and that it was definitely agreed that I was a capable and likable person and that I would be welcome back into the department after some lab experience. The feeling was, apparently, that I needed to gain some maturity and experience in the "real" world. Dr. Evans suggested that I should come back to Chicago and, with his help if necessary, obtain a technical job and then go to work on my M.S. degree. Furthermore, John wrote, that he and a group of graduate students who had rented an apartment together needed an additional person to replace one member of the group who was leaving, and they hoped that I would join them. John pointed out the obvious advantages of my living in Chicago, enabling me to keep in touch with the department, allowing me to use the university library, and taking up Dr. Evans's offer to help me find a job.

With fellow graduate student John Westley, University of Chicago, 1954

This appeared to be an excellent opportunity, and so I returned to Chicago, joined John Westley and the others in his apartment, and began to look for a job. An opening that appeared to be very promising, was for a technician at the nearby Argonne National Laboratories, in their Division of Biological and Medical Research, with Arthur Koch, who had recently earned his Ph.D. from the Biochemistry Department at the University of Chicago, and whom I knew. Through him I would be able to maintain contact with the Biochemistry Department, gain valuable laboratory experience and earn a good salary. Working at Argonne, however, required a security clearance, and for this I was turned down because my grandfather lived in the Russian Zone of Germany. Instead I was able to get a job as technician with Dr. Edith Farnsworth at Northwestern University School of Medicine. She was a friend of Dr. Evans and it was through this connection that I was hired.

Edith Farnsworth was, like Evans, a cultured person. She had studied English literature and composition at the University of Chicago, and had written several novels (none were published) and composed poetry. She also studied violin and music theory at the American Conservatory of Music and in Italy, where she also studied Italian literature and translated Italian poems. Apparently, she had intended to become a concert violinist, but because she had a slight tremor this was not possible, and so she turned to the study of medicine. Parenthetically, Dr. Farnsworth had become acquainted with the world-renowned architect Ludwig Mies van der Rohe, whose work she admired, and whom she commissioned to build a house for her in Plano, IL, along the Fox River. The glass and steel house, known as the Farnsworth House, completed in 1951, was considered one of van der Rohe's masterpieces. Farnsworth soon discovered that despite its great artistic merit, the house had major practical defects. There were also large cost overruns. She sued van der Rohe, and he counter-sued her for defamation of character, and the whole case became a cause célèbre that was featured prominently in the press.

As a physician, Farnsworth specialized in children's kidney diseases, and she had a laboratory in which she sought to follow the efficacy of the treatment regimens of her patients by analyzing steroids in their urine. My task was to conduct these analyses. The laboratory was small, with only a few employees, but well furnished with the necessary equipment. It soon became apparent to me that Farnsworth had only a limited understanding of how to conduct research and to interpret data. After only a few weeks of work, she was very pleased with my results, but soon I received word that my security clearance was approved for the job at Argonne after all, and Arthur Koch invited me to accept the job offered earlier. For all the reasons enumerated above, I was very anxious to accept, but when I mentioned this to Dr. Farnsworth she was very upset. At first, she tried to entice me to stay by offering to make me the director of her laboratory, but when I turned this offer down she told me that I was obligated to remain until the project I was working on was complete, and that if I did not, she would tell Dr. Evans that I had broken my contract with her. Clearly, this was a messy situation for me, but I agreed to stay on for several more weeks to try to complete the project. She was anxious to publish the results, and although I knew that they were too preliminary I agreed to help her to prepare a manuscript. This apparently appeased her and she agreed to let me go. I actually continued to work with her on the manuscript, meeting with her at her elegant apartment several evenings after I began work at Argonne. She sent the completed manuscript to a journal, with me as coauthor, and I hoped desperately that it would be rejected, which it was. But I had managed to leave Dr. Farnsworth on good terms.

I worked for Farnsworth for about six months and had not learned much scientifically. My job at Argonne in Arthur Koch's lab as his technician was much more interesting, intellectually challenging, and provided an opportunity to learn a lot. Also, the salary was much better. The project involved measuring protein turnover in growing *Escherichia coli*. Arthur was an excellent scientist from whom I could learn a lot. I did not receive as much guidance from him as I had anticipated but, in retrospect, this forced me to rely on my own resources and helped me to gain some self-confidence. There was a stimulating atmosphere at Argonne and I met interesting scientists. The work went well and within a year we had sufficient data to present a report at a scientific meeting and, subsequently, to publish a paper in the Journal of Biological Chemistry, on which I was co-author – my first scientific publication.

I returned to full-time study in the Biochemistry Department at the University of Chicago in the fall of 1953, two years after I failed my prelims. I was a teaching assistant and continued the research I had begun on the stereospecificity of hydride transfer in pyridine nucleo-tide-linked dehydrogenases in Birgit Vennesland's lab. I do not recall that it was ever made clear whether I should continue, assuming I would get a terminal master's degree, or whether it was assumed that I would re-take the prelims and, if I passed, continue on for the Ph.D. In fact, the latter ensued. I took the prelims again in February 1955 and passed, and in June 1956 I obtained my Ph.D.

My Ph.D. research demonstrated that the stereospecific-ity of hydride transfer catalyzed by glucose dehydrogenase and D-glyceraldehyde dehydrogenase was opposite to that in the alcohol dehydrogenase- and lactate dehydrogenase-catalyzed reactions. This was of interest because the hydrogen atoms on the position of the nicotinamide ring of the coenzyme from which they are transferred are not attached to an asymmetric carbon atom, and such specific-ity had not been observed previously. It begged the question of how an enzyme can distinguish between two apparently identical atoms, a question we addressed in the last of the articles published about my Ph.D. research, and to which my research many years later was able to provide a definitive answer (see below). My Ph.D. research was pub-lished in four articles (three in the Journal of Biological Chemistry and one in the Journal of the American Chemical Society). The JACS arti-cle is of interest because it describes the preparation, optical rotation and configuration of a pure enantiomorph of ethanol-1-d, i.e. ethanol (which is not an optically active compound) in which one of the hydro-gen atoms has been replaced by deuterium, generating an asymmetric (chiral) carbon atom and an optically active compound.

Working in Birgit Vennesland's lab was an excellent experience for me. I think, in retrospect, that one reason that I chose to work with her is that she evinced qualities as a human being that seemed to be lacking in some of the other very high-powered faculty members in the department.

Among Birgit's many fine qualities, I admired her excitement about learning, her ability to treat all students fairly, but to discern the unique needs of each one to grow as a scientist, and the importance she attached to writing clearly and elegantly. These qualities endeared her to her students and postdocs. For her 65th birthday, in 1978, I con-tacted as many of her former students and postdocs as I was able to reach, with some of their help, and assembled a book of some of their publications which we presented to her at a dinner at a scientific meeting in Atlanta. In 1993, Birgit's former students and postdocs, including I[1], wrote letters of appreciation to her on the occasion of her 80th birthday and many of us enclosed photographs. These were assembled in a booklet titled "From the Friends of Professor Birgit Vennesland In Celebration of Her 80th Birthday, November 17, 1993". This project was undertaken by two of Birgit's postdocs, Eric Conn and George Lorimer.

Failing my prelims left me miserable for many months, lacking self-confidence, wrestling with personal problems, uncertain whether a career in biochemistry was the right thing for me. On the one hand I was extremely fortunate that so many people had such strong faith in me, knowing that I would succeed in the end, but on the other, this did not really help. Ultimately, I had to find the help within myself and it came through my own increasing successes, successes that I knew were real, not those imagined by others. Once this happened, it was as if a great river was unleashed that propelled me forward and washed away all the doubts, the procrastination, the self-absorption that had held me back. It created a discipline well suited for a successful career in academic research. My experience also engendered empathy in my subsequent dealings as a professor with students who lacked self-confidence.

In retrospect, 66 years later, I believe that failing my prelims was primarily a spiritual crisis. A major factor in this episode resulted from my trying to cope with the exceedingly demanding intellectual atmosphere at the University of Chicago. I expended a great deal of mental and emotional energy in the intellectual banter and one-upmanship displayed by my fellow graduate students, trying (and generally succeeding) in keeping up with them. This took a toll, however, on the more genuine and human aspects of these relationships, which were masked behind the intellectual jostling. My relationships with fellow students lacked the warmth of friendship that would include feelings and vulnerability. Eventually, I was able to find what I needed, in an interracial group of individuals outside the university. I will return to this in Chapter 5.

By the time that I completed my Ph.D., my ideas about a career had become crystallized. The way that the professors in the Biochemistry Department divided their time between teaching and conducting research on topics that they chose, appealed to me very much, and so I decided to become an academic scientist engaged in basic research and teaching.

In the United States, the bulk of basic research takes place in academic institutions. Since the end of World War II, federal funding for basic research has been extensive, and U.S. research universities have become the envy of the rest of the world. In order to become an academic scientist, it is essential to earn a Ph.D., but in addition, to spend one or more years doing independent post-doctoral research as a "postdoc". This is a way to demonstrate that you can do independent, original research, in contrast to your Ph.D. research, which is guided by a mentor. Usually, one selects to do a postdoc in an area unrelated to that of one's Ph.D., in order to broaden one's experience. Although, as a postdoc, you work in someone's lab, in an area related to their interest, your work is independent. With my goal in mind, I therefore began to look at various laboratories for postdoc opportunities. After considering several labs, I finally chose to accept an offer from Paul Talalay at the Ben May Laboratory for Cancer Research, at the University of Chicago. Paul's research was on the mechanism of action of steroid hormones, and conducting research in this area would expose me to a whole new field and new concepts. I had spent a week or so in Paul's lab during my Ph.D. research to deal with a technical problem which Birgit's lab did not have the facilities to solve, and had been very impressed. Another advantage of taking this position was that the start date for the appointment, three months after I completed all the requirements for my Ph.D., allowed me to accept an offer from Birgit Vennesland to spend three more months, with financial support, tying up some loose ends from my doctoral research that became evident while I was writing my dissertation, and that led to another publication which described exciting work. The results from this publication re-surfaced in my research in a most unexpected way a quarter of a century later (see Chapter 7). I learned from this experience that, often the most interesting research is generated while the dissertation is being written, because it forces you to bring together your data in a coherent manner and to recognize any gaps. I later tried (not always successfully) to anticipate this problem with my graduate students at Syracuse University.

The Ben May Laboratory for Cancer Research at the University of Chicago was established in 1951 by Charles Huggins with funds provided by an Alabama businessman and philanthropist, Ben May. Huggins was a surgeon, specializing in urology, who became interested in fundamental questions about cancer. In the 1950s he gave up surgery to concentrate on research. His pioneering discoveries on the hormonal dependence of prostate cancer led to revolutionary treatments of this disease and to the rational chemotherapy of cancer. Subsequently, he demonstrated that many breast cancers were hormone-dependent and could be treated by removing the ovaries and adrenal glands. In 1966 Huggins received the Nobel Prize in Physiology and Medicine for this work.

Huggins recognized that advances in cancer research depended on basic research in many areas, and he hired biochemists, physiologists, organic chemists and others for the Ben May Lab, and gave them complete freedom to pursue their interests. He had the vision, and a canny knack of recognizing potential in these scientists. When I began my postdoc at the Ben May Lab, the members of the staff included Dwight Ingle, Elwood Jensen. Eugene Kennedy, Albert Lehninger, Frank Putnam, Paul Talalay and Josef Fried – all of whom would be elected to the National Academy of Sciences (the highest accolade conferred on American scientists), as well as Nien-chu Yang, Guy Williams-Ashman, and Samuel Weiss. Jensen was awarded the Albert Lasker Prize in 2004 for his work on estrogen receptors. Most of these scientists had joint appointments in other departments. Huggins kept a keen eye on scientists who worked with members of the staff and offered positions to those he thought would become outstanding. One such individual was Shutsung Liao, who earned his Ph.D. at the University of Chicago in 1961 and was hired by Huggins. Liao spent his entire scientific career at the Ben May Lab and became a world-renowned researcher on prostate cancer.

Huggins had some eccentric mannerisms, and he ran the Ben May Lab as a benign dictator. He was totally absorbed by cancer research, and his opinions about other matters could sometimes seem narrow-minded or bigoted. But this was something that, under the circumstances, one tended to overlook. Working at the Ben May Lab was a scientist's dream: total devotion to research and adequate funding without any other responsibilities.

Paul Talalay, with whom I began my post-doctoral research, was only six years older than I. He was born in Berlin and as a Jew, like I, fled from Nazi Germany in 1939. He was a brilliant young physician who saw patients on the clinic several days per week, conducted research at the Ben May Lab, and taught in the Biochemistry Department. He was one of the first individuals to receive a life-time award from the American Cancer Society that funded some of his research. I was his first postdoc.

Paul's research focus when I joined his lab was the mechanism of action of steroid hormones. His approach was based on the supposition that the mechanism of steroid action was based on their metabolism. The fact that this hypothesis turned out to be incorrect, did not detract from the important information his research revealed. To examine the metabolism of steroids, Paul took advantage of the fact that microorganisms can be adapted to grow on almost any chemical compound by breaking it down to generate the intermediates they need for their metabolism and growth. This breakdown is catalyzed by a series of enzymes, each catalyzing one of a series of sequential steps in the degradative pathway. Paul isolated a soil bacterium, a pseudomonad, that he grew on testosterone as its sole carbon source and named it *Pseudomonas testosteroni*. When I joined his lab, he had begun to unravel the metabolic pathway by which testosterone is degraded by *P. testosteroni*, and suggested that I focus on how the A-ring of testosterone is oxidized.

My research progressed rapidly and within six months I had sufficient data for us to publish a "communication" (brief article) in the Journal of the American Chemical Society. The subsequent isolation and characterization of the two enzymes that catalyze the introduction of double bonds into the A ring of testosterone was more tedious and took another 18 months.

The atmosphere in Paul's lab was more stressful than in Birgit's, probably reflecting that he was a young, rising star, eager to make a name for himself. Paul was very fastidious about many things, including the need for pure reagents. Commercially obtained, analytical grade steroids were further purified by sublimation. All organic solvents were redistilled. Glassware was meticulously cleaned. Instruments were maintained in prime condition and, if they malfunctioned, often repaired by Paul himself. All experiments were elegantly designed, carefully controlled, and performed only in their ultimate form after considerable preliminary work to iron out any problems. Such final experiments came to be known as "Sunday experiments", because Paul often planned them for Sundays or holidays, a strategy that his students and postdocs believed was a deliberate indoctrination into what research is all about: long working hours, not always at convenient times. When I had my own lab at Syracuse University, I retained the designation "Sunday experiments" but did not insist that my students perform them on Sundays.

Something that I soon noticed about Paul, and that became increasingly obvious with time, was that he idolized Charles Huggins. He met with Huggins every Sunday morning, in Huggins's office, where they spent hours talking. I think Huggins looked on Paul as a young protégé, to whom he could impart his life's experiences and philosophy, grooming Paul for great things. What was amusing, was that Paul began to take on some of Huggins's idiosyncrasies, such as Huggins's way of speaking and his mannerisms. Apprenticeship is a common mode of learning in science (as it is in the arts), and this can be seen in the fact that, not infrequently, Nobel laureates beget other Nobel laureates, and although Paul did not win a Nobel Prize, I believe he was under consideration for one late in his career for his work on the cancer-prevention properties of various naturally occurring chemicals. He certainly became a great scientist of international renown.

My years spent in Paul's lab were very fruitful in learning new procedures and new ways of approaching problems, and they were decisive in shaping my attitude about academic science. Not everyone in his lab appreciated the way Paul ran his lab; to some he was intolerant of their personal needs, which, they understood him to indicate, needed to be subsumed to their research. I got along well with him and we developed a good personal relationship. He met my mother and sister and took an interest in my sister's health problems. Later on, when he was at Johns Hopkins, we became friends. He invited me a couple of times to give talks there, and vice versa, and on these occasions, we stayed at each other's homes. Since then we remained in contact until he died in 2019.

My Scientific Mentors:

My Ph.D. mentor, Birgit Vennesland,
University of Chicago (date unknown)

With my post-doc mentor, Paul Talalay, Ben May
Lab for Cancer Research, University of Chicago, 1957.
University of Chicago Photographic Archive.

To jump ahead, in the late 1980s, Paul became interested in the multiple physiological roles of the steroid dehydroepiandrosterone (DHEA). It happened that one of my graduate students, Ron Raineri, had shown as part of his Ph.D. research in the late 1960s that DHEA is a potent inhibitor of mammalian glucose 6-phosphate dehydrogenase (G6PD), and that this inhibition is uncompetitive with respect to both reaction participants, a very unusual mode of imhibition. Paul wondered if the physiological role of DHEA occurred through its inhibition of G6PD, and we therefore re-connected, and I spent a week in his lab at Johns Hopkins doing some experiments with one of his postdocs to help illuminate this problem, resulting in a publication. Also, in 2003 there was a special symposium at Johns Hopkins in honor of Paul's 80th birthday, titled "Protection Against Cancer: Genes and Chemistry", a topic in which Paul had been doing seminal work for a number of years. As part of the festivities, a "Talalay Intergenerational Lab Meeting" was held, featuring 17 of Paul's former students and postdocs, to which I was invited to give a talk. I also contributed a tribute to Paul for a booklet honoring him[2].

While I was a post-doc at the Ben May Lab, Dr. Huggins asked me, on several occasions, to look after visiting scientists, including one from Israel and two from the Soviet Union. This involved taking them back and forth from their hotel, or to venues they wanted to see, and in general, attending to their needs. I remember, especially, some amusing interactions with two Soviet scientists named Barkov and Chernukh. At that time, I owned a Morris Minor, a small car I had brought with me from my postdoctoral year in London. Shortly before the arrival of these scientists, the car had caught fire in front of my apartment and I had taken it in to a foreign car garage to be repaired. The garage lent me a car while mine was being repaired – a pink Buick convertible!! It was in this car that I went to the airport to pick up Barkov and Chernukh, embarrassed to be transporting them in this gaudy vehicle – rich American scientist in huge gaudy automobile obviously seeking to impress struggling scientists from egalitarian communist republic. I tried to preempt any remarks from them by explaining what had happened, emphasizing that this was not my car, that I owned a tiny car which was being repaired, but they pretended not to believe me, though it was clear that they were being good-humored about it. In fact, we got along very well. Betty and I invited them to dinner at our apartment, where Betty cooked a fine meal, about which Chernukh commented: "This is most taste-good meal I ever had"! I had actually met Chernukh before at the International Congress of Biochemistry in Moscow, where he had joined Peter and Irene Gore and Betty and me for dinner, and I would meet him again several years later when he came to Syracuse to visit Arthur Philips. In remembrance of his visit in Syracuse, and our times together, he gave me a large pocket pen-knife.

A memorable incident during those years was James Watson's visit to the University of Chicago to give a talk. This was shortly after it was announced, in 1962, that he was a co-recipient of the Nobel Prize in Physiology or Medicine, when he was on his way to Stockholm to receive the prize. Watson had obtained his B.S. from the University of Chicago, which he entered when he was only 15, and he was invited back, as a distinguished alumnus, to give a preview of his Nobel talk. It was clear that this event would attract a very large audience, so the University's largest lecture hall, an auditorium at the Law School, was reserved for the event. The auditorium was filled to capacity well before the talk. When Watson began talking, he noticed that there was no blackboard and asked if one could be obtained. The Law School is across The Midway from the rest of the campus, but Paul Talalay rushed to the Ben May Lab to get a blackboard. Meanwhile, Watson began his talk in an almost inaudible voice, facing away from the audience. When Paul came back, maybe 15 minutes later, Watson continued and, as I recall, never did use the blackboard. It was a terrible talk and was the first of several of his subsequent behaviors, including racist remarks about the inferior intelligence of African Americans, and his condescending remarks about Rosalind Franklin, that caused me to dislike him.

After I had been in Paul's lab for about 18 months, Charles Huggins invited me to accept a research position at the Ben May Lab. I don't think I recognized what an honor that was at the time, as it indicated that Huggins thought well enough of me to consider a possible permanent position there in the future. I told him that I needed to get away from Chicago for a while, having been there since 1950, and he concurred, saying he would hold the position open for me. That was an enviable option to have. I decided to spend another postdoctoral year, and to go back to England for it, as I still had strong feelings for that country and longed to get back there. I contacted George Popják, who was one of the principal scientists reearching the biosynthesis of cholesterol, and who was then the head of the Experimental Radiopathology Research Unit at the Medical Research Council at Hammersmith Hospital in London, to ascertain if he had an opening in his lab. He did, and agreed to my spending a year with him. I applied for, and was granted a postdoctoral fellowship by the National Cancer Institute.

I travelled to England aboard the S.S. United States (and returned almost a year later on the Queen Elizabeth). The voyage was a great adventure that began with my mother, TaMa, Liz, Lore, Lore Parker, Frank Lionel, David Ostrolenk and Lois seeing me off. The food and entertainment were excellent. I won the shuffle board championship! I called Betty from the boat.

My research in George Popják's lab concerned the isolation and partial purification from pig liver, of mevalonic kinase, the enzyme that catalyzes a key step in the biosynthesis of cholesterol. Coincidentally, this enzyme had been also partially purified from yeast by T.T. Tchen, who was one of my fellow graduate students in Birgit Vennesland's lab at the University of Chicago, and who was now doing post-doctoral research in Konrad Bloch's lab at Harvard. Bloch and Feodor Lynen eventually received the Nobel Prize for their work on the elucidation of the mechanism of cholesterol biosynthesis, and Popják and John Cornforth were strong contributors to this work whose exclusion from the Nobel Prize was viewed by some as unfair. Perhaps Popják's disappointment was later compounded by the fact that Cornforth shared the Nobel Prize in Chemistry in 1975 for his work on the stereochemistry of enzyme-catalyzed reactions.

Popják, who was born in Hungary, was an energetic, internationally renowned, hands-on scientist whose work was highly regarded, and whose enthusiasm was infectious. But the lab itself was quite low-key. Many in the lab were quite laid back and the contrast with those American labs with which I was familiar was startling. Sharing my office in Popják's lab was another American, E. H. "Pete" Ahrens, a physician from the Rockefeller Institute for Medical Research who was then a leader in the field of lipid nutrition, at the center of the debate on whether dietary change could help individuals avoid atherosclerosis. As I recall, he was there to do some writing and, indeed, he started off every day with a whole batch of sharpened pencils and a yellow legal pad, wrote furiously and, as soon as one pencil was no longer sharp, took up another. We had a very amicable relationship. I introduced him to the Schlesingers, with whom he and his wife Bonnie became friends. The best thing that happened to me in Popják's lab was that I met Irene Gore, who also worked there, which led to a long and deep friendship with her and her husband Peter. Also, as I describe elsewhere, the year spent in London was a cultural feast for me. My salary from my postdoctoral fellowship was sufficient to allow me to attend many plays and concerts. In addition, I was able to reconnect with the Schlesingers and their nephew Steve Webber and his family, to visit my former school, to go to Filkins to see John Cripps, and to participate in many other enriching experiences. What the year lacked in scientific stimulation was more than offset by the cultural and personal benefits.

I returned to Chicago, and to the Ben May Lab in the fall of 1959 with the title of Research Instructor. I was now an academic scientist.

CHAPTER 5

Our Interracial Marriage

In 1958 I met Betty Samuels, my future wife, at that famous bar, Jimmy's, which caters to the intellectual University of Chicago community. I was with my friend Howard Goldfine, and Betty was with her sister Joanne and her friend, Doris. A mutual friend, Sonny, introduced Howard and me to Betty, Joanne, and their friend. At first I was attracted to Joanne, who was very outgoing and attractive, and I only subsequently recognized that Betty, who was quieter, seemed to have much more depth. Interestingly, apparently, a similar situation occurred when my father first met my mother, Charlotte. Her sister, Martha, was also present, and she, like Joanne, was much more outgoing than Charlotte, and my father was first attracted to Martha.

I had met Sonny, who was African American, and his white wife, Mary-Lou when I became involved with an inter-racial group outside the university some years earlier. As I mentioned in Chapter 4, the highly intellectual atmosphere at the University of Chicago, led me to turn to an inter-racial group off campus, where warmth and genuine feeling abounded, which included Sonny and Mary-Lou who held the group together. I spent quite a lot of time with this group, and was briefly involved romantically with one of the women. Sonny had a sports car and Betty had met him after she bought a Volkswagen in the 1950s, an uncommon car on the streets in America in those days, and her friend Doris had a BMW. They got together with Sonny and Mary-Lou through their common interest in cars. Although I didn't realize it at the time, this interracial group and Sonny were a gift in my life.

I have often thought about what attracted me so much to Betty. She was a beautiful woman, but more importantly, she was a woman of great depth, more so than any other woman I had dated. I had never admired and loved a woman so deeply, someone with whom I had so much in common. We talked about a wide range of subjects, the arts, philosophy, religion, books, our ideas about life in general -- there seemed to be nothing that we could not discuss in depth. Years later I began to search myself more deeply,

Betty and I at our wedding, Chicago, 1960

to try to uncover what other factors might have been involved in my being so attracted to Betty. Despite our different backgrounds, we each belonged to a group that had been marginalized and despised for centuries, and that had suffered monstrous atrocities. I was a Jewish boy from Germany, Betty was an African American girl from the South Side of Chicago.

Before I came to the United States at the age of 16, I had never interacted with African Americans. I knew nothing about the history of African Americans in this country, about slavery, reconstruction, or Jim Crow. The only African Americans I had seen were among American soldiers stationed in England during the war. I played the part of Koko in our school's production of Gilbert and Sullivan's *The Mikado*, and one of Koko's songs in that opera begins: "As someday it may happen that a victim must be found" and that includes the line: "There's the nigger serenader, and the others of his race"; I had no idea that the word nigger was derogatory.

Very shortly after I arrived in America I began to read things in the newspaper that were very disparaging of Negroes (as they were then called). I found this very disturbing, and began reading and collecting more articles that made me aware of racism. I soon felt deep empathy for Negroes, and identified with them from the perspective of someone who had witnessed extreme racism in Nazi Germany.

This feeling was enhanced by the fact that I had difficulty identifying with Jews, for reasons that I describe elsewhere (see Chapter 10). I had no social interactions with African Americans while I was at Rutgers, and there were none in any of the organizations I belonged to, except for one man in the drama group, Queen's Players. My social life at that time revolved virtually entirely around David and Phyllis Ostrolenk; there were no African Americans in their circle. There were no African American students or faculty in the Biochemistry Department at the University of Chicago, and none in any of the groups I was involved with there.

Betty's father James Samuels, who came to Chicago from Tennessee, was one of six siblings. He was an electrician but, as an African American, he was barred from joining the union representing electricians, the International Brotherhood of Electrical Workers, and thus precluded from most lucrative jobs. He also had his own contracting business and was an inventor, which helped to supplemented his income. He was self-taught, self-educated and fiercely independent, a trait that all his children imbibed. Mr. Samuels had a shop behind the house, containing various machines, where he had his business, worked on his inventions, and where he enlisted his two sons, Jimmy and Tony, to help him. Betty's mother, Mabel, was a homemaker, one of three children, who was born in Nebraska. After her husband died, she worked as a receptionist at Encyclopedia Britannica. The family lived in a small house on Ada Street, in the Englewood neighborhood of Chicago's South side, and they rented out the top floor.

Betty was the second of four children. Joanne, the oldest, had literary and artistic tastes and aspirations, and exquisite taste in clothes. She worked as an audiologist in the Chicago Public School system, and was deeply involved in the Civil Rights Movement in Chicago. James Jr., known as Jimmy, was the third child. He was very smart and individualistic. Already as an adolescent, Jimmy aspired to get away from home and make something of himself. He did not want to wind up becoming his father's assistant. After two years as a chemistry major at Ripon College in Wisconsin, Jimmy was called up for two years of military service. In 1960, he married Delores and they had a daughter, Lauren, who was born about a year before our daughter, Karen. Jimmy was an electromechanical engineer who earned a B.S. in mechanical and aerospace engineering and a B.S. in electrical engineering, both from the Illinois Institute of Technology in Chicago. He was devoted to keeping fit and eating well, before this became popular. The youngest of the children was Tony, who was blessed with a magnetic personality that attracted a large group of friends. He worked as an electrician and died, tragically, when he was only 29 years old, leaving three young sons.

As the relationship between Betty and me became more serious, several family members and friends talked to me about the risks of an inter-racial marriage. Some thought it could impact my career. Others warned that there might be those who would shun us. A major concern voiced by most was the difficulties our children would encounter in this racial society. At that time, it seemed that I would bear the brunt of the criticism and disdain by the members of the predominantly white society in which I was embedded, but it was also the case that many members of the African American community scorned those who married outside their race. The concern voiced by my family and friends was for our children, and for me, never for Betty. But, in fact, the difficulties that ensued were for her, not for me. In retrospect, this was not unexpected because, for our entire married life we lived in a predominantly white society. Our daughter, Karen, also faced difficulties as a bi-racial child which neither she nor we, fully understood or dealt with at the time. These difficulties resurfaced much later in her life and had a profound effect on her. We (especially I) did not fully understand those difficulties, and although we sought professional help, we probably failed to deal with them adequately. The reasons, in hindsight, were complicated. The fact that Karen became an extraordinary, gifted woman with a deeply committed, spiritual foundation and a very successful career, is a tribute to her own hard work on herself, and her resilience.

Betty and I discussed these and many other issues, and the very fact that it was necessary to do so was, I think, hurtful and demeaning for Betty. The fact that we did decide to marry was a clear (if youthful and perhaps naive) affirmation of our faith that our love, and how we lived our life together, would overcome any problems that might arise. Like most marriages, ours had its ups and downs. Many of the difficulties others had predicted did not materialize. My career was certainly not impacted. None of our friends shunned us, and if others did, we probably never knew or cared.

We also went through some very challenging times that severely strained our marriage. When we married in 1960, interracial marriages were still illegal in about half the states. Societal attitudes could not help but affect our marriage despite our love and commitment to each other, although this influence was probably subtle. A bigger strain occurred in 1963, just three years after we were married, when we moved from Chicago to Syracuse, where I accepted a faculty position at Syracuse University. This was a huge change for Betty, the magnitude of which I did not fully comprehend at the time. It was the first time that Betty left the large, predominantly African American community in segregated Chicago, where she had lived her entire life, and settled in a predominantly white community in segregated Syracuse. She had become deeply involved with African American history. It was an enormous culture shock for her, only mitigated somewhat by the fact that we lived in the University neighborhood and quickly became friends with many liberal people. Syracuse was a largely white city, segregated like Chicago, but the black community was mostly poor; there were not many middle-class African Americans, and Betty had difficulty connecting with them and she found few African American friends. I wasn't fully aware of the magnitude of this effect on her, because I was immediately caught up in establishing a biochemistry program at the University, as well as securing external funding for, and initiating my research program, so that I was under a lot of pressure myself. I have only recently come to understand just how difficult this must have been for her. The book *White Fragility* by Robin DiAngelo, made it starkly clear to me that her isolation was a constant, everyday phenomenon from which she was unable to escape. She was living in a community in which everyone assumed "white" was "normal"; she was different. This did not have to involve any overt racism, just everyday assumptions. There were instances when she would comment on her discomfort, even among our friends (which were almost all white), and some circumstances where she was actually afraid, e.g. when driving to meetings of the Black Wholeness Retreats in the Catskills, in case the car broke down and she had to try to get assistance from a (white) rural farmer. I didn't really understand her concerns, and when she expressed feelings of (subtle) racial animus from some of our friends, I would argue with her about it. As a white immigrant, I became part of the white society here, and, unwittingly part of the white privileged society. The fact that I could not understand it, which would have assured her of my love, must have helped to put distance between us.

We were very fortunate that some of the problems that are common in marriages did not arise in ours. Money was never an issue; I don't think we ever had an argument about finances. In-laws were not an issue. Although Betty's parents and my mother was very concerned before we married, they became totally supportive once we did. My mother and Betty became good friends and had a very close relationship. The same was true of Betty and my sister Liz. Likewise, the others in my family -- my aunt "TaMa", and my cousin Lore, had very good relationships with Betty. I was on excellent terms with both of Betty's parents as well as with her siblings Joanne, Jimmy and Tony, and with Jimmy's wife Delores. We frequently visited with my family and Betty's, and they visited with us.

Something else that helped to forge a strong bond between us was that we were both very committed to creating a beautiful home. Betty had exquisite taste, and from the very beginning, we agreed on the choice of furniture and art works that we purchased. Our first home, an apartment at Prairie Shores in Chicago, was beautifully appointed, something on which family members and many of our guests commented. All our homes in Syracuse were beautiful, and many of our family and friends would comment on this and on the atmosphere of tranquility. We were both devoted to our daughter, Karen, and tried to provide various life-enriching opportunities for her. Because of my job, I saw less of her than Betty, and so for some time I took her out to lunch on Saturdays so we could share some time together. When we got our second dog, Shaka, we let him sleep in Karen's room. She began to look after him, and this responsibility proved to be very beneficial for her at that stage of her life.

Both of us were deeply committed to social justice and civil rights, a commitment that was manifested shortly after our arrival in Syracuse in April 1963. That month, there was a demonstration in Birmingham, Alabama, which led to Martin Luther King's incarceration and his famous Letter from a Birmingham Jail. In May, televised news reports showed fire hoses and police dogs being turned on civil rights demonstrators in Birmingham. August saw the huge civil rights march on Washington and Martin Luther King's famous I Have a Dream speech. The country was roiled by the civil rights movement and Syracuse, too, was impacted by these events. A federally supported urban renewal project had been launched that would create new public housing, expand the facilities of Upstate Medical School, create a museum, and construct an elevated interstate highway (Route 81) through the city. The homes of nearly 1300 African-American citizens that were concentrated in this area, the 15th Ward, were being razed to make way for the project, destroying the close-knit community. Insufficient provisions had been made to relocate those threatened with the loss of their homes, who would be unlikely to find housing in predominantly white neighborhoods at a time when there was still de facto segregation, or to halt discrimination in housing. The Syracuse chapter of the Congress for Racial Equality (CORE) was headed by George Wiley, the first African-American professor hired by the Syracuse University Department of Chemistry. In 1963, Wiley mobilized a protest against the urban renewal project that became a large citizens' movement that attracted the participation of numerous students and faculty members from Syracuse University.

With Betty and Karen, California, 2003

Betty and I had already met George a few months earlier. After I was offered a faculty position at Syracuse University, we visited Syracuse in order for both of us to learn enough about the town and the University, and how it would be for an interracial couple, so that we could make the decision whether or not I should accept the offer. I learned that George was the head of Syracuse CORE, so I called him and asked whether we could meet him when we visited. He agreed, and it turned out that he was married to a white woman, Wreatha, and so a bond naturally developed, and we learned quite a lot of information from both of them that was helpful for us in making our decision to accept the offer. When we did move to Syracuse, in June 1963, George and Wreatha had a big party for us where we met many people, some of whom became our friends.

Not long after we arrived in Syracuse, we joined CORE and began participating in the protest. There were large rallies, at which George and others spoke, urging people to join in the protests, and these were very inspirational. Every day, groups of us would engage in various acts of civil disobedience, like disrupting the work by climbing onto the equipment that was being used to tear down the houses, and some of us would be arrested. More than one hundred citizens were arrested for civil disobedience, including fifty-nine Syracuse University students, twelve faculty members, and three faculty wives. Betty and I were among those arrested, and I spent one night in jail. Faith Seidenberg, an attorney associated with the ACLU, represented those arrested at their arraignments, and there were various sympathetic citizens who provided bail money when needed.

The local newspaper's editor published editorials that were hostile toward these demonstrations and George Wiley. The University's Chancellor, William Tolley, announced that students who had been arrested or detained would be placed on disciplinary probation, stating that no one was above the law and that those who engaged in civil disobedience would have to be willing to accept penalties and punishment. However, the University Senate Subcommittee on Academic Freedom, Tenure, and Professional Ethics challenged Tolley's authority in such cases, and three days later a memo titled "University Leadership in Crisis" was signed by ninety-five faculty members and sent to Tolley. It noted faculty concern for the lack of basic democratic ideals and asked for a statement protecting the rights of all members of the Syracuse community. Four days later, Tolley rescinded his previous directive for probation of the students who had participated, and two weeks later he announced that no one would suffer punitive action by the University because of their participation in the civil rights demonstrations.

Professor Marshall Jennison, chairman of my department, met with me and Roy Doi, another member of our department who participated in the protests – to voice his disapproval, but he did not threaten us with reprisals.

In retrospect, my own participation in these demonstrations, just a few weeks after I arrived in Syracuse and long before I achieved tenure, was a risky thing to do. I don't recall, at the time, being concerned about this. I was deeply committed to the protest, and excited to be able to voice my support in a small way to the larger civil rights movement that was sweeping the country. My feelings about this, and more detailed descriptions of some of the events, are contained in excerpts from letters I wrote to my mother at the time[1]. She was very concerned about my actions and I tried to allay her fears.

The urban renewal project was ultimately a failure in achieving its principal objective. It failed to eradicate slums, it simply moved them around. But it did strengthen the civil rights movement in Syracuse and, arguably, increased coverage by the local news media about the existing problems. Six decades later, a federally funded project was initiated to remove the I-81 overpass. Its objectives included attempts to redress the wrongs suffered by the Africa American community during the 1960s.

Another problem that arose for Betty and me was that we were unable to have a child. We sought help, to no avail, but eventually we decided to adopt and were both excited to have a mixed-race daughter in our lives, but probably not sufficiently prepared to deal with some of the difficulties of parenting a biracial child. Our move to Syracuse and the period of Karen's childhood was a time of great stress for Betty. I was probably not sufficiently sensitive to this, and it left some deep scars.

All these factors produced serious strains on our marriage, and we sought counselling, which was of some help. The stress all this had on me caused me to make some bad decisions and we came perilously close to getting a divorce. Fortunately, despite everything, we were still committed to each other and to staying together, which was the best decision we made since deciding to marry. The 59 years of our marriage were filled with an abundance of wonderful things, many of which we shared. We had a beautiful daughter whom we loved, and who grew into a wonderful, gifted woman with a deep spiritual core. We always had a beautiful home about which we both cared. We did some amazing traveling together (see Chapter 9). As noted above, we were deeply involved in and committed to the civil rights movement

Betty and I, in Syracuse NY, 2005

in the early 1960s and both were arrested and went to jail after participating in a demonstration. We shared a deep love of classical music, which found its most meaningful expression in our membership in the Syracuse University Oratorio Society for over 30 years, rehearsing every week during the seasons, performing concerts, mostly with the Syracuse Symphony Orchestra. We were subscribers to Syracuse Stage for many years, attending some marvelous plays together. We attended many concerts, went to numerous lectures, participated in a Book Group for over 40 years, and in a Havurah group for many years, and we had family and friends who came to stay with us on numerous occasions.

We both loved dogs. We got our first dog, a brown standard poodle we named Cocoa, in 1965. He was smart, rambunctious, and lovable, and became an integral part of our family. When we went to England for my sabbatical, 1972-73, our friend Rhoda, who is a lover of cats, but not so much of dogs, kept him for us. We had to put him down when he was 18, and Betty was devastated. She bought a little yucca plant and planted it in his food bowl. It grew until it reached the ceiling. We took a cutting and planted it, and it, too, thrived. We repeated that process several times, so we had our "Cocoa plant" for 37 years.

Shortly after we lost Cocoa, we got another standard poodle, a black one we named Shaka, who also became a member of the family, was just as lovable as Cocoa, and lived for 17 years. He, too, finally had to be put down.

We gave each other space to do many things individually. I did a lot of traveling in connection with my profession, attending conferences, participating in collaborative research at other institutions. As a member of the Association for the Study of Classical African Civilizations, Betty attended numerous national meetings and went on three amazing excursions to Egypt, West Africa, and Brazil (see Chapter 9). For several years in the 1980s, Betty was deeply involved in researching the ancient Egyptian civilization and did some lecturing and a lot of writing on this topic. We enjoyed a very rich, fulfilling life together.

CHAPTER 6

My Professional Career

Teaching

I returned to Chicago, and to the Ben May Lab in the fall of 1959 with the title of Research Instructor. I was finally on the verge of beginning my career as an academic scientist. I was situated in Paul Talalay's lab and was free to work on independent projects without any other obligations, without the need to apply for funding, but with the opportunity, if I wished, to participate in teaching courses in the Biochemistry Department. It was, in effect, an opportunity to start my own research program that I could, eventually, take to another institution for a regular faculty appointment as an academic biochemist. It would have been possible for me to get a faculty appointment elsewhere without this opportunity, but it was undoubtedly beneficial for me because I was slow to develop true independence.

I developed two projects that grew out of some of Paul's interests, one on fatty acid synthesis and one on the enzyme glucose 6-phosphate dehydrogenase, both in the lactating rat mammary gland. I devoted most of my time to these projects, but I also did some teaching in the Biochemistry Department and found that I enjoyed and was good at that. I also had access to a technician who worked in Paul's lab, but spent some time on my projects, giving me the opportunity to direct someone else's work.

After two years, I was promoted to Research Assistant Professor, an indiction that I was doing well. However, by the fourth year I was becoming impatient to strike out on my own, to obtain my own research grant, and to become involved in teaching courses and training my own graduate students. I discussed with Paul my desire to look for a faculty position and he was supportive. He was, at that time, being considered for the position of Chair of the Department of Pharmacology at Johns Hopkins University Medical School in Baltimore, which he subsequently accepted, so it was a propitious time for me to move. Also, shortly after I talked with Paul, he received a letter from Arthur Phillips, a former classmate of his at MIT, who was then a professor at the Department of Bacteriology and Botany at Syracuse University, indicating that his department wished to hire a biochemist, and asking Paul if he knew anyone who might be interested. I had never heard of Syracuse, and was not excited at the prospect of being in a Department of Bacteriology and Botany – the name conjured up 19th century science – but I thought it would be a good opportunity to be interviewed for a job and decided to apply for the position. (The Department of Bacteriology and Botany was combined with the Zoology Department in 1970 to become the Department of Biology, a much more acceptable name for me.) I was asked to come to Syracuse to give a seminar and to be interviewed for the position, which I did in October 1962.

Several things about that visit stand out in my mind. First, it snowed when I arrive in Syracuse. Chicago had not yet had any snow, and Jay Smith, a faculty member of the Department of Bacteriology and Botany who met me at the airport, assured me that snow this early was unusual for Syracuse. Second, everyone I met on my visit was very friendly and appeared to be eager for me to come to Syracuse. This included not only faculty from the Department of Bacteriology and Botany (B&B), but also faculty from the Department of Zoology, including the chairman, Fred Sherman. Third, the Biological Research Lab building was under construction. This new, state-of-the-art lab facility, funded by the NIH, was a much-needed addition to the Department of Bacteriology and Botany, which was attempting to expand its research focus as a necessary prerequisite to hiring research-oriented faculty – of which I was one of the first. I was taken to the space, not yet finished, which would become my lab, and was very impressed. Fourth, I would be the first *bona fide* biochemist at Syracuse University, and it would be my responsibility to develop biochemistry courses and a biochemistry program. Finally, I was told that the department was negotiating to hire two other young assistant professors from first-rate laboratories in the relatively new area of molecular biology. The latter was a key aspect in my considering their offer seriously, as it indicated that the department was genuinely interested in modernizing. What had begun as a chance to practice my interviewing skills turned into an enticing job opportunity.

I discussed all this with Betty and we agreed that it looked promising, but that Betty should come back with me for another visit to see how she saw it. As I discuss elsewhere (see Chapter 5), we had a useful meeting with George and Wreatha Wiley on this visit. I also learned that the two other scientists who were being hired were Roy Doi, then a postdoc in Sol Spiegelman's lab at the University of Illinois, and Elias Balbinder, then a postdoc with David Bonner at the University of California San Diego, both outstanding labs. I received an official offer from Syracuse University, which I accepted. I returned for another visit that April, to participate with Roy Doi in writing a grant proposal. On that visit it also snowed, and, again I was told that this was unusual. Neither was true, but neither dissuaded me from accepting the offer. I am forever grateful to Art Phillips, not only for his efforts that led me to Syracuse, but for his imaginative leadership in modernizing the Department of Bacteriology and Botany, including his participation in obtaining the funding for constructing the Biological Research Labs. His efforts represented the early underpinnings of the development of the current Department of Biology's impressive Life Sciences Complex. In June 1963, I began my appointment as Assistant Professor of Biochemistry in the Department of Bacteriology and Botany at Syracuse University.

To advance in their academic institution, scientists are evaluated in three areas of endeavors: teaching, research, and service. At Syracuse University, this is

With Roy Doi, Syracuse University, 1964

accomplished in two stages: first by a departmental committee and then by a college committee. The committees' recommendations then go for approval to the dean and then to the vice chancellor for academic affairs. One's teaching is judged by examining the courses taught, and their evaluations by students. Research is generally judged by productivity, i.e. the number and quality of publications, and by outside evaluations solicited from scientists in the same area of research. One's recognition by scientists in one's area of expertise is also noted. Service is a measurement of the individual's participation in departmental, college and university committees.

My principal teaching duties at Syracuse University were in the areas of Biochemistry and Enzymology, but I also taught some other courses, two of which are described below. Setting up the Biochemistry program was a challenge that I enjoyed. I taught the first Biochemistry lecture course jointly with Tom Fondy, who joined the Zoology Department in 1965, and we also set up a lab course. For this we had to devise suitable experiments and purchase the necessary equipment and reagents within a tight budget. The lecture course was initially for one semester, carrying 3 credits, but it soon expanded and, eventually became a two-semester course, 3 credits per semester. The course was always team-taught and other, regular participants included Jim Florini, Joe Merrick and Sam Chan. The lab course was eventually taken over by Sam Chan.

Developing the lecture course in Biochemistry involved deciding which aspects of this vast and growing field to emphasize, which text book to use, as well as numerous other details. This task was facilitated by the fact that we were familiar with the field and had a selection of available texts to draw on.

I developed and taught a graduate course in my research specialty, Enzymology, and subsequently also in Enzyme Regulation. For these I relied, for the most part, on the research literature, and I always updated my lectures to reflect the latest research results. With Jack Bryan, I taught a graduate seminar on proteins and enzymes, in which students learned how to read research papers from the literature critically. Tom Fondy and I developed a course on Biology and Human Values, in which we attempted to make Biology relevant to non-science majors. I enjoyed teaching and, apparently, was good at it and I especially enjoyed interacting with students on a one-on-one basis.

This occurred frequently with both undergraduate and graduate students working in my laboratory, but I also encouraged students in the classes I taught to make appointments to see me.

I engaged in several kinds of teaching. The Biochemistry Lecture course involved almost exclusively giving lectures, which is the least satisfactory, and least effective way to teach, but the only one appropriate for a course enrolling such a large number of students (up to about 120). Before each exam, I had voluntary review sessions, in which I answered questions and engaged in some discussion, which was quite effective. For my Enzymology course, and the one on Enzyme Regulation, I also relied primarily on lectures, but because these classes were smaller, there was more opportunity for discussions in class. In my "Mellon" course (see below) I gave no lectures. Each session involved discussions with the students. This was a far more effective, and enjoyable form of teaching. For my graduate and undergraduate students engaged in research in my lab, the mode of teaching was, effectively, apprenticeship, and this is by far the most effective mode of transmitting information. I usually met these students at weekly research meetings, but was available to them on a daily basis and often met with them informally this way.

Some students expressed their gratitude by sending me notes or cards after they left Syracuse University and were in their career, or in Medical School or some other program, and this was very gratifying. Several students made donations to the Biology Department in my honor. Ghaleb Daouk, who engaged in independent research in my lab as an undergraduate (see Chapter 7) endowed the "H. Richard Levy - Ghaleb H. Daouk Undergraduate Student Support Fund" in my honor in 2001. In 2021, my Ph.D. student Peter Robison (see Chapter 7) made a major gift to set up the "H. Richard Levy Endowed Biology Research Fund". Several former students have contributed donations to this fund: Mark Davino, who was an undergraduate research student in my lab in the 1990s, and whose outstanding work garnered him co-authorship on one research publication as well as being named a Syracuse University Scholar, made his gift "in honor of H. Richard Levy, the most influential teacher in my life". One student, Sriram ("Krish") Krishnaswamy who was Jack Bryan's graduate student, but on whose Ph.D. committee I served, has called me every year around Christmas time since 1988, for a long chat. My last two graduate students, Ted Lee and Michael Cosgrove, have become friends. I follow the careers of my former students with great interest, and relish their accomplishments as much as those of my daughter.

In 1998, I was honored by being awarded the William Wasserstrom Prize for the Teaching of Graduate Students. This award is given annually in memory of Professor William Wasserstrom of the English Department, who died in 1985. I knew him and his wife, Rose. The award was presented to me at the Doctoral Dinner and reception of the Graduate School to which Betty and I were invited, but I had no idea that I was to be the recipient. Robert Jensen, who was the Dean of the College at the time, presented the award to me after the dinner[1].

A Novel Molecular Biology Course

Within a few months, in 1962 and 1963, three young faculty members trained in biochemistry and molecular biology at leading laboratories in the United States joined the Department of Bacteriology and Botany at Syracuse University: Elias Balbinder, Roi Doi, and I. One decade earlier, in 1953, Watson and Crick published their seminal paper on the structure of DNA, one of the most important publications in all science, and one that created a paradigm shift in biology. Since then, a cascade of discoveries had changed the science of biology. The protein, insulin was sequenced by Fred Sanger, the first protein to be sequenced; Jacob and Monod published their model of the operon; Crick, Brenner and Jacob proposed the concept of a messenger molecule; and an unknown biochemist, Marshall Nirenberg, elucidated the first mRNA codon, cracking the genetic code; Kendrew reported the first three-dimensional structure of a protein, myoglobin, followed shortly by Perutz's report on the three-dimensional structure of hemoglobin. In 1965 Monod, Wyman and Changeux published their concerted model for allosteric proteins, followed in 1966 by Koshland's sequential model. The significance of these discoveries can be judged by the fact that Watson, Crick, Sanger, Jacob, Monod, Crick, Brenner, Nirenberg, Kendrew, and Perutz all received a Nobel Prize for their work.

The ramifications of these revolutionary discoveries had not yet penetrated the curriculum in the Department of Bacteriology and Botany at Syracuse University. This fact, and Elias's, Roy's and my scientific backgrounds that had incorporated the latest findings in biochemistry and molecular biology, created our strong desire – accompanied by not a little hubris – to propel the department into the era of modern biology. A professional and personal bond was established among the three of us. Over a period of several weeks during the summer of 1963 we met for lunch to plan a course that could accomplish this. (This was, incidentally, at the same time that I participated in civil rights demonstrations, described in Chapter 5). I had taken a course as a graduate student at the University of Chicago in which prominent biochemists from across the country presented their latest findings to us students. I suggested to Elias and Roy that we should collaborate to present a course in the Department of Bacteriology and Botany, based on this idea, as a means of bringing the latest concepts in biochemistry and molecular biology to the department. They agreed enthusiastically, and the result was a proposal for a course entitled "Regulatory Control Mechanisms", that included inviting outstanding molecular biologists and biochemists at the cutting edge of specific areas of the field. We met with Professor Marshall Jennison, chairman of the department, to describe our idea. He shared our enthusiasm for the concept and asked me to present it at the next faculty meeting, where the faculty approved it. The fact that molecular biology was then an exciting new field, which had never been taught in the department, helped to make our idea appealing to everyone.

The course was organized as follows. Each of us presented lectures on a specific topic in preparation for one of the visitors. Shortly before the visitor's arrival, we distributed reprints of one or more articles suggested by the visitor, to prepare the students for the specific topic they were going to present. Each visitor spent two days at Syracuse University. On the first day, they talked to the class about their work, followed by an extensive discussion period. On the second day, each visitor gave a public lecture open to the scientific community at Syracuse University, the College of Forestry, Upstate Medical University, and others. On the first evening, the visitor attended a dinner hosted by Elias, or Roy, or me, at our homes, to which we invited other interested scientists. Financial support for the course, to cover the cost for the participating visitors, was provided by an NIH training grant that Roy had submitted earlier that year.

The first time we gave the course, in the Spring of 1965, we had the following visitors. Arthur Pardee from Princeton University, who received the Pfizer Award in Enzyme Chemistry in 1960 and the Sir Hans Krebs Medal in 1973, talked about feedback inhibition of enzymes; Phil Hartman from Johns Hopkins University discussed regulation of gene expression in bacteria; Ernest Borek from Columbia University discussed transfer RNA and its methylating enzymes; and Gordon Tomkins from NIH described the concept of allosteric proteins and the latest models that described their mode of action. Two years later the course was repeated, using the same format, with Jim Florini replacing Roy Doi, who had left to take a faculty position at the University of California at Davis. The four visitors that year were Robert Holley from Cornell University, who talked about the structure of transfer RNA, work for which he received the Nobel Prize the following year; Werner Maas from the NYU School of Medicine, who talked about the mechanism of repression of arginine biosynthesis in *E. coli*; Jean-Pierre Changeux from the Institut Pasteur in Paris who spoke about cooperativity in allosteric proteins, and who received the Wolf Prize in Medicine in 1982; and Daniel Atkinson from the University of California at Los Angeles who discussed the adenylate control hypothesis, a novel mechanism for the regulation of metabolism that he had developed.

Both years, the course was met with great enthusiasm by the students as well as the faculty. It succeeded in acquainting students and faculty with many of the core concepts in molecular biology, and succeeded in their incorporation into the curriculum. It also forged a strong sense of accomplishment among Elias, Roy, and me and a deep and lasting friendship.

The Mellon Project

As a biochemist, and as an enzymologist, the greatest proportion of my teaching was in those disciplines. As enjoyable as this was, one of the most rewarding and exciting activities during my 37 years on the Syracuse University faculty was my involvement in an interdisciplinary project sponsored by the Mellon Foundation that came to be known as "The Mellon Project", and the course that evolved from it. The objective of the project was to lower the barriers between professional and liberal education, initially by engaging a group of faculty from both the College of Arts and Sciences, and from the professional colleges within Syracuse University, in an extended seminar that would enhance mutual understanding of and appreciation for one another's disciplines; and then for the participants to develop courses that crossed the liberal-professional divide, ideally team-taught by a liberal arts and a professional faculty member.

In 1984, I was invited to participate in this endeavor. Although the details of what was to take place, or how long the project would last, were not specified, the fact that it was interdisciplinary very much appealed to me. I had always been interested in many other things besides biochemistry. For about a decade I participated in an organization, *Orbis Scientiae*, a faculty group from different disciplines from Syracuse University and the adjoining College of Environmental Science and Forestry and Upstate Medical School (both state institutions). *Orbis Scientiae's* objectives were to stimulate the research spirit in all fields of knowledge, to encourage research, to foster the interchange of ideas by discussion, and to recognize attainment in research. Members were research faculty from the three institutions who were chosen on the basis of scholarly attainment. The organization met four times per year for dinner and a lecture by one of its members. These meetings were always stimulating and educational and I enjoyed them very much.

I accepted the invitation to participate in the Mellon Project. The seminar was led by Peter Marsh, Professor of History, and included twenty faculty members from the Departments of Physics, English, History, Biology, Fine Arts, and Sociology and the Writing Program in the College of Arts and Sciences; and faculty from the College of Visual and Performing Arts, College of Engineering, School of Management, School of Nursing, Maxwell School of Citizenship, and Newhouse School of Public Communications.

We met over a two-year period, occasionally on weekends, except during May, when we met for a three-week period daily, both in 1986 and 1987. The discussions were wide-ranging, but were kept in focus by Peter Marsh, who proved to be an outstanding leader. Initially, each of us provided reading material for the whole group, introducing our area of expertise to the broader audience. Those of us, like I, from the College of Arts and Sciences, sought to make this relevant to the professional college to which it was related – in my case, to the Medical

School (which, however, was a separate institution in Syracuse, and thus not represented in the seminar). Those from the professional schools sought linkage for their material with liberal arts departments. A detailed account of the whole experience is found in a book, to which several of us contributed, titled *Contesting the Boundaries of Liberal and Professional Education: The Syracuse Experiment* edited by Peter Marsh (Syracuse University Press, 1988). The book was a collaborative effort. Each of us wrote a draft of our chapter, the drafts were circulated back and forth to the other participants, and critiqued during four long, intensive weekend meetings.

The discussions became deeper and more probing once we overcame these initial forays, and several concepts became central to our discussions, such as objectivity, embeddedness, enculturation, and the impact of seeing. Embeddedness, we defined as "the ways in which thinking within the framework of any discipline or profession is shaped, limited, constrained, or enriched – often unconsciously and invisibly – by influences impinging from outside itself." (Melville & Segall, *Contesting the Boundaries...*, p. 116). Within our own field, we tend to minimize its embeddedness. Our "expertise" is often narrowly guided by our discipline, discounting other influences. Enculturation is "the recognition that every pattern of thought and action is shaped profoundly by the culture in which it arises." (Marsh, *Contesting the Boundaries...*, p. 112). The profound impact of seeing was brought home to us by our varied responses to the Norman Rockwell poster *Freedom from Want*, a scene showing a family Thanksgiving dinner, as well as our response to the civil engineer's showing of a film about the Brooklyn Bridge, allowing many of us, for the first time, to see the aesthetic dimensions of an engineering feat. (Radke & Melville, *Contesting the Boundaries...*, p. 99).

My course proved to be possibly the best example of the power of these concepts in the relationship between science and medicine. "The course says more than that there would be no [Western] medicine without science. It considers the possibility that science and its technological offshoots not only inform medicine, but constrain and distort it. The course makes the student consider that science and technology reflect a broader culture, and that medicine informed by science and technology is not the only conceivable medicine. It suggests that medicine as a profession has a culture of its own, with hard-to-bend rules governing doctor-patient relationships, norms governing physicians' modes of behavior, and economic considerations tied to the broader culture in which the profession exists. The course demonstrates as well that the conduct of medicine impacts, in turn, on that broader culture." (Melville & Segall, *Contesting the Boundaries...*, p. 124).

Our interactions were stimulating and fruitful. Hearing others' comments on our own area of expertise, was revelatory and had the power to make us aware of how insular some of our views were. This happened to me when I reported on Thomas Lewis's book *The Youngest Science: Notes of a Medicine-Watcher*, which I had suggested as relevant material to the group. I had been blinded, by Thomas's engaging writing style, to the fact that his focus on the scientific underpinnings of Western medicine made him insensitive to its human dimension. It proved to be an eye-opener that helped to generate my focus for the course that I would create.

A principal goal of the seminar was for us to generate honors courses that permeated the boundaries between professional and liberal arts education. My goal was to create a course in the Department of Biology that would help pre-medical students (a substantial proportion of our majors) confront some of the dilemmas of contemporary medicine. A dozen courses were, in fact, created, but for a variety of reasons, especially administrative ones, few survived. I taught my course ten times over a thirteen-year period.

As I began to read widely in an area that I had not previously explored, the outlines of a course emerged. I realized that such a course would be particularly relevant to students who intended to enter a career in the health professions, during a time when they still had the opportunity for reflection, an opportunity that would become lost once they entered medical school (or other health career-related post-graduate education), when such reflection would be impossible in their busy professional education. I sent this outline to the following physicians whose writings seemed especially relevant to what I wished to convey, explaining my goals and asking them for some feed-back: Lester King, a medical historian, author of *Medical Thinking, a Historical Preface*, formerly senior editor of the *Journal of the American Medical Association*; Edmund Pellegrino, Professor of Medicine and Medical Humanities, Director of the Joseph and Rose Kennedy Institute of Ethics, Georgetown University, author of

Humanism and the Physician; and George Engel, Professor Emeritus of Psychiatry and Medicine, University of Rochester Medical Center, author of numerous articles expounding on his biopsychosocial model of medicine. Each of these physicians wrote back enthusiastically about the need and importance of a course such as the one I had outlined, encouraging me to proceed.

Dr. Engel invited me to come to Rochester to discuss my ideas with him in greater detail. Over the years, we became friends and he was a guest participant in my course one year. He and I remained in contact over the next dozen years with an exchange of numerous letters, until his death in 1999. He remained interested in, and engaged with my course, providing support, encouragement and generous praise. I referred him to articles in the press and provided him with scientific information that he found useful for his writings. I sent him essays my students had written, which he read with great interest, encouraged by the fact that the concepts of humanistic medicine were being absorbed by students interested in pursuing medical careers. On two occasions, I described to him interactions with my physician about some puzzling symptoms I had experienced. His incisive responses to these encounters provided clear examples of missed opportunities in this patient-physician relationship. Our friendship was stimulating, intellectually rewarding and mutually beneficial.

The success of the Mellon Project was mixed. On the one hand, our in-depth discussions, mutual engagement in the endeavor, and exposure to new ways of thinking about teaching, undoubtedly made us better teachers. Yet, the administrative procedures and structures within universities constitute powerful constraints to breaking down the barriers between professional and liberal education. Departments and professional schools are domains with deeply entrenched procedures and expectations, and with limited resources. The Mellon courses would, necessarily require limited enrollments and would shift responsibility of the faculty members who teaches them from their normal, essential curricular assignments. Thus, they were viewed as a threat to the existing curriculum. I noted this in our book:

"Our aim is not to *supplant* the usual kind of courses with Mellon courses, but to *supplement* the curriculum with an array of Mellon courses so that, eventually, all students will have some understanding of the embeddedness of their field, or profession, in the rest of the world. This should not be viewed as a threat in any way to the conventional curriculum; without the conventional curriculum, Mellon courses would not exist. My course, for example, does not in any way lead to the conclusion that physicians should be exposed to less science, but rather that they should reflect on the impact science has on their profession". (Levy, in Marsh, *Contesting the Boundaries...*, p. 254).

My "Mellon" Course: The Impact of Science on Medicine

The first descriptions of my course, titled "The Impact of Science on Medicine", appears in our book (p. 130). Later, I changed the title to better reflect the content, to "The Impact of Technology and Culture on Medicine" and in 2002 I published an article about it in *The Advisor*, published by the National Association of Advisors for Health Professions. Many of the following comments about my course are taken from the article in *The Advisor*, and from my chapter in *Contesting the Boundaries of Liberal and Professional Education: The Syracuse Experiment*.

My principal goals in this course were to enable students to reflect on what it means to be a physician; to engage them in an examination of how technology affects the practice of medicine; to sensitize them to some of the predicaments of contemporary medicine; to illuminate the centrality of the patient-physician relationship in medicine; and to consider how culture influences our concepts of illness and disease. My premise was that by far the best time to do this is in college, before students become consumed by the relentless pressures in medical school, where they will have little time for reflection. Although the course was directed toward pre-medical or pre-health professional students, it was open to others and invariably benefitted from their participation. My primary objectives were to stimulate reflection and broaden thinking, not to impart facts to memorize. These goals were reflected in the ways in which I conducted the course and evaluated the students. The course met for two 90-minute sessions per week and the format entailed extensive reading and writing. Typically, we read major portions of six books as well as about 100 articles that I assemble in a course reader, and that included brief articles from the popular press, some that were contemporary illustrations of topics covered in the books, as well as articles form such journals as Perspectives in Biology and Medicine, Science, Nature, Journal of Medicine and Philosophy, Journal of the American Medical Association, and New England Journal of Medicine. It consisted virtually entirely of discussion; I only lectured briefly to explain concepts and to provide background. This format necessitated that enrollment be limited to about 12 students. There were no examinations. Students were graded on the basis of: 1) four short essays; 2) my subjective assessment of the quality of their discussions in class; 3) my evaluation of a journal they kept, in which they wrote about the readings, discussions, and their reflections; and 4) a term paper on a topic of their choosing but requiring my approval. My principal criterion in grading them was the extent and quality of their reflection about the subject matter, but I also paid attention to grammar, spelling, and style in the formal writing, because of the importance of these for clear thinking and communication.

The topics varied somewhat over the years, but the course remained focused on the goals above. The following topics were included in the final year I gave it: Essentials of Medicine; Impact of Technology on Medicine; Predicaments of Modern Medicine; The Biopsychosocial Model and Humanistic Medicine; Alternative and Complementary Medicine; Medicine and Culture. A brief summary of each of these follows.

Essentials of Medicine. A brief account of some of the ideas that pervaded medicine in the past used Lester King's book *Medical Thinking: A Historical Preface* to illustrate the fact that, while the physician's tools have changed dramatically during the past two centuries, their goals have remained unchanged. King describes these goals by listing those fundamental questions that physicians have always posed: What is the disease from which the patient suffers? How can we identify it? What can we do for it? How can we prevent it? How much confidence can we place in our assertions and judgments? How do we know if we are right? Physicians in the past were as intelligent, diligent, and concerned as are today's doctors. Although their actions may seem quaint and foolish today, we must not judge them by the standards of today's technologies and thinking, but in the context of those prevailing at the time. I pointed out that, in the future, some of our current medical ideas and practices will seem as strange as some of those from the past do today. I asked them to think of current practices that might appear as outlandish then as bloodletting does today, and upon reflection they could usually cite several. Bloodletting and the use of leeches were practiced because they often worked, although their over-use proved fatal. Students read about a plausible, current rationale for bloodletting and why leeches are sometimes used today in conjunction with microsurgery. Physicians who used bloodletting in the past did not understand its physiological basis, they did so on the basis of current, incomplete understanding. It surprised students to learn that today's physicians also use some medications and techniques with an incomplete understanding of their mode of action. What has characterized good physicians at all times is their ability to exercise good judgment.

The Impact of Technology on Medicine. This section utilized Stanley Joel Reiser's *The Impact of Technology on Medicine*, which begins by recounting how physicians who examined patients in the seventeenth and eighteenth centuries relied almost exclusively on the patient's narrative. Subsequent discoveries of various instruments and clinical techniques facilitated physicians' diagnosis of disease, some of which allowed them to see inside the body (e.g. X-ray machines) and appeared to diminish the need for the patient's participation in the clinical encounter. Yet, each new technique brought its own unique problems and, importantly, none eliminated the need to select and evaluate data, despite initial expectations to the contrary. Physicians can answer questions better with their new tools, but they need to rely on critical judgment as much as earlier physicians did, and students read articles on the evaluation of medical evidence. The advances that Reiser describes have led to profound changes in the practice of medicine and in the physician-patient relationship: "...the physician in the last two centuries has gradually relinquished his unsatisfactory attachment to subjective evidence – what the patient says – only to substitute a devotion to technological evidence – what the machine says. He has thus exchanged one partial view of disease for another".

Predicaments of Modern Medicine. After a brief discussion of several problems: operating room errors, assessing health risks, excessive performance of hysterectomies in the United States, and problems that arose after the diet pill Redux was approved by the FDA, we focussed on three predicaments in detail: the administration of diethylstilbestrol (DES) to pregnant women, the development and implantation of the artificial heart, and the swine flu immunization program. All three are described in Diana B. Dutton's *Worse Than the Disease. Pitfalls of Medical Progress*, but we read about the DES problem in *To Do No Harm. DES and the Dilemmas of Modern Medicine* by Roberta Apfel and Susan Fisher. I used Apfel and Fisher's book because the authors, as psychiatrists, focus not only on the physiological effects of DES, but on the emotional impact on the mothers and daughters, and the disruption of the relationships between mother and daughter and physician and patient. This viewpoint added a unique dimension, helping students to better understand the impact of traumatic, unintended medical intervention. Dutton's book devotes several chapters to a penetrating discussion of the lessons, questions, and challenges posed by these (and other) predicaments. My expectation was that reading and discussing these books would equip future health care professionals to deal with other predicaments that will surely arise in the future. We concluded this section by discussing some articles on managed care taken from the popular press.

The Biopsychosocial Model and Humanistic Medicine. This section served as the core of the course, because it highlights what lies at the core of medicine, i.e. the physician-patient relationship. Invariably, it engaged the students deeply, especially the book *Medicine as a Human Experience* by David Reiser and David Rosen. Underlying the successful treatment of his or her patients is the physician's understanding of the problems for which they seek relief. This is not limited to their diseases, but includes the subjective perception of their illnesses. Engel's biopsychosocial model has provided a paradigm that promises to restore balance to the increasing distortions in clinical medicine resulting from the emphasis, both in teaching and practice, to the technologies of medicine. Reiser and Rosen's book includes two chapters by George Engel that describe the clinical application of the biopsychosocial model. Students also read his classic article in which he first proposed the model, as well as articles that extend his ideas. The prologue in Reiser and Rosen's book, describing a medical student's painful passage through the often-dehumanizing rituals of medical school, made a deep impression on students.

The prevailing model in Western medicine, the biomedical model, rests on the assumption that diseases are the manifestation of one or more biological abnormalities in the patient. Spectacular advances in the application of biochemistry, genetics, molecular biology and related disciplines to medicine have led to the success of this reductionist approach to the diagnosis and treatment of many diseases. The biopsychosocial model, emphasizing the complexity of human beings and the multitude of interactions among the various levels of their being that comprise this complexity, postulates that persons may be ill because of malfunctions at any one of these levels, or of the interactions among them. It seeks scientific understanding of the person who feels ill, whereas the biomedical model searches for scientific explanations of the disease he might harbor.

In this section, we also read some essays from a collection, first published in the Journal of the American Medical Association, consisting of personal vignettes by medical students, interns, residents and patients that provide insights into their daily confrontation with medical problems. We also discussed articles on the placebo effect, the problem of pain and suffering, the linkage between emotion and reason, and the physiological effects of stress.

Alternative and Complementary Medicine. The emergence of alternative and complementary medicine as an enormous enterprise enthusiastically embraced by a large proportion of the American public, has had a major impact on health care in this country, and physicians need to understand the reason for its great appeal, and what this implies for the medical profession. The establishment of the Office of Alternative Medicine at the National Institutes of Health in 1992 (later the National Center for Complementary and Alternative Medicine), and the devotion of an entire issue of the Journal of the American Medical Association to this topic (in November, 1998) attest to the impact of alternative and complementary modes of treatment on contemporary medicine in the United States. We read some editorials from this issue of JAMA and then read Mehmet Oz's *Healing from the Heart. A Leading Heart Surgeon Explores the Power of Complementary Medicine.* A graduate of Harvard and the University of Pennsylvania School of Medicine, Oz directed the Columbia Presbyterian Medical Center's heart-assist device program. He combined his surgical skills with complementary treatments, and his western education with oriental techniques reflecting his Turkish ancestry. Students found this to be a revealing book that expanded their ideas about healing.

Medicine and Culture. The final section of the course explored the idea that the practice of medicine is inextricably linked to the culture in which it takes place. Lynn Payer's *Medicine and Culture. Varieties of Treatment in the United States, England, West Germany, and France* illustrates the surprising differences in medical practices in these four western countries that share a common medical heritage and similar life expectancies. Students found it astonishing that what is recognized as a clinical entity in one country does not exist, or is treated as an entirely different disease, in another. How can that be when we have scientific evidence for the etiology and clinical course of a disease? Reflection on and discussion of this and similar questions provided a broadening experience for future health care professionals.

Most years I included a session in which a health care professional visited the class. These visitors, who included physicians (including Dr. George Engel), a chiropractor, a pediatrician who also practiced homeopathic medicine, a medical ethicist, and a medical student, provided opportunities for students to interact with someone within the profession about which they are learning.

Impact of the Course

Most faculty members at Syracuse University are required to gather student surveys after a course is completed. We are pleased when students provide positive feed-back, as I certainly was when comments such as the following appeared among my student evaluations for this course. "Dr. Levy is an understanding, intellectual professional - an almost extinct species." "Class discussions and debates were especially productive, because we were able to challenge what we were reading to develop a better and stronger opinion for ourselves." "The professor was always well prepared and very enthusiastic about what he was saying. I admired him. Up to now I haven't had a role model yet, until now." "I was always coming out of class enthusiastic to argue with my friends about what was brought up in class." "There is an element to Dr. Levy that motivates a student to perform to the best of his/her abilities. I can't quite explain what it is. It may be because I always felt I was getting his best, and felt compelled to do the same in return."

As gratifying as these comments were, they did not reveal whether the students had learned anything, and if so, whether it would prove to be useful later in their lives. I attempted, therefore, to ascertain whether my course did have a more lasting effect. My article in *The Advisor* included the results of a survey I sent to 65 former students in the course, 30 of whom replied. Of these, 5 were currently medical students, 13 were physicians, 3 were in other health professions, and 9 were "other". All but two (and they were "other") found the course, in retrospect, had been very useful (31) or somewhat useful (13). They also provided comments that I had invited them to submit about the course which expanded on their replies and which confirmed my impression that the course did, indeed, have more than just a transitory benefit.

I believe that my participation in the Mellon Project, and designing and presenting the course were the best thing I did at Syracuse University. It was totally original – I don't believe there existed another course like it in the United States – and I felt a sense of real accomplishment in having created it through my own efforts. In addition to helping the students, this course also had an unexpectedly beneficial, lasting effect on me. It opened me up to new ways of thinking, sensitized me to different viewpoints about established opinions, and generally broadened my outlook on a variety of topics ranging well beyond those in the course. There was also a spiritual component to my creating and teaching this course which spilled over into other areas of my life.

CHAPTER 7

My Professional Career

Research

In this chapter I will describe, briefly, the results from the principal research findings by my students and me in Syracuse. To do so, I will need to employ scientific language and concepts in some sections, but will try to make them as brief and clear as possible and avoid using biochemistry jargon. The reader without some background in biochemistry may wish to skip this chapter, except for the final section, Science is a Human Endeavor, which is widely accessible despite containing a few biochemical terms.

My research spans four time-frames: my Ph.D. in the Biochemistry Department at the University of Chicago (1950-56); post-doctoral research at the Ben May Laboratory for Cancer Research at the University of Chicago, and at the Experimental Radiopathology Research Unit, Hammersmith Hospital, London, England (1956-59); independent research at the Ben May Lab in Chicago (1959-63); and research conducted at Syracuse University (1963-2000). My Ph.D. research – as well as virtually all my research since then – was in the area of Enzymology. A summary of my Ph.D. and post-doctoral research is included in Chapter 4. This chapter focusses on our research at Syracuse University.

With my first group of M.S. and Ph.D. students, Syracuse University, 1964

Regulation of fatty acid synthesis in the lactating mammary gland

One of my first independent research projects, while I was still at the Ben May Lab in Chicago, was to study fatty acid synthesis in the rat lactating mammary gland. I took this project with me to Syracuse, and it was the subject of the first paper I submitted from Syracuse, a short note sent to *Biochimica et Biophysica Acta*. It described experiments demonstrating that the enzyme acetyl-CoA carboxylase catalyzes the rate-limiting reaction in mammary gland fatty acid synthesis under physiological conditions. The experiments were performed by my first graduate student, Peter Howanitz, who earned an M.S. before going to medical school and becoming a physician. What happened to this paper provided an important lesson for me. The manuscript was returned as unacceptable, the editor commenting that the reviewer had found that our principal conclusion was not supported by the data and that the changes in enzyme activity that we reported during lactation, and which were critical to our argument, had been reported previously. This was not the last time that I was upset about an editorial decision about one of our manuscripts, but it hit me hard as I felt this work was important for the direction our research was taking. I was certain that no one had published these results previously and that our conclusions were correct. I wrote to the editor, stating that the reviewer had not read our paper carefully, and that if the work had been published previously, to provide the citation for me. The editor replied that our conclusions were, indeed, well founded; that the reviewer was incorrect: the "previously reported" results were actually in press, i.e. not yet published; and that our paper was accepted for publication. It turned out that the paper "in press" never appeared, so the reviewer was wrong on both of his assertions. This experience taught me not to be intimidated by the comments of reviewers or editors, and served as a guide when I subsequently became a reviewer and editor. Incidentally, although I was often upset with editorial comments about the papers I submitted for publication during my career, the fact is that, on the whole, such comments proved to be helpful in improving the quality of our papers.

The mammary gland becomes a highly active "factory" for producing the necessary components of milk, including fatty acids for milk fat, as soon as the young are born and begin to suckle, so this was a useful organ in which to study fatty acid synthesis. I minced the mammary glands and measured fatty acid synthesis *in vitro*, and noticed that it diminishes rapidly in extracts prepared from rats shortly after the young are weaned. Mammary extracts from these rats are engorged in milk that is retained in the gland.

Previous attempts to explain the cessation of milk production after weaning attributed it to a complex mechanism that involved the cessation of the suckling stimulus. My hypothesis was that the milk contains a constituent that inhibits fatty acid synthesis. As long as the milk is withdrawn by the suckling baby rats, fatty acid synthesis continues, but once suckling ceases, this compound (or compounds) accumulates and inhibits fatty acid synthesis.

To test this hypothesis, I painted collodion (nail polish) on the five nipples on one side of a lactating rat, leaving the nipples on the other side exposed. I put the rat back with her young for ten hours. At this time, the mammary glands with the obstructed nipples appeared engorged in milk, whereas the ones on the other side appeared normal. I prepared separate extracts from the mammary glands on the two sides and measured fatty acid synthesis in each. Fatty acid synthesis in the extract from the obstructed side was only 10% of that in the extract from unobstructed side. This experiment, demonstrating that diminished fatty acid synthesis could be explained by a local phenomenon, was consistent with my hypothesis.

Next, I milked a rat whose young had been weaned, allowing milk to accumulate, added the milk to a mammary gland extract prepared from a lactating rat, and measured its effect on fatty acid synthesis. The milk produced strong inhibition, again consistent with my hypothesis. This result showed that the cessation of fatty acid synthesis has nothing to do with the lack of a suckling stimulus.

I now wished to establish what it was in the milk that caused the inhibition of fatty acid synthesis, and which step(s), in the multi-step process of fatty acid synthesis was being inhibited. These questions were the subject of a Ph.D. dissertation by one of my first graduate students, Arnie Miller, with some additional work by my technician at the time, Mary Geroch. The short answer is that the inhibitor(s) are certain, specific fatty acids present in the milk, which inhibit the enzyme acetyl-CoA carboxylase, which catalyzes the first step in the biosynthesis of fatty acids. This is an example of the well-known concept of feed-back inhibition, in this case occurring both on the molecular and the physiological level: the final product of fatty acid synthesis inhibits the enzyme catalyzing the first step in this process, and the accumulation of milk after weaning shuts off more milk production. Milk production by the mammary gland is a complex phenomenon, involving biochemical, physiological and endocrinological processes. There are, undoubtedly, other factors that participate in the cessation of milk production upon weaning. Our studies elucidated one component of what may be a multi-faceted regulatory process. Arnie Miller eventually became a Professor of Neuroscience at the University of California in San Diego.

Glucose 6-phosphate dehydrogenase

The problem described above began with a broad, physiological question, and ended up focusing on an enzyme, acetyl-CoA carboxylase. Almost all of my research, beginning with my Ph.D. dissertation, has involved enzymes, which have always fascinated me. Enzymes are catalysts that expedite biological reactions. Like all catalysts, they enhance the rate of the reaction they catalyze without being used up during the process. They differ from ordinary catalysts in their enormous rate-enhancement, their extraordinary specificity, and in their ability to have their rate regulated. They do so under mild physiological conditions of temperature, pressure and pH, using amino acids that are components of their protein structure, employing chemistry that is quite ordinary. Elucidating the mechanism of enzyme catalysis, the reasons for their specificity, and the ways in which their activities can be regulated for physiological purposes has engaged many biochemists, including me.

My research has utilized several enzymes, but the principal one has been glucose 6-phosphate dehydrogenase (G6PD). Fifty of my 81 publications concern various G6PDs; 31 of these deal with G6PD from the bacterium *Leuconostoc mesenteroides*, which exhibits some unique characteristics that have interested me for many years. I will describe, briefly, some of these, as well as some other research projects my students and coworkers have conducted over the years.

Dehydrogenases comprise a class of enzymes that catalyze oxidative or reductive reactions. When they catalyze the oxidation of a compound, they utilize a coenzyme, either nicotinamide adenine dinucleotide (NAD^+) or nicotinamide adenine dinucleotide phosphate ($NADP^+$), to take up the hydride ion removed from that compound. When they catalyze the reduction of a compound, the reduced form of the coenzyme, NADH or NADPH, donates a hydride ion to the compound being reduced.

Those dehydrogenases that catalyze oxidations tend to utilize NAD rather than NADP. They play important roles in metabolic pathways (catabolic) that capture the energy involved in breaking down compounds, e.g. sugars and fats. Dehydrogenases that catalyze reductions typically utilize NADPH rather than NADH, and these enzymes are involved in biosynthetic (anabolic) pathways, e.g. the biosynthesis of fatty acids.

G6PD from the lactating mammary gland

The G6PD that I investigated initially is from the mammary gland, which becomes very active during lactation, where it participates in the vigorous synthesis of milk fat by catalyzing the donation of the hydride ions needed for fatty acid synthesis. I isolated and purified

G6PD from lactating rat mammy glands, and on investigating some of its characteristics I discovered that it could also utilize NAD, and that the properties of the NAD-linked reaction displayed interesting differences from those of the NADP-linked reaction. It was unclear whether this NAD-linked activity, which was much weaker than the NADP-linked activity, had any physiological importance. The vast majority of dehydrogenases utilize either NAD or NADP; dual nucleotide specificity is very rare and investigating such an enzyme, I thought, would be especially interesting. I asked a graduate student who had just started to do his Ph.D. research with me, Chuck Olive, to search the literature for G6PDs in other organisms, that interact with both NADP$^+$ and NAD$^+$, and where both activities might play physiological roles. Among a few that he found, the G6PD from the bacterium *Leuconostoc mesenteroides* looked promising and so Chuck isolated and purified it and began investigating some of its properties. This *L. mesenteroides* G6PD, which became the principal focus of much of the research in my laboratory for 35 years, is described below.

Steroid inhibition of mammalian G6PDs

Mammalian G6PDs are inhibited by certain steroids, and we performed detailed studies of this inhibition using G6PD from lactating mammary glands. My graduate student Ron Raineri examined a large number of steroids in order to elucidate the structural features that caused inhibiton. He also confirmed and extended previous studies that demonstrated that the mechanism of inhibition is uncompetitive with respect to both glucose 6-phosphate and NADP. Uncompetitive inhibition is rare, most enzyme inhibitors are either competitive or non-competitive, and is interpreted, on theoretical grounds, as occurring when the inhibitor binds to the enzyme-substrate complex. Since steroid inhibition of G6PD is uncompetitive with respect to both glucose 6-posphate and NADP, this implies that the steroid inhibits by binding to the ternary enzyme complex, i.e. that its binding occurs only after both glucose- 6-phosphate and NADP are bound.

A quarter of a century after Ron Raineri's work, our interest in steroid inhibition of G6PD was renewed by some work being performed by my former post-doc mentor, Paul Talalay. Ever since the discovery of steroid inhibition of mammalian G6PDs, scientists have been

puzzled about the possible physiological significance of this phenomenon, in part because of the discrepancy between the concentrations
of circulating steroids and the concentrations necessary for them to
cause inhibition. Talalay and his coworkers drew attention to the fact
that the steroid dehydroepiandrosterone (DHEA), shown by Ron
Raineri to be one of the most potent inhibitors of G6PD, is one of the
principle steroids in the circulation, and that its concentration drops
with age, coincident with increased risk of developing age-related diseases such as cancer and heart disease. Administration of DHEA to
animals leads to a decrease in the development of atherosclerosis and
spontaneous and chemically-induced cancers. The mechanism of this
effect was not understood, but Paul Talalay and his coworkers provided evidence that it is associated with the inhibition of G6PD.

These considerations prompted Gary Gordon, in Paul Talalay's
lab, and I to collaborate in a study that confirmed our conclusion that
inhibitory steroids bind to the enzyme ternary complex. We studied
this inhibition in the reverse reaction catalyzed by human G6PD and
showed that it is uncompetitive with respect to both substrates for the
reverse reaction. Thus, inhibitory steroids bind to the ternary complex
formed in the forward (physiological) reaction, or the ternary complex
formed after catalysis, or both. Such inhibition is extremely rare and it
would be of interest to elucidate how the steroid binding site is formed
upon binding of both glucose 6-phosphate and $NADP^+$, and how this
information might further illuminate the physiological role of steroid inhibition of G6PD. In order to understand how steroids such
as DHEA inhibit G6PD, it will be necessary to solve the three-dimensional structure of the enzyme with bound steroid. This will require
preparing crystals of the enzyme and solving the structure, probably
using X-ray crystallography. Since our kinetic studies demonstrated
that the steroid binds to a ternary complex, and since a catalytically
competent complex would preclude performing such studies, probably
a complex using glucose 6-phosphate and NADPH will be required. I
suggested, a few years ago, to my former students Ted Lee, then a professor at the State University of New York in Fredonia, and Michael
Cosgrove, who was a professor at the Upstate Medical University in
Syracuse, that this might be an interesting and important problem for
them to collaborate on, and they did do some preliminary studies, but
both are busy with other projects and I doubt that they will be able to

actually do it. It is my regret, that I was not able to solve this important problem before retiring.

G6PD from *Leuconostoc mesenteroides*. Early studies

L. mesenteroides is a relatively primitive microorganism that has only limited ability to synthesize what it needs to survive. To grow it in the laboratory, one must supply it with many nutrients. This is in marked contrast to *Escherichia coli*, bacteria that are widely used in biochemical, genetic, and molecular biological research studies, and which can synthesize everything they need to grow and survive, if they are supplied with only glucose and an ammonium salt. Previous studies had shown that G6PD is the only NADP-linked dehydrogenase present in *L. mesenteroides*, catalyzing the generation of the NADPH needed for fatty acid synthesis, whereas its utilization of NAD^+ is linked to catabolic reactions (those involved in the oxidative breakdown of nutrients). Thus, *L. mesenteroides* G6PD is unique as it plays crucial roles in both anabolic and catabolic reactions, which made it an inviting target for probing several important questions.

Although the structures of NAD^+ and $NADP^+$ are very similar, differing only by a phosphate group, most dehydrogenases have evolved to bind only either NAD^+ or $NADP^+$, so their active sites must be designed to bind NAD^+ and exclude $NADP^+$, or *vice versa*. I wondered whether *L. mesenteroides* G6PD has two separate sites for binding NAD+ and $NADP^+$ (very unlikely) and, if not, how the active site of *L. mesenteroides* could bind both coenzymes. It appeared likely, to me, that the enzyme must undergo different conformational changes (changes in three-dimensional shape), depending on which coenzyme is bound. It also suggested that these two roles, catalyzed by the NADP-linked and NAD-linked reactions, respectively, must be regulated to enable one or the other activity to predominate under appropriate physiological conditions. I was also interested in trying to elucidate the catalytic mechanism of this enzyme, i.e. which specific amino acids are involved in catalysis. Although G6PDs had been isolated from many other sources, the catalytic mechanism of the enzyme had not been described.

Initially, techniques available to probe these questions could only lead to tentative conclusions. My graduate student Michael Milhausen provided evidence that the enzyme contains an essential lysine residue, and that its probable role was to bind glucose 6-phosphate. Some years later, my graduate student Bahram Haghighi, from Iran, in collaboration with Geoffrey Flynn, at Queens University in Kingston, Canada, isolated a peptide from the enzyme containing this essential lysine, and confirming that it binds glucose 6-phosphate. Michael Milhausen and another graduate student, Arman Ishaque, from India, showed that G6PD from *L. mesenteroides*, does not contain any cysteine residues, which is unusual for any protein, and which led, many years later, to some complications when we began X-ray crystallographic studies. Adeyinka Afolayan, a visiting professor to my laboratory from the University of Ife in Nigeria, showed that the enzyme contains an essential arginine residue and that this residue is also involved in glucose 6-phosphate binding. Bahram Haghighi also conducted fluorescence studies, suggesting that the binding of NAD^+ induces different conformational changes in the enzyme than does $NADP^+$ binding. My decision to spend one year of sabbatical leave, in 1972-73, in George Radda's laboratory at Oxford University, who had expertise in utilizing various techniques to measure protein conformational changes, was prompted by my desire to provide further evidence for different conformational changes by NAD^+- and $NADP^+$-binding to *L. mesenteroides* G6PD.

In his thorough characterization of *L. mesenteroides* G6PD, Chuck Olive included an extensive analysis of the kinetic mechanisms of the NADP- and NAD-linked reactions, and showed that the two mechanisms were different. Enzyme kinetics is a relatively specialized research area which provides information about the exact sequence of events during catalysis. The information we gained from these studies proved to be critical in our understanding, years later, of how this enzyme is regulated.

The dual-wavelength assay

By the late 1970s, our studies on G6PD from *L. mesenteroides* had confirmed our assumption that NAD and NADP bind to the same site on the enzyme, and that each of the coenzymes appears to induce a different conformational change upon binding. We had also established that the steady-state kinetic mechanisms of the NAD- and

NADP-linked reactions differ: coenzyme and substrate binding is ordered, with $NADP^+$ binding first, for the NADP-linked reaction, but random-order for the NAD-linked reaction. The significance of this apparently esoteric difference in the kinetic mechanisms eluded me until we discovered, using a novel method described here, that it was, in fact, the key to the way in which the enzyme regulates which one of the two coenzymes it uses. Our previous attempts to show differential effects of various ligands on the NAD- and NADP-linked reactions had measured these effects separately on each of the reactions, but *in vivo* both coenzymes are present. It was necessary, therefore, in order to simulate *in vivo* conditions to measure the effects on both reactions simultaneously. Because the absorption spectra of both NADH and NADPH are identical, with a maximum absorption at 340nm (which is how the reaction is measured), this cannot be done using the conventional assay. The thionicotinamide analogs of NAD^+ and $NADP^+$, however, upon reduction, absorb maximally at 400nm. By using the thionicotinamide analog of one coenzyme plus the other natural coenzyme, e.g. NAD^+ plus $S-NADP^+$, one could measure both reactions simultaneously by rapidly alternating the wavelength between 340nm and 400nm. I called this the dual wavelength assay.

Just as I had worked this out, a new undergraduate student, Ghaleb Daouk, inquired if he could do some research in my lab. Ghaleb came from Lebanon and had just completed two years of college education in Paris, but had not had a course in biochemistry. Because of this, I dissuaded him from joining my lab. He was very insistent, however, coming back several times to see me, and his Gallic charm persuaded me to give him a chance. We both agreed that, initially, this was on a trial basis, and only if it turned out that he was capable of handling the techniques in my lab would he be able to continue.

I never regretted that decision. Ghaleb turned out to be very talented and quickly worked out the details of the dual wavelength assay. Before we could use this new technique to try to measure differential effects on the two reactions we had to measure kinetic constants with the thionicotinamide analogs, and to ensure that the kinetic mechanisms with the analogs were the same as with their corresponding normal coenzymes. Once this preliminary work had been completed we tested for differential effects on the two reactions proceeding simultaneously. Our results can be summarized as follows.

1. Increased glucose 6-phosphate concentration increases the NAD-linked relative to the NADP-linked reaction. High glucose 6-phosphate concentrations inhibit the NADP-linked reaction.

2. Increased $NADPH/NADP^+$ concentration ratios inhibit the NADP-linked, but stimulate the NAD-linked reaction.

The selective effects of increased glucose 6-phosphate concentration and increased $NADPH/NADP^+$ concentration ratios can only be demonstrated with the dual wavelength assay; they cannot be detected in the conventional assay. These effects are explained in terms of the different kinetic mechanisms for the NAD-linked and NADP-linked reactions for *L. mesenteroides* G6PD. They explain how this enzyme can regulate its utilization of NAD^+ or $NADP^+$, depending on its need for the anabolic and catabolic roles of the enzyme, respectively, and are consistent with the physiological needs of the bacterium, *L. mesenteroides*.

Ghaleb Daouk was a cultured young man with interests in music, philosophy, and literature. We had many interesting discussions during the time that he worked in my lab, and remained in contact thereafter. After he graduated from Syracuse University in 1979, he studied medicine at the American University in Beirut in his native Lebanon, obtaining his M.D. in 1983. He then returned to the United States, conducted postdoctoral research at MIT, where he also obtained a S.M. in Management of Technology, and did his residency in pediatrics and pediatric nephrology at the Mass. General Hospital, Harvard Medical School. During those years, we continued to remain in contact, and he came to visit us a couple of times. He was appointed assistant professor at Harvard Medical School in 2006, and from 2005 was the Director of Extramural Services, Nephrology, at Children's Hospital, Boston. He was a member of the Board of Trustees at American University, Beirut, and of the Board of Visitors, College of Arts and Sciences at Syracuse University. Ghaleb's involvement with Syracuse University began when he became a member of the Biology Department's Alumni Advisory Board (see Chapter 8). In 2001, Ghaleb established the "H. Richard Levy - Ghaleb H. Daouk Undergraduate Support Fund" in my honor in the Biology Department.

In my lab, Syracuse University, approximately 1984. Photo by Steve Sartori, Syracuse University

An "Aha" Moment

In the early 1980s I read about a relatively new nuclear magnetic resonance (NMR) technique, transferred nuclear Overhauser enhancement (TRNOE), that enables one to determine the conformation of small molecules bound to macromolecules. A specific proton on a molecule is irradiated, and the effect on other protons in the same molecule are measured, enabling one to determine the distance between the two protons. For example, one can irradiate the H1 proton on the ribose component of NAD$^+$ and measure its effect on the H8 proton of its nicotinamide component, and obtain a measure of the distance between these two protons. Rotation about the bond between the N on nicotinamide and C-1 of the ribose can result in two limiting conformations of this portion of the NAD$^+$ molecule, *syn* or *anti*, in which this distance differs.

The technique had been applied to examining the conformation of NAD$^+$ and NADP$^+$ bound to two different dehydrogenases, and it occurred to me that it might be a useful tool to help us understand any differences in the way NAD$^+$ and NADP$^+$ bind to *L. mesenteroides* G6PD. There were excellent NMR facilities in the Syracuse University Chemistry Department, run by Dr. George Levy (no relation). I approached him with this problem to see if he could help us. He agreed and asked a Polish postdoc in his lab, Andrzej Ejchart, the husband of my technician at the time, to work on the problem with me. I did the experiments, Andy did the NMR analyses.

Two significant conclusions emerged from our results. First, there are significant differences in the conformations of NAD$^+$ and NADP$^+$ bound to *L. mesenteroides* G6PD, and also in the conformations of NAD$^+$ and NADP$^+$ bound to another dual-nucleotide specific enzyme, rat liver glutamate dehydrogenase. This difference may be a reflection of the difference in the protein conformations of the enzyme-coenzyme complexes, as revealed in *L. mesenteroides* G6PD by our earlier studies using fluorescent probes.

The second conclusion came from our finding that the TRNOE measurements, in which specific protons on the coenzyme were irradiated, were completely different for G6PD than the corresponding measurements reported previously for NAD$^+$ bound to lactate dehydrogenase or alcohol dehydrogenase, and for NADP$^+$ bound to dihydrofolate reductase. This was surprising and puzzling at first and it took me some time to understand it, which occurred in one of those rare, exciting "aha" moments that researchers relish. I suddenly recalled the experiments I did in Birgit Vennesland's lab 25 years previously, after completing my Ph.D. research, and before embarking on my first postdoc in Paul Talalay's lab (see Chapter 4). Those experiments were directed toward trying to understand the stereospecificity of dehydrogenases, i.e. why some dehydrogenases catalyze the addition of a hydride ion to, or its removal from one side of the nicotinamide ring of NAD$^+$ or NADP$^+$, while others use the opposite side. All dehydrogenases are absolutely specific as to which side they use. Our explanation at that time was cast in the context of the scientific knowledge in 1957. During the intervening quarter century our understanding, especially of protein structure, had advanced greatly, and someone else had offered a different explanation for the absolute stereospecificity of dehydrogenases, based on very limited data. The previously reported TRNOE studies had all been performed on A-stereospecific dehydrogenases, whereas G6PD is a B-stereospecific enzyme. I realized at once that this stereospecificity probably resulted from the conformation of the bound coenzyme, and that the technique that we had employed to answer a specific question about *L mesenteroides* G6PD could rapidly and easily answer a much broader question about all dehydrogenases. I performed TRNOE experiments on several other dehydrogenases and, just as I predicted, the results fell into two clear, non-overlapping classes: A-stereospecific dehydrogenases, in which the conformation of the nicotinamide-ribose bond in the bound coenzyme is *anti*, and B-stereospecific dehydrogenases in which the conformation of this bond is *syn*. Our method provided a facile method for distinguishing between dehydrogenases that are A- and B-stereospecific.

We sent our manuscript to the journal *Biochemistry* and the editors returned it and requested us to submit it for accelerated publication because of its general importance. This experience was a powerful demonstration for me of the fact that problems that are answered with the limited tools available at one time can be better resolved at a future date, provided that one recognizes the applicability of a new technique. This experience also demonstrates the importance of collaborative research. During my tenure at Syracuse University I benefitted from numerous collaborative research endeavors with other scientists at Syracuse, the SUNY Medical University, Rochester, Cornell, Notre Dame, Johns Hopkins, McMaster and Queens Universities in Canada, and Oxford University.

Cloning and sequencing the gene for *L. mesenteroides* G6PD, solving the three-dimensional structure of the enzyme, and creating mutant forms of the enzyme

To gain a detailed understanding of the mechanism of *L. mesenteroides* G6PD, its regulation, and the role of conformational changes, it was necessary to perform X-ray crystallographic studies, which allow one to see the three-dimensional structure of the enzyme and to monitor changes of the structure under various conditions, e.g. when ligands (small molecules like NADP or glucose 6-phosphate) bind to it. As I had no expertise in this area, I contacted Margaret Adams at Oxford University, whom I had met while on sabbatical in George Radda's lab (see below), and who had performed X-ray crystallographic studies on other dehydrogenases. I asked if she would be willing to collaborate with me on X-ray studies of *L. mesenteroides* G6PD. She said she would be willing, if I would furnish her with suitable crystals of the enzyme. She provided me with instructions on methods of protein crystallization, which is as much an art as a science, and I set about to obtain crystals. After some weeks, I obtained what looked like enzyme crystals and sent her a picture. She assured me that these were very likely enzyme crystals and arranged to come to Syracuse. When she arrived, she contacted Keith Moffatt, a protein crystallographer at Cornell University, in nearby Ithaca, and arranged to go there to examine the crystals at their synchrotron source. The crystals proved to be protein, and were suitable for structural studies. Thus began, in 1983, a very long and difficult collaboration that led, eleven year later, to the elucidation of the three-dimensional structure of *L. mesenteroides* G6PD.

My decision to collaborate with Margaret Adams proved, in retrospect, to be partially responsible for the long time it took to obtain a structure. An excellent crystallographer, Margaret was extremely deliberate and perhaps too cautious in her approaches. There were more serious difficulties, including the fact that the crystals were sensitive to radiation. The principal difficulty, however, was the fact, alluded to above, that the enzyme contains no cysteine residues. In order to obtain crystals suitable for X-ray diffraction, one usually has to prepare heavy metal atom derivatives, and metal atoms prefer to bind to cysteines. Attempts to prepare heavy metal atom derivatives of the *L. mesenteroides* G6PD were unsuccessful.

Fortunately, a few years previously, my graduate student Ted Lee had cloned the gene for *L. mesenteroides* G6PD. This proved to be a difficult task, complicated by the fact that a publication purporting to have cloned this gene appeared after Ted had initiated his studies. It turned out that, whatever the authors of this report had cloned, it was not the *L. mesenteroides* G6PD gene, a fact that Ted proved convincingly. My colleague Ernie Hemphill in our department helped considerably with this work. Ted went on to sequence the gene, in collaboration with Geoff Flynn at Queens University in Kingston, Canada.

This was a huge advance in our research, and it allowed us to deduce the amino acid sequence of the enzyme. Ted had also succeeded in constructing a suitable strain of *Escherichia coli* that lacks its own G6PD gene. He inserted the *L. mesenteroides* G6PD gene into it, where it was expressed, enabling us to isolate large quantities of *L. mesenteroides* G6PD much more easily, and in greater yield, than from *L. mesenteroides* itself. These important advances in our research now enabled us to move far beyond the findings of our earlier studies by using the techniques of molecular biology. We prepared mutant forms of the enzyme containing a cysteine residue, allowing Margaret Adams to crystallize and solve the three-dimensional structure of G6PD. We also prepared several other mutant forms of the enzyme, which allowed us to deduce the mechanism of the enzyme-catalyzed reaction, to identify which amino acids residues were responsible for binding glucose 6-phosphate, NAD^+ and $NADP^+$, and which ones catalyzed the reaction itself. We were also able to confirm that different conformations of the enzyme were generated by the binding of NAD^+, $NADP^+$ and glucose 6-phosphate. This work involved continuous collaboration between Margaret Adams's lab and mine. In my lab, the principal individual responsible for carrying out this work was my final, very gifted Ph.D. student, Michael Cosgrove. Important contributions were also made by my excellent technician, Valarie Vought, and by several undergraduate students who worked for varying periods of time in my lab. During the course of his Ph.D. studies in my lab, I arranged for Michael to spend several weeks in Margaret's lab in Oxford during three separate visits, where he performed experiments included in several publications. His time in Margaret's lab convinced him that structural studies on proteins would be something he would pursue during his career, and that has proved to be the case.

Some of the important findings that resulted from these studies include the following.

To generate a form of the enzyme that could provide a three-dimensional structure, we resorted to site-directed mutagenesis in which either a serine or a glutamine residue was replaced by a cysteine. All of these mutant G6PDs possessed specific activity and NAD/NADP activity ratios similar to the wild-type enzyme. For one of these, S215C (S = Serine, C = Cysteine, and 215 is the position of this amino acid in the enzyme), we prepared a mercury derivative, crystallized it, and its three-dimensional structure was solved in Margaret's lab. The structure of the coenzyme-binding domain proved to be similar to that in other dehydrogenases. The substrate binding site revealed several possible amino acid candidates for substrate binding. The probable position of the active site could be elucidated from this structure, and candidates for catalytic residues were deduced. Subsequent studies confirmed many of these.

L. mesenteroides G6PD consists of two identical subunits, each containing 485 amino acids. The amino acid sequences of several G6PDs, including the human enzyme, as well as the *L. mesenteroides* G6PD are remarkably similar in their active site region. Lysine-21 of the *L. mesenteroides* G6PD is involved in binding the substrate, glucose 6-phosphate via charge-charge interaction. This lysine residue is highly conserved among G6PDs from many sources.

The elucidation of many details of the reaction catalyzed by *L. mesenteroides* G6PD, and likely of G6PDs in general, are described in six articles that we published between 1996 and 2002, all made possible by Ted Lee's cloning of the gene for the enzyme, enabling us to perform site-directed mutagenesis. Briefly, the following are some of the details we were able to describe.

Arginine-46, which is conserved in all G6PDs, plays a key role in binding $NADP^+$, but not NAD^+, by contributing a positively charged, planar residue that interacts primarily with the 2'-adenosine portion of the coenzyme. The mechanism of the reaction catalyzed by the enzyme involves Histidine-240 acting as a general base to abstract the proton from the C-1 hydroxyl group of glucose 6-phosphate, while the carboxyl group of Aspartate-177 stabilizes the positive charge that forms on Histidine-240 in the transition state, enhancing its ability to abstract the proton from the substrate. Histidine-178 participates by binding the phosphate moiety of glucose 6-phosphate. Lysine-182 and Lysine-343 are important residues for binding the substrate both to the free enzyme and during catalysis. Threonine-14, Glutamine-47, and Arginine-46 are involved in coenzyme binding and in discriminating between the binding of NAD^+ and $NADP^+$. Lysine-343 also participates in coenzyme specificity. Different inter-domain hinge angles are involved in NAD- and NADP-binding, enabling *L. mesenteroides* G6PD to utilize both coenzymes.

The detailed description of the G6PD mechanism, and the roles of various amino acids in the mechanism, stand in stark contrast to the more general conclusions we were able to derive from earlier experiments, and demonstrate the powerful tools that the techniques of molecular biology and X-ray crystallography have brought to the field of enzymology, enabling us and many other scientists to describe the details of the catalytic mechanisms of many enzymes.

The three-dimensional structure of L. mesenteroides G6PD and the catalytic mechanism we proposed are shown below.

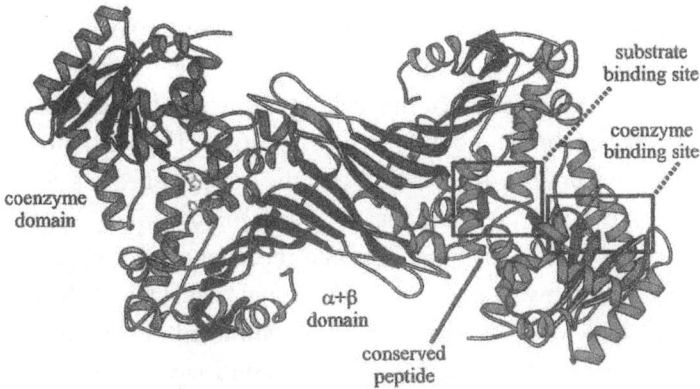

A ribbon diagram of the three-dimensional structure of L. mesenteroides G6PD, *showing some key features.*

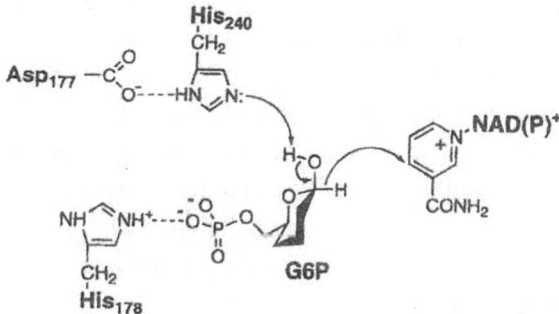

Proposed catalytic mechanism for the reaction catalyzed by G6PD. Histidine-240 acts as a general base to abstract a proton from the C1 OH of G6P, allowing the transfer of the C-1 hydride to the C-4 position of the nicotinamide ring of NAD or NADP. This is facilitated by Aspartate-177, which forms a catalytic dyad with Histidine-240, stabilizing the resulting positive charge in Histidine-240. Histidine-178 participates by binding the phosphate group of G6P.

These figures are reprinted with permission from Biochemistry Vol. 37, pp 2759-2767. Copyright 1998, American Chemical Society.

Sabbatical Research. Glyceraldehyde 3-Phosphate Dehydrogenase

In late 1971, I read some papers about the introduction of paramagnetic molecules into enzymes in order to measure conformational changes. The reports, which were from the laboratory of George

Radda at Oxford University, aroused my interest because I had postulated that conformational changes were involved in the ability of *L. mesenteroides* G6PD to utilize both NADP and NAD, and we had at our disposal only limited techniques for measuring such changes. I wrote to Prof. Radda to inquire whether it might be possible to spend some time in his lab to learn the techniques he was using. He replied, inviting me to join his group for a year. I obtained approval for a sabbatical leave from the department, and the College of Arts & Sciences. I would receive my full salary for half a year, or 50% of my salary for a full year's sabbatical. I applied for, and received a fellowship to cover the other half of my salary from the National Institutes of Health.

I will briefly describe the research I conducted in George Radda's lab. I was joined, in this project, by Raymond Dwek, a senior scientist in George's lab who was an expert in nuclear magnetic resonance measurements, and John Seeley, one of George's graduate students. We used rabbit muscle glyceraldehyde 3-phosphate dehydrogenases because its crystal structure was known, so that we could compare our structural information from paramagnetic studies with the crystallographic data. We studied the effects of the paramagnetic gadolinium ion on the nitroxide spin resonance signal of iodoacetamide spin label covalently bound to Cysteine 149 of the enzyme. This enabled us to calculate the distance between the bound metal ion and the spin label. We also carried out similar studies with human glyceraldehyde 3-phosphate dehydrogenase.

This experience exposed me to a great deal of new science, and new experimental techniques and theory. It provided the background that enabled me, ten years later, to utilize transferred nuclear Overhauser effects to compare the conformations of NAD^+ and $NADP^+$ bound to *L. mesenteroides* G6PD, and to collaborate with other scientists in applying this technique to two other enzymes. I heard some excellent seminars, especially from members of the Oxford Enzyme Group, including Margaret Adams who would later become a collaborator in my research, and had some very fruitful interactions with George's and other graduate students - some of whom came to visit us in subsequent years in Syracuse, as did George.

Anthranilate Synthetase

Beginning in 1973, I participated in a collaborative research project with my friend and colleague, Elias Balbinder, who had joined the department the same year that I arrived. Elias was a geneticist studying the biosynthesis of tryptophan in *Salmonella typhimurium*, especially the regulation of the genes controlling the multi-enzyme complex which catalyzes the first two steps in the biosynthetic pathway, anthranilate synthetase-anthranilate phosphoribosylpyrophosphate phosphoribosyltransferase (hereafter referred to as anthranilate synthetase). We applied for, and received a grant supporting his genetic and my enzymatic studies on this complex. Two of my graduate students, Tom Grove and Peter Robison, did their Ph.D. research on anthranilate synthetase. We developed a method for purifying the enzyme complex and undertook various kinetic and mechanistic studies.

When Tom and Peter began their work on anthranilate synthetase my lab was fully occupied by two other graduate students, Michael Milhausen and Armana Ishaque and my technician, Joann Ingulli working on G6PD. We set up the anthranilate synthetase project in another lab, two doors down from mine and I also hired another technician, Roberta Sheffer, to assist with this project. Together with our dishwasher, Roberta Goldstein, plus several undergraduate students who participated in various short-term projects, we had quite a large group for several years.

Tom went on to do post-doctoral research with George Radda. Later, he became president and CEO of BioCentrex, a food safety and food biosecurity testing products company in California. After post-doctoral research, Peter worked in the oil industry as a researcher, environmental manager and fuel quality advisor. As noted in Chapter 6, In 2021, he made a major gift to Syracuse University in my honor to create the H. Richard Levy Endowed Biology Research Fund.

Science is a Human Endeavor*

This section deals with an episode in my research that is broadly relevant. Although it describes some biochemistry, the reader need not

---

* A slightly edited version of this essay appears in the December, 2021 issue of *ASBMB Today*, a publication of the American Society of Biochemistry and Molecular Biology.

understand the few technical terms in order to comprehend the events described.

The general public may think of science as a cold, heartless endeavor, and scientists as individuals concerned with cold facts, but of course this is not true. Many of us are passionate about our work. We exhibit the same foibles as non-scientists – hubris, jealousy, competition, exhilaration, disappointment. Much of what we do depends on human interactions, and our work is affected by the lives and deaths of our colleagues and peers.

One of the most frustrating periods of my research career occurred in the early 1980s. During the course of reviewing the scientific literature in the late 1970s for a review that I was writing about the enzyme glucose 6-phosphate dehydrogenase for *Advances in Enzymology* [1], I read a paper published in 1974, by Eggleston and Krebs [2] that aroused my interest. It purported to describe a novel mechanism for the regulation of hepatic glucose 6-phosphate dehydrogenase (G6PD) by an unidentified factor. In March 1977, I wrote to Krebs asking whether any further, unpublished work had been done that I could cite in my review. He replied that since Eggleston had died the work had been in abeyance, but that he had recently taken it up again and was trying to identify the factor. He would keep me apprised of any progress. In September, he wrote again that he had nothing new to report; a few attempts to identify the factor had been unsuccessful. I decided that we would try to take up this problem in my lab. We did so and encountered baffling difficulties that took long to resolve, and that eventually included some personal tragedy.

Hans Krebs, one of the giants of twentieth century biochemistry, was born in Hildesheim, Germany, in 1900. As a Jew, he was forced to resign his position in the Department of Medicine at the University of Freiburg shortly after Hitler came to power in 1933. He went to the University of Cambridge in England, and then to the University of Sheffield [3]. It was in Sheffield that he produced his most widely recognized work, the elucidation of the metabolic pathway that became known as the Krebs cycle. In 1953, he was awarded the Nobel Prize in Physiology and Medicine.

While I was a graduate student in the Biochemistry Department at the University of Chicago, Krebs came to spend a month in the department. This was in 1954, one year after he received the Nobel Prize. We graduate students had a Biochemistry Club and that year I was its president (the title was actually "dictator"). We invited him to give a talk, which he did. This is how I first met him. I met him several times subsequently and was always impressed by the fact that he remembered me, and details about me. When I was on sabbatical leave at Oxford University in 1973-74, Krebs had a position in the Department of Clinical Medicine at the Radcliff Infirmary and I talked with him on several occasions. He had been Professor (i.e. Chair) of Biochemistry in Oxford until his mandatory retirement in 1967.

I thought, correctly as it turned out, that the research following up on Krebs's work would be too risky a problem for a graduate student so I asked my technician, Melody Christoff, to undertake it. The essence of Krebs's finding can be summarized briefly as follows. G6PD plays an important role in carbohydrate and lipid metabolism in several tissues including the liver. It catalyzes the oxidation of glucose 6-phosphate using the coenzyme $NADP^+$, which is thereby reduced to NADPH. NADPH is a potent, $NADP^+$-competitive inhibitor of G6PD and in mammalian tissues it is present in concentrations 100 times greater than that of $NADP^+$. Under these conditions G6PD should be totally inhibited, yet it is known to be highly active. Krebs's experiments sought to resolve this paradox. The paper of Eggleston and Krebs reported that rat liver extracts contain an unidentified, macromolecular, highly unstable cofactor, which together with oxidized glutathione overcomes this NADPH inhibition, thus providing a physiological explanation for this paradox. My goal was to identify this cofactor.

First, though, we had to repeat Krebs's experiments. Despite devoting enormous time and effort to this problem, we were unable to confirm certain of Eggleston and Krebs's key findings. I consulted with several colleagues but to no avail. Ultimately, by following minutely every facet of the experimental protocols in the paper by Krebs and Eggleston we found two, mutually reinforcing errors in their work that allowed the authors to make their interpretation. The first error was one in basic enzyme kinetics: a large correction they made for the reaction rate in the absence of glucose 6-phosphate. Because of the saturating glucose 6-phosphate concentration they used, this correction was unnecessary and incorrect. The second error was that their use of $ZnCl_2$ to inhibit endogenous glutathione reductase led to an interfering absorbance at same wavelength used to measure the enzyme activity. It was critical to inhibit glutathione reductase in their experiments because this enzyme catalyzes the oxidation of NADPH in the presence of oxidized glutathione, thereby removing the inhibitory NADPH, but because of its interfering absorbance, $ZnCl_2$ was an inappropriate choice. When we took these two artifacts into consideration we were able to reconcile the data of Krebs and Eggleston with ours, but proved that their conclusions were incorrect.

In September 1980, I wrote a detailed letter to Krebs about our findings and conclusions. I mentioned that I would be in England the following year and would be pleased to meet with him, if he were interested, to discuss our data. He replied that he was intensely interested in our work and to get in touch with him when I come to England, hoping very much that we could meet. We met on July 28 for an hour. He was impressed with our work, said that the problem was important, and urged me to publish it, but agreed it would be best if we understood it better first. He conceded readily that the "cofactor" of Eggleston and Krebs could well be the result of a constellation of artifacts.

I told him that two Spanish workers had repeated his findings using mussel hepatopancreas and claimed to have isolated the cofactor [4]. He asked me whether they were from the laboratory of Alberto Sols. They were not, and Krebs said that Spanish scientists were only rarely first-rate; Sols was one of the few exceptions. He told me about a book by C.D. Darlington that deals with world history from the viewpoint of genetics, in which the author states that Spain has not yet recovered from the expulsion of the Jews in the 15th century. Krebs believed that Germany was currently facing the same problem.

Upon my return to Syracuse I wrote to Krebs to thank him for talking with me, and enclosed reprints of a recent article by my former Ph.D. advisor, Birgit Vennesland and one by Efraim Racker, both of which I had mentioned to him at our recent meeting, as well as reprints of two recent articles we had published [5]. I said that I planned to do a little more work on our study and would then write it up for publication, and that I would send him a copy. His reply, dated 24th. August 1981 was as follows:

Dear Dick,

Thank you very much for your very kind and appreciative letter, and for the enclosures. I find it all very interesting.

Birgit's lively and robust style of writing is quite new to me – very different from the style of the many conversations I have had with her.

I am somewhat sceptical of Racker's interpretations but I have to read the full papers before arriving at a more definite assessment. I do not think that his ideas properly explain the high air aerobic glycolysis of cancer cells.

Studying your excellent two 1979 papers brings home to me that you have gone a very long way since I first met you in the spring of 1954 when I spent a month in the Department of Biochemistry as a visiting professor.

With kind regards,
Yours sincerely,
(signed) Hans Krebs

Two months later, Krebs died unexpectedly.

Meanwhile, Melody and I wound up our research. In February 1983, I submitted the manuscript to the Biochemical Journal, the British journal in which Eggleston and Krebs's paper had appeared. In my letter to the editor I provided some background to our work, including the interactions with Krebs, and then continued: "His death so soon after I had seen him and had witnessed his lively and vigorous intellect (seemingly undiminished from 27 years previously, when we had first met) was a great shock and I felt it inappropriate to publish at that time. In the meantime, we have reconfirmed all our findings. The continued interest in the problem of the regulation of the HMP shunt and the frequent references to the work of Eggleston and Krebs and Rodriguez-Segade *et al* has convinced me that our findings should be published. Clearly, Sir Hans would have wanted me to do so. As the initial papers of Krebs and of Rodriguez-Segade on this topic appeared in Biochemical Journal, I would like to see our paper published there also."

In their response, the journal's editorial report included the following comments. "The authors appear to have disposed convincingly of a misleading artifact. Their covering letter reveals some anxiety about challenging the work of an eminent scientist so soon after his death, but there can be little doubt that the scientist in question would have wanted to see this matter cleared up and would have been intrigued by the explanation." The paper was accepted for publication, with minor revisions, and appeared later that year [6].

There is yet another fact to add to the long saga concerning this work. When Melody Christoff first came to work for me in the early 1980s she told me that she had suffered from leukemia, but that it was now in remission. In the fall of 1982 she began to experience signs of a relapse. She was admitted to the Roswell Park Cancer Institute in Buffalo to receive a bone marrow transplant. While she was recovering there in an isolation unit, in which she was placed because of her compromised immune system, we continued to correspond about the manuscript. In March 1983, I received a letter from her, which ended as follows: "I hate to end this on a gloomy note but the doctors just came in and told me that there is a spot on my left lung, which has about doubled in size since Monday. It could be a fungus or bacteria and definitely means...". She ended her letter in mid-sentence, clearly recognizing the import of what she had written, and shortly thereafter, on April 3, she died. All the bone marrow transplant patients at Roswell Park died because the isolation ward had become contaminated with a fungus, and with their drastically compromised immune system none of the patients were able to withstand the infection. This resulted, later, in a class-action suit against the Institute. Melody left behind a husband and two daughters. She had been a superb technician and a wonderful human being. Thus, of the four individuals associated with this study – Eggleston, Krebs, Christoff and Levy – I was now the sole survivor. And just as the Eggleston and Krebs paper contained a footnote about Eggleston's death, so now our paper included a footnote about Melody's death.

Although not directly pertinent to the events described here, the paper by Racker that I sent to Krebs, and about which he expressed skepticism in his letter to me, represents an example of another, darker human dimension in scientific endeavors. Racker, like Krebs, was one of the leading biochemists of the 20th century. Also, like Krebs, he was a Jew who had escaped Nazism, leaving Austria, first for Britain, then settling in the United States. (I, too, am a Jew who escaped Nazi Germany, in my case as a nine-year-old boy). The paper I had sent Krebs [7] claimed to provide support for Racker's hypothesis that ATPase plays a key role in cancer. It had aroused intense discussion in the scientific community, primarily because the rapidity with which the lead author, Racker's graduate student Mark Spector, had purportedly done the experiments, strained credulity. Mark Spector was a brilliant, exceedingly talented graduate student, who appeared to have answers for all the criticisms levelled at him at numerous scientific meetings. Eventually, it turned out that his publication was based on completely fabricated data, one of the most spectacular cases of scientific fraud in the second half of the twentieth century [8]. Spector's deception was cleverly fabricated, fooling many, including Racker, whose reputation suffered a severe blow, but the fraud was eventually exposed.

The saga of this work contains several important lessons. First, it bears out the oft-mentioned dictum that science is self-correcting. Errors occur even in peer-reviewed, published papers and can be corrected provided they are noticed and pursued. Second, the pursuit of such errors can be dogged. Melody and I devoted a great deal of effort to solving this problem because we were convinced that something was wrong and because the problem of G6PD regulation was an important one. Third, even eminent scientists can make mistakes, and one of the great things about the ethos of science is that it cares about the truth, not the reputation of those pursuing it. Fourth, although science is objective, it is carried out by human beings, and thus subjective factors can impinge. The tragic deaths of Melody Christoff and Hans Krebs as this story unfolded will be forever linked with this work in my mind. Finally, a lasting impression from this episode is the kindness, graciousness and humility of Hans Krebs, as reflected in all his interactions with me, and displayed in the letter quoted above. I have met other famous scientists in my life, but few share these attributes with Krebs.

For references cited see Notes[1].

CHAPTER 8

My Professional Career

Service

Of the three areas comprising an academic scientist's work – research, teaching, and service – most academic scientists regard the latter to be the least desirable. Service involves working on various committees – at Syracuse University these include department, college, and university committees. They may also include professional committees outside the university. During my years at Syracuse University I served on about 50 different committees and chaired about a quarter of them. Some were constituted to deal with a specific, temporary problem and others were long-standing committees required to deal with ongoing situations. Unlike the majority of my colleagues, I enjoyed very much serving on most committees, which provided a wide variety of interesting tasks.

Departmental committees on which I served included those dealing with departmental functions such as the executive committee, long-range planning, graduate student recruiting, graduate student education, and organizing departmental seminars. Others were for immediate, specific tasks, such as search committees for new faculty or chairman review committees.

Departmental Chair. My biggest service contribution to the department was serving as departmental chair, for which I was elected by my colleagues, and which I held for two three-year terms from 1993 to

1999. A few months prior to becoming chair I spent some time trying to decide whether I would really want to assume this major responsibility. To clarify my thinking, I wrote down my thoughts. We had read a book in our Book Group recently, Stephen Jay Gould's *Wonderful Life. The Burgess Shale and the Nature of History*, which describes an epochal discovery, at the beginning of the twentieth century, of an astonishingly rich collection of fossils in a small limestone quarry in Canada. The man who made the discovery, Charles Walcott, interpreted these fossils within the context of the current ideas about evolution, though he had to strain these ideas to do so. Some four decades later his work was totally reinterpreted in a manner that revolutionized evolutionary concepts.

Gould's book brilliantly describes not only the fossils and their discovery, but the intellectual constraints on Walcott, and how these were removed by the team of scientists who reinterpreted his work. Walcott was the leading American geologist of his time, and his views were shaped by the times and by his character, as is true for all scholars. Gould notes that Walcott was a fine geologist, but an even greater administrator, and as such, one of the most powerful scientists at the time. He was the administrator of the Smithsonian Institute, president of the National Academy of Sciences and the American Association for the Advancement of Science, and he knew every American president from Theodore Roosevelt to Calvin Coolidge. Yet, his name was largely forgotten before Gould wrote his book, and Gould argues persuasively that this is largely because, despite his great power, his principal accomplishments were administrative, not intellectual. "Since administrators are usually recruited from the ranks of successful researchers as they reach mid-life," Gould writes "Walcott's story of intensely conflicting demands, and consequent internal stress, echoes a pervasive and honest refrain heard from the helm of scientific institutions. Administrators are chosen because they understand research – meaning that they both love the work and do it well...You begin with a promise to yourself: I won't have as much time for research, but I will be more efficient. Others have fallen by the wayside, but I will be different; I will never abandon my research; I will keep working and publishing at close to full volume. Slowly the perverseness of creeping inevitability takes over. Research fades. You never abandon the ideal, or the original love. You will get back to it..." Walcott consoles himself by a claim (disingenuous, in Gould's view) that he did not enjoy administration and did it out of a sense of duty. Gould notes, perceptively I believe: "I do not believe that most people are sufficiently self-sacrificial to spend the best years of their life on something that they could put aside with no loss of respect, but only of power. The ethos of science requires that administration be publicly identified as done for duty, but surely most people in such roles take pleasure in their responsibility and influence."

These were my thoughts about all this at the time:

I do not wish to compare Walcott with myself. He was a powerful, nationally known administrator. His administrative work was done at the same time as most of his scientific work, including the discovery of the Burgess Shale. Times then were very different. Nevertheless, Gould's account struck a chord with my ambivalent feelings and helped me, I believe, to come to terms with my decision. What I feared most was the loss of my scientific reputation. I have no illusions about my stature, but am confident that I have a very solid reputation among my peers, and there are few things that I value more. A reputation is earned slowly with hard work, but it can be destroyed rapidly. I also have to be honest with myself: I would like to be chairman, I think I would be good at it, and would mostly enjoy it. The ethos of science that Gould describes, and which I have imbibed with my own scientific development, naturally led to my ambivalent stance, but as I thought more about it I had to admit that my real stance is not ambivalent at all. Unlike Walcott, I have made whatever reputation I have prior to embarking on my administrative role. What I have published so far will not be affected by becoming chairman. I have come to terms with the fact that the likelihood of achieving major future accomplishments is remote.

Also, weighing on my decision was the fact that I did not have an excellent technician or graduate student at that time, which would greatly influence how smoothly our research would continue. What I did not know then was that, just after I decided to become chairman, I hired Valarie Vought, who would turn out to be the best technician

I ever had; and Michael Cosgrove decided to do his Ph.D. research in my lab, arguably the best graduate student ever to work with me. They played a major role in continuing the research, and in participating in what was probably the best series of publications ever to come from my lab. Thus, my fears turned out to be unfounded, which I could not know at the time. And my belief that I would be good at being chair, and enjoy it, turned out to be true.

The chairman is responsible for overseeing and directing all the functions of the department, including the departmental staff, the budget, hiring new faculty, evaluating faculty performance, determining faculty salary raises, and interacting with the college dean and with other departmental chairs. In addition to these major responsibilities, as chair one is required to deal with a myriad of daily problems of a wide variety, many of which require immediate attention.

Two actions I took as chair that proved to have important and unforeseen consequences were,

1). the creation, in 1995, of a departmental newsletter, BIO@ SU; and as a direct outcome of this, 2). the creation of the Syracuse University Biology Alumni Advisory Board (SUBAAB). BIO@SU was produced and edited by my friend and Associate Chair, Jack Bryan, and sent to thousands of departmental alumni and friends. Clearly, it filled a need, because the feedback was gratifying, both in regard to providing information about them, and in generating financial contributions to the department. SUBAAB consisted of eminent alumni whose dedication to the department's welfare was extremely beneficial in many ways, including the important role they played in garnering approval from the administration for construction of the Life Sciences Complex. My most important contribution, as chair, to the department's future was my role in securing this approval.

The need for such a facility became increasingly urgent ever since the merger, in 1970, of the Departments of Bacteriology & Botany and Zoology into the Department of Biology. The department's facilities were housed in two buildings -- Lyman Hall, constructed in the first decade of the 20th century, and the Biological Research Labs (BRL), built in two stages in the 1960s. These buildings were at two ends of one block on College Place. Not only was this inconvenient, it necessitated duplication of some facilities and it split up faculty and students, diminishing opportunities for interaction. Increasingly, during the 1980s and 1990s, the two departments were cramped for space. Under the chairmanships of Judith Foster and David Sullivan some significant improvements and enlargements of the facilities in Lyman Hall took place, and additional space was secured in Sims Hall, but these changes were not sufficient and they did not address the fact that the facilities were still not under one roof.

The following narrative for securing the approval for the construction of a new building is taken from my book "Biology at Syracuse University 1872-2010".

A number of factors came together in the late 1990s to catalyze the university's decision to construct a new building to house the Department of Biology. Dick Levy, chair, and Jack Bryan, associate chair, developed a statement to that end. In October, 1998, they met with College of Arts and Sciences dean Robert Jensen and Associate Vice Chancellor Michael Flusche to discuss facilities needs and related issues. At this meeting, it became clear that no options would be excluded, including a new building. Levy and Bryan were asked to develop a concise document within two weeks outlining a preliminary assessment of departmental space needs and the rationale for such needs. The vice chancellor and chancellor would review this document.

In November 1998, Levy sent a letter to Dean Jensen, accompanied by a detailed assessment of present and future departmental space needs, prepared by Bryan. The letter emphasized the nationwide explosion in interest in biology; the large increase in enrollments in biology courses at SU; the needs of faculty, undergraduates, and graduate students in a modern biology department; the importance of creating flexible space and facilities to adapt to shifting research directions in the future; and the need for both large lecture halls and small conference rooms as well as common core facilities. The letter urged the university to engage professional laboratory consultants with extensive experience in developing plans for biology departments. One week later Flusche responded: "We have accepted your thoughtful space program and I am eager to bring in a laboratory consultant to help refine the statement of needs for biology research and teaching. Vice Chancellor Vincow has accepted the program that you submitted as a very useful first step in moving toward this goal."

Consultants were hired and the architectural firm Ellenzweig was awarded the contract. SUBAAB played a significant role in discussions with the administration, and in March 1999, John Hanlin, SUBAAB's chair sent a letter to Chancellor Shaw outlining their recommendation to erect a building by adding onto the existing Science and Technology Center, which housed the Chemistry Department, facilitating interdisciplinary interactions with their faculty and students. My pending retirement in 2000 necessitated finding a replacement, preferably from outside the department. An excellent candidate, John Russell, was identified. His interest in assuming the position strongly depended on assurances that the building would be constructed. In November 2002, the SU Board of Trustees gave their approval for the construction of the building, and John Russell accepted the chairmanship position. Groundbreaking for the building, which would be joined to the existing Science and Technology Center via a large atrium, took place in April 2006. Extensive consultation among interested parties continued throughout construction. The building, encompassing approx. 230,000 gross square feet, opened in August 2008 and has proved to serve the department needs extremely well.

Among the various **College of Arts & Sciences Committees** on which I served were ones that dealt with plans to develop the Life Sciences, with curriculum changes in various departments, the Faculty Council, scholarship and research, and the Biophysics Committee.

University Committees on which I served included my first assignment when I arrived, the Biochemistry Committee, which oversaw the Biochemistry program, and of which I soon became chair. I was also on the Board of Editors of the Syracuse Scholar, a magazine published by the University, the faculty editorial committee of Syracuse University Press, the Honors Council, the Departmental Chairs Steering Committee, and the University Senate.

I was chair of the Academic Committee when we instituted a major change in recognizing outstanding graduating students. Up to that time, like most colleges and universities, at every Commencement Syracuse University honored a valedictorian and salutatorian, students who were selected based solely on the best and second-best grade-point average. In 1982, the Academic Committee proposed changing this to recognizing outstanding graduating students as "Syracuse University Scholars". Each College within the University would be able to select two S.U. Scholars based on the following criteria.

"In addition to demonstrated skill in the use of the English language, criteria for selection shall include: outstanding performance in course work; exceptional academic attainment such as publication of original research, literary work, critical essays etc., or public performance or exhibition of artistic work; recognition or acclaim by the wider community for academic attainment."

These provided much broader and more sensible criteria for excellence, and the recommendations were approved by the Vice Chancellor for Academic Affairs. Their application has been very successful.

Other committees on which I served included the Senate Committee on Academic Freedom, Tenure and Professional Ethics which adjudicated cases of perceived violation of academic freedom or ethics as well as tenure decisions; and the Overseas Fellowship Committee, which evaluated the credentials of outstanding students who were nominated to apply for Rhodes or Marshall Scholarships. While I served on this committee we nominated Elliot Portnoy for a Rhodes Scholarship, which he won in 1986. He went to Oxford University for his Ph.D. and then to Harvard Law School, where he graduated *cum laude* in 1992. While at Oxford, Elliot and his wife founded an organization "Kids Enjoy Exercise Now" (KEEN), a non-profit organization that provides sports opportunities for children with severe disabilities. Portnoy is a top Washington attorney recognized as one of Washington's "Legal Elite".

The various **Professional Committees** on which I served included Scientists and Engineers for a Livable World, which had as its members, scientists and engineers from Syracuse University, Upstate Medical University, the College of Environmental Sciences and Forestry, and several local industries. My recollection of my participation in this organization, of which I was president from 1970 to 1971, is that we gathered to discuss scientific and technical issues that impacted the community and the population at large. In 1978, I initiated the Syracuse Enzyme Club and acted as its first chairman. This was for those of us at the University and Medical School who were interested in discussing problems in Enzymology. In 1985, Geoffrey Flynn of Queens University, in Kingston, Canada, J. Ellis Bell at the University of Rochester, and I founded the Northeast Enzyme and Protein Group which had annual meetings for six years at our three home venues, where students, post-docs and faculty presented talks about their latest research. These meetings were quite successful and drew participants not only from our own institutions, but from others in the Northeastern United States. The three of us took turns organizing the meetings and garnered institutional support for them (see Chapter 7).

Editorial Service. In 1986 I was invited to join the editorial board of the journal Archives of Biochemistry and Biophysics. I served as one of its editors from 1986 to 1999. This involved reviewing manuscripts submitted to the journal and recommending whether to accept for publication, ask authors to revise or provide additional experimental evidence, or reject the manuscript.

Grant Reviews. I reviewed several grants and was a member of a couple of National Science Foundation *ad hoc* committees appointed to review specific grants.

Having summarized my teaching, research, and service, I will now try to do an honest self-evaluation. How well did I perform in these tasks? How good a scientist was I? How successful was my career? What are the characteristics of a successful scientist -- of a great scientist?

As an academic scientist, my teaching featured some novel courses, was recognized by an award, and included supervising the research of numerous undergraduate students, M.S. theses, and Ph.D. dissertations. My research led to 81 publications (see Appendix) and was supported virtually continuously by grants from the National Institutes of Health and the National Science Foundation.

To be a successful scientist requires several characteristics, including curiosity, imagination, and willingness to take risks. You have to have discipline and the persistence to overcome obstacles. You have to be able to recognize a good problem and pursue clear goals. You must be able to deal with failure and have confidence in yourself. I believe I possessed these characteristics to a substantial degree. Great scientists have these characteristics in abundance. They are the ones who create what Thomas S. Kuhn calls paradigm shifts in his book *The Structure of Scientific Revolutions*. They are willing to sacrifice everything in the pursuit of their goals. They immerse themselves in their work single-mindedly and nothing else, including family, has greater importance for them or gives them greater joy and satisfaction.

Kuhn defines a paradigm as a "universally recognized scientific achievement that, for a time, provides model problems and solutions for a community of researchers." The success of a paradigm rests on its ability to succeed in explaining problems. Most scientists work within a paradigm. Much of this work is fascinating and productive and constitutes normal science. Great scientists are often those whose work does not fit within, or is difficult to fit into a prevailing paradigm, and who are thus forced to establish a new paradigm to accommodate their results. Invariably, this paradigm shift is met with criticism, even derision, by the scientific community, but its success is assured when others recognize that the new paradigm explains more and better than the old one. An example of a paradigm shift in enzymology is the replacement of Emil Fischer's "lock-and-key" hypothesis of enzyme specificity with Koshland's "induced-fit" hypothesis. Science mostly moves incrementally and cumulatively; sudden shifts, as in paradigm shifts, are crucial but rare.

I believe that I was good scientist, engaged for the most part in normal science. None of my work resulted in paradigm shifts, and probably no one, a hundred years from now, will point to any of my publications as having altered the course of enzymology. That is not to say that some of my publications weren't important.

I had a successful career as an academic scientist, a career that gave me tremendous satisfaction. That career encompassed more than research, it also involved teaching and service, including administration. Great scientists are usually primarily great researchers, sometimes also great teachers. Not everyone has the same qualities, or derives joy and satisfaction from the same activities, and if your goal is to be happy in your career you must recognize what gives you the greatest satisfaction. The German poet Goethe wrote:

> Eines schickt sich nicht für alle.
> Sehe jeder, wie er's treibe,
> Sehe jeder, wo er bleibe,
> Und wehr steht, daß er nicht falle!

Which, loosely translated, is:

> The same thing is not fit for all.
> Let everyone look to himself,
> Let everyone decide where he dwells,
> And he who stands, let him not fall!

I think that early in my path toward becoming an academic scientist, the models I aspired to were great scientists in the rarified atmosphere at the University of Chicago, like Paul Talalay and Charles Huggins. But, slowly I recognized that I was not willing to sacrifice everything to rise to the level of those models, that I wished to pursue other interests that I enjoyed. That realization has allowed me to derive enormous satisfaction and joy from my career and my life.

CHAPTER 9

Travel

My travels as a child, and in my teens, were described in earlier chapters.

While I was a graduate student at the University of Chicago, I drove to California twice to visit my friend Pierre Joske. Returning to Chicago from one of these visits with my sister Liz, we saw the Northern Lights. This occurred in Aurora, Illinois - the Aurora Borealis in Aurora! While in California, Pierre and I went camping in Yosemite National Park. In this chapter I describe trips with my wife and by myself, but begin with an adventure I shared with my friend Howard Goldfine.

European Trip, 1959.

In 1958, at the conclusion of my post-doc year in England, Howard Goldfine and I toured Europe for four weeks with the Morris Minor I had bought in England. Our journey began in Calais, and proceeded through Germany and Austria to Italy. In Venice, we took in the canals and palaces. In Florence, we were awed by the glorious art and sculpture. We happened to arrive in Siena on the day of their Palio Festival. This features an exciting horse race, where jockeys dressed in colorful costumes representing the contrades (wards), ride horses bareback at break-neck speed three times through the Piazza del Campo. The race is preceded by a spectacular pageant featuring beautiful medieval costumes.

We spent a few days in Rome, taking in the artistic wonders of that city. Driving back north we stopped in Pisa and in Lerici, where we spent some time with my friends, the Gores, who were vacationing there. Much of the Renaisance art we admired in Italy I revisited with Betty two years later, so will not detail it here.

On our return trip through France we stopped in Montbard, to eat at a restaurant that was advertised en route as "La deuxiéme table du France". It was at the railway station, quite unpretentious-looking, but had a truly outstanding, varied menu and a very large selection of wines. We spent a few days in Paris, visiting many of its landmarks and enjoying gourmet meals.

We returned to England via ferry and spent several days there meeting with the Schlesingers and Mrs. Jeffries (my landlady during my post-doc year), and seeing some plays.

Not long after returning to the United States, Howard married an English girl, Norah, who was a biochemist. They had two children. Howard and I remained friends for the rest of our lives, now over 65 years. He first met Betty the same day as I did and was present at our wedding, and at Betty's memorial service. Howard earned his Ph.D. in biochemistry at the University of Chicago the year after I. He was one of my apartment-mates in Chicago, and he, too, became an academic scientist, at the University of Pennsylvania. His research specialty was the structures, functions and formation of bacterial lipids and fundamental issues about membrane biology and lipid biosynthesis. He was the most intellectual of my friends, with wide-ranging interests in music, art literature politics, history, and science. In recent years, we have carried out a correspondence via email about a broad range of topics, titled "Continuing Conversation". Although it is not as voluminous as my E PEGORILE correspondence with Peter Gore (see below), it is as stimulating.

Some of the many travels Betty and I took together are described below.

Mexico honeymoon, 1960

Our honeymoon was divided into two parts. We had arranged to begin with a tour, but then to strike out on our own. We flew to Mexico City, stayed at a small, unostentatious hotel, where the proprietor was a

White Russian who had fought in the Czarist army, and who hated communists with a passion. We were met the next day by Mr. Garcia of Happiness Tours. It turned out that, instead of a tour bus, we had a Cadillac and Mr. Garcia to ourselves! We spent the first day sightseeing in Mexico City.

Our guided tour included Querétera, a picturesque colonial town of historical importance for Mexico's independence; San Miguel Allende, where we had lunch at the charming Posada de San Francisco with a beautiful courtyard; and Guanajuato, built in a canyon along the hillside, full of tiny, narrow twisting streets. Here, I got very ill at night and we had to call a doctor. He gave me a prescription, which I took to a pharmacy in the morning, where I had to take down my pants to get a shot in my buttocks!

In Morelia, we visited the oldest university on the American continent, founded in 1540, and spoke with some of the students. We drove via Tzintzuntzan to Lake Patzcuaro, a primitive-looking town with a large, quaint market place crowded with Indian women and small children. We took a boat ride to the Island of Janitzio in the middle of the lake. The ride began in a swamp, with floating flowers, cattle submerged to their necks, cranes walking on the floating foliage, water snakes and little Indian boys swimming naked.

Mr. Garcia drove us to San Jose de Purna via the Sierra Madre, on steep roads with many curves and beautiful views. We stayed at a fabulous hotel, built on the side of a canyon, with winding paths connecting the many different levels, open corridors providing an airy atmosphere, lovely flowers and trees, and a large waterfall cascading down from a mountain above, through a natural cave, where one could dance on a glass floor with the waterfall rushing below. There were mineral baths with radioactive waters of reputedly great curative powers, which we tried. The following day we left for Toluca, driving over high mountains, then back to Mexico City where we were welcomed back at our hotel like royalty.

For the rest of our honeymoon we were on our own. We took a guided tour of Xochimilo, including a ride on the floating gardens, and went to some bullfights which I did not enjoy. We visited the Shrine of Guadalupe and the Pyramids of the Sun and Moon at Teotihuacán. Many sick people at the shrine were walking on their knees, a pitiful sight. Our drive afforded excellent views of Popocatepetl and Ixtasiuatl.

Roberto, a jolly, fat, talkative guide, told us his version of the legend of these mountains. We saw the cathedral and the national museum, with its Aztec calendar and wonderful murals by Diego Rivera. At the Museum of Fine Arts there were more murals by Orozco, Siqueiros and Rivera, one of which was intended for the Rockefeller Center in New York, but rejected because the socialist theme was considered too controversial.

We visited Taxco, a very beautiful town with steep cobblestone streets, a lovey colonial church, houses scattered on top of each other with flowers growing up the walls. We stayed at the Posada de la Mission, a beautiful hotel with an airy openness, rooms with balconies, open stairways, a quaint bar, and a swimming pool with a mosaic by Juan O'Gorman. We took a bus to Acapulco, where the Hotel Aloha was air-conditioned, but otherwise had lots of bad features: many insects, the toilet and water didn't work at first, no hot water, and the food and service were bad. Like everywhere else in Mexico, we were constantly surrounded by small children trying to sell us something.

We flew to Mexico City, stayed at the Hotel Prince again, then flew back to Chicago.

Moscow, International Congress of Biochemistry, and Europe, 1961

This trip was the result of my being invited to give a talk at the 5th International Congress of Biochemistry in Moscow. It was a rare opportunity to visit the Soviet Union during the height of the Cold War. As this was Betty's first trip to Europe, we decided to include other countries. Prior to the Congress we visited France, England, Italy and Switzerland. After Moscow, we went to Denmark and Sweden before returning home.

We took a special charter flight for those attending the congress, from Idlewild International Airport in New York. Prior to departure, we were briefed on what to expect in Russia. We flew to Paris, where we went sightseeing, visited the Jeu de Paume museum to see their collection of Impressionist paintings, then to see some of the sculptures at the Louvre, and to the Cité, where we admired the stained glass at Ste. Chappelle, and Nôtre Dame. We heard some very good jazz at Les 3 Mailletz, and went to L'Abbaye to hear African-American folksingers

Lee Payant and Gordon Heath, the latter a very angry young man, with whom we spent some time talking.

Then we flew to London, where we visited Mrs. and Mr. Jeffries, with whom I had stayed during my postdoc year in London, and who were delighted to meet Betty. We went to the theater with Bernard Schlesinger, Susan, Hilary, Roger and his wife Gabriel, to see John's latest film, "Billy Liar". Afterwards, we had an excellent and very pleasant dinner at the Caprice, joined by John.

We drove a rented car to Lewes, in Sussex, to visit Steve and Mary Webber (Steve was Win and Bernard's nephew), who were attending the Glyndebourne Festival, and then to visit Win and Bernard at their home, St. Mary Woodlands. Hilary and Susan were there, as was Kap (Dr. A. Kappas), a physician-scientist whom we knew from Chicago, and who had become friends with Bernard. There was an excellent dinner with animated discussion, mostly about Cuba, where our views were in the minority. We also visited the Gores for an excellent dinner, and met their daughters.

We flew to Geneva, rented a Volkswagen, and drove to beautiful Turin. Among the interesting sights en route was the Sacra di San Michelle, an 11th century monastery perched atop a 3000-foot mountain. In Venice, we enjoyed travelling on the canals in vaporettos. We saw the Doges Palace, and took a gondola ride. We saw the collection of Tintorettos, Titians, and Veroneses at the Academia, and bought a beautiful vase at Venini's. Then we drove, via Padua, Ferrara, Ravenna, Cesna and Perugia, to beautiful Assisi, where we saw the Church of St. Francis with lovely cloisters, beautiful Giotto frescoes, and went up a perilous drive to the old castle at the top of the city for a superb view. We drove to Rome via Foligno, Spoleto, Terni, and Narni. Our hotel was rather dirty and decrepit. We walked to Piazza di Spagna, had a very good dinner at the Taverna Margutta, where we were serenaded by a singer, and met a very nice New Zealand couple – she's an actress -- with whom we had a long and interesting talk.

We went to the Vatican Museum to admire the Sistine Chapel, with its wonderful Michelangelos, and to St. Peter's Square, but were not allowed into the basilica because Betty's arms were uncovered! We saw the Trevi fountain, and took a 4 ½ hour tour of Rome by night. We visited a good night club, Villa dei Cesari on the Appian Way, where the waiters wore Roman garb, and a fabulous night club in Borghese with a superb floor show that included an act with chimpanzees and a midget from Mexico named Tun-Tun, who was a singer and comic actor. We saw the Forum, Colloseum, and Michelangelo's Moses at S. Pietro in Vincoli. We found driving in Rome to be a perilous venture!

We left Rome, after finding that the hotel tried to cheat us, and drove to Florence, stopping in Sienna for a couple of hours on the way. I climbed the 286-ft. tower of the Palazzo Publica, from which there is a glorious view of Sienna and its surroundings. The Hotel Universo, with its friendly staff, was much nicer than the one in Rome. We had an outdoor supper on Piazza della Signoria, then viewed the city at night from Piazza Michelangelo.

At the Medici chapels, we admired Michelangelo's David, the powerful, *non-finito* Prisoners or Slaves and St. Mathew. After dinner at Al Lune di Candela we went to hear La Bohéme at the lovely, modern Teatro Communale. We spent time at the Uffici, seeing some of the highlights, followed by a walk in the Boboli Gardens, where it was very hot.

Our drive via Bologna, and Milan, took us to Como, where we had lunch along the lake. In Switzerland, we drove to St. Moritz, Celerina and on to Zuaos where we spent the night at a charming little hotel annex. The food was excellent, everything spotlessly clean. We took a beautiful route to Davos, and then to Zürich to return the car.

From Zürich, we flew to Prague, where the airport was very dreary. We were scheduled to wait seven hours, but many of us from the congress managed, with a lot of fuss and red tape, to get on an earlier flight on a Russian TU-104 two-engine jet, with very curious, almost Victorian appointments. The stewardesses were neither attractive nor courteous. After a smooth 30-minute flight we landed in Budapest where it was extremely hot. We had to wait about two and a half hours at the airport without any food. When we boarded the plane again, it was stiflingly hot. After 40 very uncomfortable minutes, we took off. The air conditioning was turned on, it got freezing cold, moisture condensed and it actually rained inside, so we all got wet! The flight, once we got going, was very smooth and a good lunch/dinner was served.

We arrived in Moscow at 8 p.m. local time at a large airport decorated for the Titov celebration. The airport at which we were supposed to land was taken over by the celebration for Juri Gargarin, the first astronaut to fly in space, so things were very confusing. My suitcase was missing, which set off another series of frustrating events. We were finally driven to Moscow University, where we were to stay, much to the chagrin of many of the congress participants. But we found the University to be an impressive building, and a beehive of activity involving registration. Our accommodations were austere but quite nice – two small bedrooms with closets, chairs, table, desk and radio, which was tuned to one station and could not be changed, and a bathroom with a shower.

We spent the following morning in seemingly endless, almost motionless lines registering, exchanging money, registering for tours, etc. We pestered the authorities about my lost luggage. Trying to find buses was futile, we had to take taxis. We met Paul Talalay, Peter and Irene Gore and arranged to have dinner together. A Russian man and woman escorted us (and insisted they pay) in the Metro, which was elegant and clean, to the Praha Hotel, where there was a lavish reception with lots of caviar, wine and vodka. We were introduced to many Russians, all very nice, notably Lieberman and Lapin. The former, a Jewish man from Leningrad, an interesting character, very sharp, spoke excellent English. I met Bela Khuskivadze, a girl from Moscow studying steroid metabolism who will act as interpreter in the steroid session, and with whom I had a long, interesting discussion about education in the USSR vs. USA. After dinner, we took a congress bus back to the University, with mostly Russians, some of whom were obviously fascinated by Betty. At the University, a pleasant surprise awaited us: my luggage was there! We were given tickets to an all-Beethoven outdoors concert the following evening, but as it rained, we didn't go.

My paper at a symposium went well. Betty came to listen and talked with a Moroccan student. We had a very pleasant lunch with Mrs. Popják at the Moscva Hotel. I went to a meeting, Betty and Mrs. and Dr. Popják went to the GUM department store and Red Square. In the evening, we met with friends and walked to a well-known restaurant on Pushkin Square, but it was closed, so we walked to the Peking Hotel to try to eat there. We were told we needed to have reservations, but managed to talk our way in. All this took about two hours. Although the food was only mediocre, the conversation and camaraderie were wonderful and we had a great time. Lieberman was very entertaining and witty, and he proposed a very nice toast.

Next morning, we took a tour of the Kremlin. At the museum there, we had to put on felt slippers over our shoes. There was an impressive collection of armor, jewels, handicraft, carriages, etc., some of which were gifts to the czars from many countries. We visited several of the churches on Red Square ("red" is a corruption of a word that meant "beautiful"). Everywhere there were large crowds, and they all stared at us Westerners as though we were from outer space. We walked around the Kremlin and visited Stalin's and Lenin's mausoleum, a small marble structure in grey, black and red. There were huge lines waiting to get in, that apparently begin every day at 8 a.m. Once inside, one files past the two bodies, looking completely life-like, encased in glass caskets, lit by an eerie amber light. It was a very strange experience. After the mausoleum, we filed past numerous graves or commemorative stones representing The Great of the Revolution. On the bus back, I had a fascinating conversation with a Dr. Edozian, a Nigerian, who spoke of his visits to Lumumba University (formerly Freedom University), and with Nigerian and other students. The USSR was giving five years' free education to hundreds of Asian and African students. The students receive about $500 when they arrive, and a Russian teacher for every two or three students for six months, so they can learn the language. They can go home every summer for holidays at USSR expense. Apparently, they get no Soviet indoctrination, but are inculcated with great pride for their own country.

On another tour of Moscow, we saw some impressive new housing in districts that each had their own school, shopping district, etc. Many of the streets were very wide, seven lanes in each direction, but traffic was light. We visited the Pushkin Museum, which displayed some excellent French Impressionists, Picassos, and reproductions of sculptures by Michelangelo, Donatello etc. As many others had done in Moscow, a woman guard came up to Betty and asked if she was from Africa. We joined Peter and Irene on a long bus ride to Ostankino Palace, which was built and furnished entirely by serf artisans in the 18th century, supposedly the finest example of serf craftsmanship. Again, we had to put slippers over our shoes to go in. There were beautiful inlaid wooden floors, a theater, many rooms, a garden, and a church nearby. We had dinner at the Moskva Hotel, excellent soups, fair main dishes, huge quantities, very slow service. A band consisting of some strange-looking characters played schmaltzy music and some music pretending to be jazz.

Betty took a very interesting tour to a Research Institute for Handicapped Children, where they showed laboratory apparatus for teaching the blind, deaf and dumb. They had perfected instruments to allow blind children to read ordinary books by an auditory system, and a method to teach deaf and dumb children foreign languages and Russian. The emphasis was on having each child learn a trade or craft to be a useful member of society, professional as well as labor jobs. There were several short lectures by a psychologist, psychiatrist, teacher and instrumentalist. We visited the fascinating GUM Department Store. It is a huge building with a glass roof. Inside there are lots of separate shops selling all sorts of things usually found in department stores, linked by little bridges and paths (it was a forerunner of our malls!). It was very crowded, with Russians of all kinds, and plentiful merchandise. The displays, especially at food markets, were often very attractive. There were lots of book shops, some right on the street, with people eagerly grabbing large numbers of books. We were invited for a reception at the Hall of Science for all Symposium participants. The wine, vodka and caviar were plentiful. Popják and his wife were hosts and held forth splendidly! We talked to several Congress participants, including Bela Khuskivadse (the girl who studies steroid metabolism) with whom we discussed American political institutions.

At the conclusion of the Congress, we took a long ride to the international airport. Along the way, we saw numerous roadwork gangs, with men and women doing the same hard work. Our plane was a Russian TU-104 again, but this one was more modern than the one we had taken previously, and the hostesses were very nice, English-speaking. The arrival in Copenhagen was beautiful because the plane came down low over Sweden, skimmed over the water, and afforded a lovely view of Copenhagen before we landed. We went to our hotel, the Missionshotellet, driving through lovely Copenhagen, very refreshing after drab Moscow. Copenhagen and its people are very gay with all sorts of amusing statues of fantastic animals, dogs chasing each other, etc. We went to the store Den Permanente and were bowled over by all the beautiful, Danish furniture, glassware, wood, ceramics, glass, art, silver etc. In the evening, we went out to Wivex Populaer at the Tivoli entrance for a superb dinner, very cheap. We spent the rest of the evening at the Tivoli Gardens, an enchanting place full of cafés, amusement places, a concert hall, open-air stages, various kinds of children's rides, tiny kiosks selling all kinds of things, a little lake, fountains, etc. There is beautiful lighting and everything is in exquisite taste; there were many people, all of whom seemed to be laughing and enjoying themselves. A visit to Tivoli should cure any depression – what a change from Moscow!! We went on some of the rides, listened to a band, watched a man making tiny clay animals. Tivoli was like a true fairy land!

The next morning, after a superb breakfast (the food was excellent everywhere!) we walked to Illum's Bolligus, another fantastic shop, like Den Permanente, but containing items from elsewhere as well as Denmark. Then we had a lunch of open-face sandwiches at a tiny restaurant followed by an interesting tour of Copenhagen by bus with an excellent guide. We saw the Carlsberg Museum at the breweries, had some beer there, stopped to see the famous little mermaid and the king's palace, and had dinner near the Tivoli, where we went for the evening to see a western ballet.

We saw the old fish market, took a boat tour around Copenhagen canals, then walked to picturesque Ny Havn, stopping en route at a fascinating place decorated in a most imaginative manner with tubes, wires, bottles, instruments, chemical flasks etc. We had dinner at Skandia, a really lively place, where we heard an excellent jazz band and danced a little.

The next day we saw Tivoli by daylight, took a bus tour, with an excellent female guide, to North Zealand. We stopped at Christenborg Castle, Kronberg castle (Hamlet's castle) in Helsingor, which is most impressive and beautifully situated, with a view of Helsingborg in Sweden across the water. Copenhagen provided so many beautiful things, enticing us to do a lot of shopping.

The final destination of our European tour was Stockholm. The express train from Copenhagen crossed via boat at Helsingor to Helsingborg. The journey was through beautiful countryside with many lakes. In Stockholm, the nasty, cold, rainy weather exacerbated my cold. Our hotel room was huge, with a high ceiling, enormous desk, ornate mirror, bay window, tiny built-in wash room and closet. We went on a rather dull bus tour with an uninteresting guide, in nasty, cold, damp weather.

At dinner, an American Negro parked himself next to us and talked to us. An unpleasant man, a Howard graduate in social science named George Wilson, who had been in Europe for five years, working around, disenchanted with USA, who all but asked us to buy his meal. He said he always hitch-hiked, only lived at places where lodging was free. He felt American Negroes weren't doing enough to end discrimination, that Martin Luther King's approach was wrong, etc. Very cynical, with a big mouth.

The next day we met a Canadian physiologist, Vincent Blockley, who talked to us about the Berlin crisis. He was excited, reactionary, and interesting. Our waiter, Carl Freeman, was left-wing, most engaging and also interesting. He had done lots of odd jobs while travelling all over, and we found him to be very likable. We went to Nordiske Kompanie, a large department store with a superb collection of glass, pottery, ceramics etc. We bought quite a few things and had lunch there (my parents had done so 24 years earlier!). For our departure from Stockholm, we were all taken to dinner at a very nice restaurant called Valingehus, where we had a good dinner and spoke with some others from the International Congress. Our flight was delayed 3 hours, landed in Brussels where we witnessed an almost complete eclipse of the moon. From there we flew to Shannon, and then to New York.

Canada, 1964

We drove to Montreal via the Adirondacks, stopped in North Ellba to see John Brown's grave, and up Whiteface Mountain. In Montreal, we heard Oscar Peterson at Le Jazz Hot, went to see "Tom Jones", and saw an outstanding exhibition of African, pre-Colombian and Eskimo art at Lippel Gallery.

In Quebec, we drove to Lac Beauport, a resort area with beautiful scenery, and Île d'Orleans in the St. Lawrence River. We visited two 17th century farm houses preserving all the charms of that era, including a horse and buggy drive up to the door. We sampled the delicious soup made over the hearth in a large cauldron, and a huge piece of home-made bread covered with pure maple sugar and heavy cream, plus a glass of cider. A highlight of our visit to Quebec was the evening we heard 17th - 20th century flute and piano music, form Bach to

Poulenc, at l'Atre at the Île d'Orleans. The lovely harmonies in cozy surroundings contrasted with a fierce storm outdoors.

We had some superb meals in Canada, including crêpes suzettes and coq au vin at Kerhuku; coq au vin at Le Caveau in Montreal; onion soup at La Soupière in Montreal; calves' livers at Le Vendôme; and filet mignon flambeau cognac at La Chammiere. They were all lubricated with excellent, mostly French wines,

Japan and Hawaii, 1967

The purpose of this trip was to attend the International Congress of Biochemistry in Tokyo. We stopped in Hawaii on our way home.

We flew to Chicago to leave Karen with Betty's mother, then flew to Los Angeles. From there we flew to Tokyo via Hawaii and Wake Island, and took a bus to our hotel, the new wing of the Tokyo Imperial Hotel. Next morning, we heard on the radio that there had been a riot in Syracuse! We looked at the fabulous old wing of the Imperial Hotel, built by Frank Lloyd Wright. This hotel withstood the great earthquake in 1923, which destroyed most of Tokyo, because of Wright's genius and insistence to adhere to his plans to make the building earthquake-proof.

We went to "New Center", a modern round building with a revolving restaurant lounge on top, affording a lovely view of the city. While I went to a plenary session, Betty attended the opening ceremonies for wives, including a traditional Tea Ceremony. We took the Congress bus to Nippon Budokan, a very impressive looking building built for the Olympics, for a welcoming reception.

One evening we went to dinner with our friends the Dois and Merricks, and met with several Japanese who had been postdocs in Syracuse, who took us to the exquisite Happo-En Garden restaurant, where the food was cooked at the table. After dinner, we took a walk in a beautiful peaceful garden, with a tea house, old stone lanterns, miniature trees, etc. It was one of the highlights of our trip.

While I attended scientific sessions, Betty learned wood-block printing and went to flower arranging, and to an interesting visit to a Japanese home. One evening we went, with my friend John Westley, to see Bunuraku, an ancient Japanese puppet show, which appeared very strange to us.

We took an air-conditioned train to Nikko, passing through fascinating countryside with steep little hills, rice paddies with women picking rice. Nikko is a charming little town, in the foothills, with steep, narrow streets. The bus took us up a very steep road with 48 hair-pin turns, breathtaking views. We had an excellent, knowledgeable guide. After lunch, we went to the 300-years-old Toshogu Shrine, which we found gaudy, and which is actually a collection of many shrines, some designated as National Treasures of Japan.

We took the super-express train to Kyoto, travelling at over 100 m.p.h. At the Kyoto Hotel, we had a charming room, and took a walk through the lovely, quaint town. From there we took an all-day bus tour to Nara, with an excellent, informative guide. Nara was the first capital of Japan, built in 712. We were at a deer park, at Todaiji Temple, the world's largest wooden building, housing the world's largest bronze Buddha. We also saw Kasuya Shrine, with its 3000 stone and bronze lanterns, and visited Momoyama Castle and Fushimi Inzari Shrine, before returning to our hotel.

Among the many beautiful sights in Kyoto were the Higashi Hoganji Temple; the Zen Buddhism temple with its garden of Daisen-In, featuring lovely stone arrangements, abstract depictions of waterfalls, rivers, mountains and the sea, over 400 years old; Gold Pavillion, Nijo Castle with decorated rooms used by Shogun to receive nobles; the Sanju Sangendo temple with 1001 Buddhas, each one different, created by many artists, that took 50 years to complete; and Kiyomiju Temple. We watched pottery being made in the basement of a little shop. We also saw Ryozan Kannon, with large Buddhas in the hillside, dedicated to unknown soldiers from World War II, and Heian Shrine with its beautiful walk-through garden. Our taxi drive to the station featured a taxi driver who drove like a mad man, angry at another driver. We took the super express back to Tokyo.

There were big differences between the International Congress in Moscow in 1961, and the one in Tokyo. The former was poorly organized, technically unsophisticated, often frustrating, and took place in a grim, gloomy city. The one in Tokyo was efficiently run with excellent technology in a city and country where everything was displayed beautifully. In both events, however, the scientists were friendly and warm.

Our flight to Honolulu crossed the date line, so we arrived on the previous day!

In Hawaii, we visited Maui, Hilo on Hawaii Island, where we visited the rainbow falls, orchid nurseries, and Volcano National Park, where we had lunch right on the edge of a crater. We drove through a volcanic landscape to the Black Sand Beach, then to Kailua on the Kona coast. We visited the Captain Cook monument, went on a glass-bottom boat viewing coral and sea urchins, and had a brief swim. We took a plane back to Kuai, where we went swimming under the stars at a magnificent beach.

We took Smith's river boat up the Wailua River to the Fern Grotto where the Smith family sang the Hawaiian Wedding Song and entertained us on our way back. We saw Opaikaa Falls on our way to the airport, where we took a flight to Honolulu. After flying back to Los Angeles, we spent the evening with Betty's Uncle Wilbur, then flew back to Chicago to pick up Karen, and the following day to Syracuse.

Sabbatical in England, 1972 - 1973.

Betty and Karen accompanied me for my one-year research leave to Oxford University. Before we left, there were three critical problems we had to solve: what to do about the house, the car, and our dog Cocoa. We solved all three most satisfactorily.

We rented the house (our first house in Syracuse, at 200 Kensington Place) to some medical students from SUNY Upstate Medical School. There were four men, but they were, apparently, joined by two women later. Several friends warned us that renting to students was not a good idea, that they tend to ruin the carpets and furniture, but we both had the impression that these students were mature and responsible, and we were right. They took good care of the house, even fixed the humidifier, and it was in excellent condition when we returned.

We asked our neighbor to sell our car, a relatively new Dodge Dart, for us, which he did several weeks after we left, at a reasonable price, sufficient to allow us to purchase a car in England, a little red Hillman Imp which served us very well.

Our good friend Rhoda agreed to take Cocoa for the year. This was an act of great kindness, and loyalty, especially as she was a cat lover who didn't own a dog. Rhoda lived in the country outside Ithaca, but for most of the year she was working in New York, so Cocoa got to experience both country and city living. He adapted to both very well and apparently really liked Rhoda. Nevertheless, when we returned he was ecstatic to see us again and, when we went to visit Rhoda a few weeks later, and took him with us, he wouldn't get out of the car!

Rhoda was one of the first persons we got to know in Syracuse, in 1963. She and Betty both worked at the Huntington Family Service Center. She played a large role in many aspects of our life and became a very good friend. When we wanted to adopt Karen, she wrote a letter, testifying to our suitability as parents. When we went to England in 1973 for my sabbatical, she kept our dog Cocoa for us, and she visited us there. When Karen and I went to Leipzig in 2009 (see Chapter 11), she stayed with Betty. When we moved from our apartment to our first house, in 1965, she rented our apartment for a while. She participated in Betty's memorial service in 2019. We have frequently attended her annual Labor Day picnics, held, at first, in her A-frame and then at her geodesic dome, both of which she built with the help of her brothers and father near Ithaca.

Rhoda's family owned a farm near Ithaca, and we got to know her brothers and parents, as well as her many nieces and nephews. Rhoda was a community organizer, but she also worked at Cornell University, was a faculty member of the Free University, and for many years spent several months, mostly as a Fulbright Fellow in Burma, where she had spent time as a missionary in her youth, organizing women. She had many women friends in and around Ithaca and beyond, who attended her annual picnics. She is a highly intelligent, interesting, committed, independent-minded woman and our friendship with her has been very rewarding. She has known Karen ever since we adopted her, and when Karen moved back east in 2018, and then began to work at Cornell University, a friendship developed between her and Rhoda.

Packing for our departure to England was a huge job, especially as we also had to get the house in order for the medical students. The hours before departure were hectic, and we had to cancel our 12:30 flight to New York as we weren't ready, and took a 6 p.m. flight instead. My graduate student Mike Milhausen and technician Connie Hyde took us to the airport. We had a lot of luggage, but had also shipped a trunk. In New York, we arrived in plenty of time for our flight to

England, and as we prepared to wait, an airline employee asked us if we would like to leave on an earlier flight, on a Boeing 747, due to depart very shortly. We agreed, had a good flight and were met by Win and Bernard Schlesinger who drove us to Oxford, to our flat, which we had rented with the help of Henry Tedeschi. Henry was a physiologist who was a graduate student at the University of Chicago when I was there, and who had been on sabbatical at Oxford for the past year, and was living in the downstairs flat until the end of August. Win and Bernard left us at our flat, having brought lots of food, including a large roasted chicken.

Our flat was in a nice Tudor house at 321 Woodstock Road with a lovely garden. For much of the year we enjoyed the garden, the birds, and Karen had a tree she climbed. That part of Woodstock Road has beautiful gardens and houses. The interior of our flat was quite comfortable, but the furniture and rugs were very ugly, and the kitchen was tiny. We rented a TV and radio, which were very good investments as there was a lot of good programming on both. The stove and refrigerator were very small, and there were no washer or dryer, so we had to take the laundry out to a commercial laundromat.

Soon we encountered a problem: our trunk did not arrive. There had been a strike in the shipyards, and it took over three months, and a lot of angry letters from me, and intervention of my attorney, before it came. Our winter clothes, and a lot of my scientific stuff was in the trunk, but we did get used to getting along with what we had.

We enrolled six-year-old Karen in the Wolvercote school, a ten-minute walk from our house. There were children from other countries in her class, and she had a very nice teacher.

After a while we bought a little red Hillman Imp, and bicycles for me and Karen, which she loved (she had one in Syracuse). Routinely, I bicycled to the lab, which was about two miles toward downtown. I discuss my scientific experience in Chapter 7. Here I will briefly describe some of the highlights of our year in Oxford.

We visited many of my friends and family on numerous occasions - the Schlesingers, the Gores, Steven Webber (the Schelsinger's nephew) and his wife Mary and their children as well as Steven's sister Barbara (Bar) and their mother Meg; my friends from Leipzig, Walter and Renate Weg and their families; Eva, John, and Anthony Glees (see Chapter 2); my mother's friends the Tanners; Mrs. Jeffreys, my landlady while I was a postdoc in London, who was then living in a retirement home in Brighton; and I visited John Cripps (see Chapter 2). We became good friends with Bunny and Rose Chukwukere. He was a graduate student in anthropology, from Nigeria, she was from Jamaica, they had a little daughter Nekka.

We took trips to some beautiful villages, animal parks, Windsor Castle, Blenheim Palace, and we went to many concerts, ballets and plays, including at Stratford-on-Avon, the Royal Festival Hall where we heard several concerts and saw the Ballet Folklorico of Mexico. We took Karen whenever appropriate.

We spent Christmas with Steve and Mary Webber and their children. It was a lovely, warm visit with this beautiful family. In February, we had booked a short trip to the costa del Sol in southern Spain. That turned into a big disappointment. We got up early, took a bus to Heathrow, got processed, and then waited. After a long time, and many announcements, the flight was cancelled. The French air traffic control personnel had gone on strike, and since they also controlled the air space over Spain, all flights were cancelled. We had to make our way back to Oxford, where we had a nearly empty refrigerator. We brought in some Chinese food and spent a cold weekend in Oxford instead of a warm one in Spain.

A much more successful trip was our fantastic one to East Africa, which is described below.

Quite a lot of visitors came to see us in Oxford. During the first week, Clara Mitchell (Betty's childhood friend Helen Lamb's sister) and her husband Norman came from London. We had visits from Debbie Apter, a Syracuse friend, who stayed a few days but got sick; Mina Ostrolenk and one of her grandsons; Rhoda, who stayed several weeks; Liz's friend Ronnie Coleman; my mother, who stayed a couple of weeks; Tess Denov from Funference days; and Howard, Norah, Cynthia and Sarah Goldfine. While my mother visited, we met with my cousin Ora and her husband Moshe Moskovic from Israel.

We were invited by several faculty members of the Oxford Biochemistry Department, including George Radda and his wife, to their respective colleges for dinner at High Table.

It was an extraordinary year for all of us.

Betty took a train to London every Thursday and spent time at the British Museum, where she saw the Tutankhamun exhibit, which was one of the events that set her off on her long journey of discovery about ancient Egyptian civilizations. She also made all the arrangements for our trip to East Africa. She participated in a graduate seminar on Ethnic, Cultural and Racial Studies at Oxford University and took courses in photography, pottery making, and expository writing at a Community College. She joined the Oxford Africa Society, which presented interesting lectures.

Karen took ballet and recorder lessons. She looked after the school gerbil during Spring break, and then we got her one for herself. She became more independent, and quickly picked up an English accent, which she soon lost after our return to Syracuse.

I went to an Old Newburians' Dinner at my old school. Quite a lot of former students recognized me, and I saw several of my former class mates, and spoke with several of my former masters. It was a wonderful, nostalgic experience, 27 years after I left. I also drove to Cambridge to see David Ellar, a former student in our department in Syracuse, who was on the faculty at Cambridge University.

I went to the Oxford Museum of Natural History, which I had enjoyed as a young boy, and saw an exhibit that had so impressed me then: the sun and all the planets of the solar system, made to scale, with the distances of the planets' orbits also made to scale. I went to the Bodleian Library and saw a fascinating exhibit about books: the first printed book, illuminated Hebrew bibles, Shakespeare's first play, the first edition of Dante's Inferno, Chaucer, Egyptian writings, Mendelssohn's works, including his paintings and drawings. I also had a disturbing talk with Raymond Dwek, who was a senior staff scientist in George Radda's lab, about the difficult experiences of being a Jew at Oxford. I learned a great deal of new science in George Radda's lab, which I describe in Chapter 7. I heard some excellent seminars, especially from members of the Oxford Enzyme Group, including Margaret Adams who would later become a collaborator in my research, and had some very fruitful interactions with George's and other graduate students, some of whom came to visit us in subsequent years in Syracuse.

East Africa - Kenya and Tanzania, 1973.

This was a once-in-a lifetime vacation to end our year in England.

We drove to Heathrow, left our car at a garage near the airport, and made our way to our flight, a huge E. African Airlines VC 10, but with only about 30 passengers. We left at 8 p.m. and, since there was lots of room, we each took a 3-seat bench so we could stretch out. We arrived in Nairobi eight hours later.

Nairobi had modern, western architecture, including our hotel, the Nairobi Hilton. After lunch, we took a short stroll and were appalled by the signs of terrible poverty among western-style splendor. Many poor people were begging and peddling their wares. The city seemed to be like a shanty town, with shops crowded along alleys, contrasting with splendid hotels and other buildings at the center. The University had magnificent buildings, attractively landscaped, and some stunning sculptures scattered about.

The next day we took a bus to the National Museum where we visited the Snake Park with a fascinating collection of snakes, lizards, turtles, and crocodiles. We visited Judith Heyer, the daughter of John and Ursula Cripps who became my sister's good friend (see Chapter 2), at her suburban home. She very much resembles her father. We met her three children, and there were two dogs and three black servants who lived in separate housing. The house was beautiful, in rolling grounds. Her husband, Sujit, arrived later, we had good conversations, and Karen got along well with the children. Sujit drove us back to our hotel.

We decided that Kenya was too western, and that Tanzania was bound to be better. We bought safari boots, visited some arts and crafts shops, took a taxi to the East African Airline terminal, and flew on a small, 2-prop engine plane to Arusha, landing at Kilimanjaro airport. We were driven in a mini bus to Arusha, the New Arusha Hotel, arriving after dark. We had a very attractive, rustic room.

When we awoke, we saw that the hotel was rambling, partly open-style, in a garden with bright, tropical trees, full of white-naped ravens, hornbills and other birds. As we went out to see about tours, we were besieged by boys trying to sell us all sorts of jewelry, carvings, etc., terribly crippled men and boys, many colorfully dressed women and men, Maasai, some with sticks, some carrying loads on their heads. Arusha gave the impression of a frontier town. We took a five-hour tour of Arusha National Park which is 20 miles outside Arusha, driven by a guide in a large Toyota limousine, accompanied by an elderly German couple. We went past native huts, banana trees, coffee bushes, first on a tarmac road, then on a bumpy dirt road. We drove to Leitony, at 6080 feet elevation, overlooking Ngurdoto Crater at 4700 ft. There was a sensational view - lakes, mountains, and the crater floor, with buffalo, hippopotamus, flamingoes and giraffes. On the way we saw, at close range, waterbuck, wart hogs, colobus monkeys, bushbuck, and reed buck. We continued on to various lakes and saw hippopotamus, rhinoceros, buffalo, giraffes, baboons, black monkeys, dik-dik, ibis, bush buck, white pelicans and eagles. We had some marvelous views of Kilimanjaro and Meru, one of the most magnificent was from a point overlooking Small Momela Lake. In bright sunshine to our left was Kilimanjaro. In front of us was the lake, with many hippos bathing. At the other shore were giraffes and a rhinoceros and many different birds. To our right was Mount Meru, enveloped in dramatic clouds. Behind us, not far away, were waterbuck. Seeing so many animals in the wild was amazing, and I decided I could never go to a zoo again.

The next day we packed, leaving one trunk and bag at the hotel for our return. We were driven by Mr. Moshi to Lake Manyara, seeing Maasai with their herds of cattle on the way, and villages with grass huts. The land was mostly semi-arid. There were lots of large termite hills, occasional acacia and baobab trees. We climbed an escarpment which afforded fantastic views of the lake and the Maasai plains we had just traversed, to the Lake Manyara Hotel. It was another beautiful, rambling hotel, built on the open plan. Our room, with a balcony, overlooked the lake below with a fantastic view. After lunch in a large, airy dining room, Karen and I went swimming in the pool. Later, Mr. Moshi drove us to Lake Manyara National Park, another fantastic experience, where Karen took her first photographs. We saw elephants, rhinos, zebras, giraffes, impala, dik-dik, buffalo, fisher eagles, storks, vultures, a snake that darted off the road, a lizard, baboons, vervet monkeys, ground hornbills, flamingoes, crowned cranes, water hogs, and a troupe of banded mongoose, but not the tree-climbing lions for which the park is famous. All the animals were easily seen and not frightened by cars. It was another extraordinary experience and the profusion of flora and fauna was astonishing. The drive was hot and dusty, but at night it got cool, and the weather was very pleasant. We noticed that, whereas the tourists in Kenya seemed to be mostly English, here they were American and German. The night sky, with bright stars, was spectacular. Karen always led when we moved around the complicated paths in the hotel, and she always found the way!

The next morning, after a howling wind storm during the night, we were joined by a man who worked at Ngorogoro Wildlife Lodge, and asked if he could have a lift. That turned out, later, to be very fortunate. Today's drive went through fertile lands, past cultivated fields. The soil was a dusty red color everywhere. Maasai herdsmen were all about. As we got closer to Ngorongoro, we started to climb and it became very foggy. The man whom we had given a lift said that Forest Lodge, where we had planned to stay, was not nearly as nice as the place where he worked, Wildlife Lodge. Indeed, when we got to Forest Lodge, it was quite dismal and there were no other guests. We decided to take a chance - we might not get a refund, and there might not be any rooms at Wildlife Lodge - but our decision proved to be a good one. The hotel was spacious, beautifully designed, right on the edge of Ngorongoro Crater. We had an excellent lunch there and then a driver guide took us in a 4-wheel drive Land Rover down into the crater. It was an incredible drive, with many hair-pin turns down steep, rocky dirt tracks. The crater comprised about 100 sq. miles, full of all sorts of wild life, most abundant were wildebeest and zebras, but we also saw rhinos, hyenas, jackals, two types of gazelle, hippos, Kori bustards (the largest flying birds in Africa), secretary birds, an elephant, and we drove up to within few feet of eight lions. They were presumably sleeping after a feast of buffalos last night. On a lake, there was a vast profusion of pink flamingos, packed tightly together - an incredible sight. Later, we could make them out as a pink patch from our hotel window. When we first entered the crater, we stopped near a Maasai village, and several Maasai came out and wanted to have their picture taken (for money). As was true at Lake Manyara, at the hotel there was a telescope through which one could observe the wildlife below.

We were awakened at 3 a.m. by a noise outside our window. It was a buffalo, who was grazing and had stopped to rub himself against a tree right outside our room.

Later, we left in a chilly, thick fog, but that cleared as we descended from the crater's edge and soon we were riding in hot sunshine with a clear sky. Our entire trip today was over the most rough, bumpy roads we experienced, through desolate country reminiscent of a moonscape. Our car rattled and bounced along, sending up a trail of dust which seemed to get right under our skins. We drove to Olduvai Gorge, where we took a tour down into the gorge, where Mary Leakey had discovered the *Zinjanthropus* skull in 1959. Olduvai Gorge is situated in the Olduvai Conservation Region, one of the most desolate, dusty areas we encountered. The guide took us to a place where we could overlook a cross section of the whole gorge, where there was a small, excellent museum. It was an exciting, moving experience.

We then drove to Seronera, in the middle of the Serengeti National Park, passing many strange-looking kopjes, massive collections of granite rocks, often with vegetation, many having bizarre shapes, and also some acacia trees. At the Seronera Lodge we ate some box lunches we had brought from Ngorongoro. We had seen lots of animals - Thompson's and Grant's gazelles, giraffes, ostriches, secretary birds, Kori bustards, brightly colored superb starlings, and zebras. After lunch, we drove around in the Park, saw topis and leopards resting up in some acacia trees. We drove to Lobo Wildlife Lodge, where we witnessed part of the annual great migration, passing two huge herds of wildebeest and zebra, stampeding across the road.

Lobo Wildlife Lodge was another fabulous hotel, situated atop a kopje, overlooking a waterhole and great plain below. From our beautiful room, we could see malibu storks at the water hole, and buffalo, wildebeest, zebras and topis, and an occasional waterhog, grazing below. On the rocks in the hotel grounds there were hyrax and lots of lizards. Karen and I took a quick dip in their magnificently situated swimming pool (the water was very cold), next to which there was a telescope though which one could view the wildlife below. There was a spacious bar, with a huge fireplace at one end, where we had some drinks and then an excellent dinner in a magnificently constructed dining hall with a tree rising up through its roof. After dinner, we met a nice African American couple from Atlanta, Mr. & Mrs. Anderson Davis, whose daughter was American Consul in Nairobi, and spent half an hour over coffee with them. That night, although the windows were closed, a wind was howling through them. We never thought we'd be cold in Africa!

It took us eight hours the following day to get back to Arusha, including a one-hour lunch stop at Crater Lodge in Ngorongoro. On the way, we had an exciting encounter with two lions, a full-grown male and a female, just outside Serengeti National Park, who stood in the middle of the road. We could drive right up to them, they ignored us completely, walked around the car and went about their business. The road, such as it was, out of Serengeti past Olduvai Conservation Region, was the worst and most desolate we encountered. We were amazed that the car could withstand the harsh, rocky surface, full of boulders and holes, rattling and shaking all the time. Mr. Moshi was a skillful driver. At some points the road was so bad, he had to drive along the fields alongside, which were so dusty, we sometimes seemed to sink into the sand and dust, and the windows became completely darkened by clouds of dust. The only animals we encountered on this part of our trip were Thompson's and Grant's gazelles, giraffes, and an occasional silver-backed jackal. The giraffes could be seen from far away because they are so tall, and despite their ungainly appearance, are actually very graceful. We passed a Maasai village, I took some photos of the people, many of whom came running up to the car, begging for money. After we got back to Arusha, we all took thorough baths or showers to get rid of the dust that clung to us all over.

The next day was gloomy and rainy. After lunch, I walked to the memorial to see the Arusha Declaration, written in 1967 for Tanganyika African National Union by Julius Nyerere, Tanzania's first president. It is Tanzania's political statement on African socialism, "Ujama". This concept is often expressed in Makonde sculptures, and greatly impressed Betty. I walked through old Arusha, quite a dreary town, really a trading post. Most of the shops were owned by Indians. In the public library, there were many people reading. What brought a lot of color to the town was the displays of crafts, especially Maasai beadwork, and the Maasai in their brightly colored garbs, some with babies on their backs, some carrying their wares on their heads and live chickens under their arms, presumably to take to the market; Maasai men carrying sticks, or leading goats; school children, some in uniforms; people trying to sell us something. I went to the Arusha Branch of National Arts of Tanzania Ltd., to look at their Makonde sculpture. The man who ran the shop there explained that the government carefully controls the cutting down of ebony trees and provides wood to the artists. At dinner, we talked with the chef, originally from Belgium, married to a woman from the Chagga tribe. He was a sailor for many years, and spoke five languages, including Swahili.

The next day we visited National Arts of Tanzania Ltd., and a little library with a children's section. After lunch, yesterday's guide drove us to Moshi, a town larger than Arusha, at the foot of Kilimanjaro, but the mountain remained hidden behind clouds. We walked around the town, and then drove to the airport for our trip to Dar es Salaam. We soon learned that our plane was delayed, and then cancelled, because of engine trouble. Another flight was to be diverted to Kilimanjaro to take us to Dar es Salaam, but it wasn't due until after 11 p.m. Those of us waiting for the plane, including a Columbia University professor who was scheduled to give a talk in Dar, argued with the airline officials, to no avail. We were provided a free dinner, and were at that airport for six hours without ever seeing a plane land, or take off, or on the ground. At 11:20 a D.C. 9 arrived. We flew to Mombassa, and then to Dar, arriving at 1:30 a.m. It took a long time to get our luggage, there were no cabs, so we took a bus to down town, an adventure itself as the bus took ages to get started, then lurched over a bumpy road, suitcases flying about, until it got to down town. We had to take a taxi to our hotel, the Kunduchi Beach Hotel, 13 miles away, where we arrived at 3 a.m., had to register, a cot had to be prepared for Karen, before we finally got to sleep.

When we awoke the next morning, we found we were magnificently situated, right on the Indian Ocean, with palm trees and little grass huts on the beach. We had a snack in a half-open, spacious lounge facing the ocean. We swam in the ocean and the hotel pool. After lunch, we went on an outboard motor boat to the totally uninhabited Mbudya Island, a ten-minute ride, where we swam and hunted for sea shells. Karen, who loves the water, was in her element. When we got back, we relaxed, enjoying the sea breeze. Here, and elsewhere in Africa, the stars in the moon-less sky at night were fabulous.

The next day was dull and drizzly. We took a little bus from the hotel to downtown Dar and visited the National Museum. A large portion was devoted to the excavations at Olduvai; the skull of *Australopithecus* was displayed here and some sections were devoted to the history of Tanzania and artifacts relating to the people. We went to the National Arts of Tanzania to see the Makonde sculptures. After dinner, we let Karen stay up as there was a dance, with a band and singers.

The following day was also drizzly. We took the hotel bus to the African Village Museum, which featured different types of African houses and huts, each one typical for a specific tribe. We did a little shopping down town. After lunch, we took a taxi to the University. On a tour of the Zoology Department we met a graduate student born in Syracuse, as well as a Sociology professor who earned his Ph.D. at Syracuse University! We took a taxi back to the hotel. For dinner, there was an excellent barbecue and there was entertainment provided by young girls and boys, dancing to drums. After dinner, Karen watched the film "The Boyfriend", with two girls she had befriended.

Next day started off with bright sunshine. We had ordered a car, so we could do a little touring ourselves, but after much waiting it became clear the car would never arrive. Karen made friends with the hotel manager's eight-year-old daughter, Bronwin; they were a good match for each other. I went swimming in the ocean. As it was low tide, I wandered way out, where I stepped on a sea urchin, which was very painful. I made my way back, found my foot was swollen, went to the dispensary where a medical officer put some ointment and bandages on my foot, making it very awkward to get around. Bronwin ate lunch with us, to Karen's great delight. After lunch we ordered another taxi, which took ages to get to the hotel, and went down town just as a partial solar eclipse was at its maximum. We bought some gifts at Crafts of Tanzania. Our taxi back to the hotel went past Julius Nyerere's house. Dinner was a very nice buffet around the pool, with a band and dancing.

On our last day in East Africa, we went on a tour of Dar es Salaam. We saw a large hospital, two open-air markets, the harbor, and other places, all well explained by our guide. After lunch, we went, with the same guide, to Bagamoya, driving through banana and cocoanut plantations, past cashew trees, mango trees, and papaya trees, and past places where artists were making Makonde sculptures (we bought a couple). In Bagamoya, a sleepy, picturesque town, we saw carved doors along narrow streets; a museum devoted to the explorers Stanley and Livingstone, who started their journeys here; memorabilia from both the German colonial time and the slave trade. This was a point of departure for slaves, and we saw the very place where they were shackled and transported. Later, our guide drove us to the airport. He helped us to locate a currency exchange and shepherded us through a lot of bureaucracy. Our flight on a V.C. 10 to Nairobi took just over an hour. Then we left for Rome, a 6 ½ hour flight, had a 40-minute stopover there, and then flew, in bright sunshine, over the Swiss Alps to London. We picked up our little Imp from the garage and drove to Oxford. Our memorable East Africa visit was a unique adventure that brought us many new experiences and was filled with unforgettable encounters with many kinds of beauty.

Postscript. When Betty arranged our Africa trip in London, the man at the travel bureau told her to be sure not to pay our bill in Dar es Salaam, but to tell them to charge it to them. Apparently, the travel bureau doesn't get their cut unless it is done that way. Once we got to Oxford, I called the travel bureau in London, to tell them we were back and had charged our Dar es Salaam stay to them. I reminded him that we were leaving for the States in a few weeks. After a month, I still had not received our bill, so I called the travel bureau again to remind them to bill us. I also gave them our Syracuse address. I wrote to them again from Syracuse twice, not having received a bill. WE NEVER DID GET A BILL!! Our 5 day sojourn in that luxurious Kunduchi Beach Hotel outside Dar es Salaam was free!!

Trinidad and Tobago, 1989.

This was planned as a warm vacation from cold, snowy Syracuse in January. We flew to Newark, then on to Trinidad. In Syracuse, the plane had to be de-iced in a snow storm; in Trinidad, the temperature was 85 degrees. Our room was very small, right by the pool, with primitive plumbing and noisy air conditioning. Kiskide birds made a terrific screeching noise every morning.

The next day, we rented an old Nissan with 106,000 miles on it, drove around Port of Spain, where the inhabitants seem to be mostly African or African mixture, but also lots of East Indians. After an excellent dinner at the hotel restaurant, La Fantastic, a mix of French and Trinidad cuisine, we went to the Carnival Expo '89 Festival where we saw some excellent calypso performers, visited many stalls with crafts, different foods, etc.

Driving to the beach at Maracas the following day was an adventure, trying to understand directions from natives, with poorly marked roads, partly through very mountainous terrain with hair-pin curves, but breath-taking vistas. When we finally arrived, there was not enough time to swim.

We drove to town the next morning, to exchange some money. When we returned from the bank, our car was gone! We had unknowingly parked in a no parking zone, so our car was towed. We had to take a couple of taxis to get the car from the police station. It cost me $85 Trinidad (ca $20 U.S.) to retrieve it. On the following day, we returned our car, which had a bad clutch, rattled, and had bad springs, and, rented a nice Toyota Corolla.

We set off for Chaguarams on the Gulf of Paria, where we found a bearded man who took us by boat to Gaspar Grande Island, and saw pelicans and a view of the coast of Venezuela en route. We walked to find the caves, a steep path, in the hot sun. We were joined by a little dog who seemed to lead the way. We came across a house with a notice about the cave, where a young, black man became our guide. His name was Sheldon Ian Antoine, he was 19, bright, enthusiastic, and very engaging. We took some stairs to the cave, Sheldon explaining everything as we went. There were lots of stalagmites and stalactites, a clear pool of water with fish, lots of bats and large cockroaches. Sheldon told us that he hopes to visit the States, we invited him to visit us, and exchanged addresses. Our bearded man with the boat was waiting for us, and took us back, with Sheldon coming along. Back in Trinidad, Sheldon told us about social and political troubles in Trinidad. He wrote down some local foods we should sample and places to see in Tobago. We went to the Café Savanah for a superb meal, chicken with bananas, coconut shrimp curry, shark paté, and coconut ice cream.

We were awakened at 4:30 a.m. the next morning to drive to the airport. When we asked for directions, a man asked us to give him a lift, which we did, and we enjoyed chatting with him. We had a light breakfast at the airport, took a jet, which took twelve minutes to get to Tobago! We joined a tour, were driven by minibus to Pigeon Point, a lovely beach dotted with palm trees and little huts. We made friends with a lovely, interesting black girl, Bunny, who was there with a German man. She worked for British West Indian Airlines, spoke fluent German and Chinese. A group of us went on a glass-bottomed boat for a tour to Buccoo Reef, where we got out to snorkel (my first time) and saw lots of fantastic, colored fish swimming among the corals. It was breathtakingly beautiful! I also got out in the Nylon Pool, a shallow pool of water, quite warm, in the middle of the sea. We went back to Pigeon Point for lunch and then a 2 ½ hour tour of beautiful, hilly, busy Scarborough and its surroundings, conducted by a woman driving a taxi. School children wore uniforms and seemed more immature than in the U.S., more like children in Europe. We saw cocoa fruits, breadfruits, cattle egrets, pelicans, tethered little sheep and goats. We learned that Tobago was trying to build a tourist industry.

Back in Trinidad the next morning, we went to take our car back and see about a tour, but the proprietor said we could keep it the rest of the day free of charge! So, we drove down to the south of Trinidad through San Fernando to La Brea, the site of Pitch Lake. Roads there were terrible: even when they get repaired, they buckle again, houses have to be jacked up every few weeks, because everything lies over pitch beds. A guide at Pitch Lake took us onto the lake, which is about a half mile in diameter. It was originally owned by a black woman, who had it taken from her by a British company. There is an endless reserve of pitch, which forms a skin that one can walk or drive on, but can't leave a car on it for long as it will sink. The pitch contains fossils, and the water on the lake contains tiny fish which don't live anywhere else. Gas forms constantly and escapes from little vents. Betty slipped into some pitch, but our guide cleaned up her shoes. He was very enthusiastic and had lots of information, charged us $120 Trinidadian. We drove back to return the car.

The following day we got up early, put on our winter clothing, and were driven by taxi through a beautiful mountain route to the airport. We took a flight to San Juan, then Newark, then Syracuse, where Karen picked us up, but our luggage didn't make it! At midnight, they called to say it had arrived, we got it late next morning. It had been a wonderful trip.

The Southwest, "Four Corners", 1993.

We flew to Denver, rented a car, visited my cousin Lori and met her new boyfriend, John. We also visited Lori's son Steve and his wife Meg at their house and met their daughter, Sarah. In the evening, we went to Elias and Gloria Balbinder for dinner, joined by Clark Bublitz and his wife and one other couple. Elias was my former colleague at Syracuse University (see Chapter 6), Clarke was a fellow graduate student at the University of Chicago, Gloria is an interior decorator and the Balbinder house is beautifully appointed and decorated.

We drove to Taos, a lovely town with every building covered with terra cotta adobe. We had a tour of the Taos Pueblo, which has been consistently inhabited for more than a thousand years. We saw the Gorge of the Rio Grande and visited a museum housing Native American and Hispanic art and artifacts.

We then drove to Santa Fe via a picturesque route. Santa Fe has many art galleries. We stopped at the Fine Arts Museum, saw some Georgia O'Keefe paintings and Dorothy Lange photos. We visited Connie Hyde, one of my former technicians, and her family in Cedar Crest, NM, where we had dinner and then set off for Albuquerque. From there we drove to Flagstaff the next day, visiting the El Moro National Monument on the way, an interesting configuration of rocks with Indian petroglyphs. We visited the Painted Desert and Petrified Forest; both had spectacular, beautiful colors.

We drove through the absolutely spectacular Oak Creek Canyon and to Sedona, both having a spiritual aura about them, with amazing red colors, to Flagstaff. We visited the Grand Canyon at Yarapai Point. No pictures can do justice to what one experiences when one first looks across the Grand Canyon - the majesty and splendor are awesome!! We took a shuttle bus tour to different locations to get different views - they were all magnificent! In the afternoon, we went back to Yarapai Point to watch the sun set over the canyon, an awesome display of different colors. What a grand, beautiful experience this day was! The next day we went back to watch the sun rise over the canyon - also spectacular, but the sunset was more beautiful. We also watched an Imax film of a helicopter ride through the canyon and white-watering on the Colorado River. We went to Desert Point to see a different configuration of the Canyon, also spectacular. I climbed into a watchtower, from where one gets a grand view, all the way to the Navajo Mountain in Utah, 120 miles away.

Next, we drove to Bryce Canyon via Zion National Park. Zion is another magnificent, beautiful place, with strange configurations unlike any others we've seen, the road through it is also spectacular, with hair-pin turns and magnificent views. We took the scenic drive, stopping every once in a while, to admire the striking views, including the strange hoodoos, which are tall, thin spires of rock with less easily eroded rock on top that forms a sort of cap. We heard a ranger talk about the geology of Bryce. The panoramic views at Bryce were magnificent, unrivalled among those we've seen. The air was thin, as the elevation was quite high (8 - 9,000 ft.), the skies were bright blue. We saw prairie dogs, magpies, ravens and other wild life.

Our trip to Mesa Verde proceeded through Arches National Park, with its fantastic, bizarre rock formations and natural arches, and through mountains brightly colored yellow, pink, purple and green. The last part, from the park entrance to our hotel, was 14 miles of hairpin curves and spectacular views, but it was very scary because I hadn't filled up the gas tank and it read "empty"; there were no gas station on the way!! Luckily there was one at the top. We visited a museum that had an interesting exhibit about the Anasazi Indians who used to live here. We drove past many cliff dwellings, did not go inside as they were only accessible by difficult climbs, and visited the Four View Ruins. We drove to Montezuma Valley Overlook for beautiful vistas.

The following day we drove to Salida, stopping in Durango for lunch. We took the Million Dollar Highway, where silver and gold mining occurred, a scenic road over the San Juan Range involving two passes over 11,000 feet, and then over the Monarch Pass, also over 11,000 feet, at the Continental Divide.

Our drive to Denver the following day took us across the Colorado Rocky Highlands, with passes at 9,000 - 10,000 feet. In Denver, we spent the afternoon at the Tattered Cover Book Store - the biggest in the U.S. It was fascinating, with armchairs for people to read, maps, posters, historical editions of newspapers, and an enormous collection of books, covering four floors. This was heaven for Betty, who found quite a few books in the African American section. In the evening, we went out to dinner with Lori and John, and a tour of Denver. The next morning, we turned in our car at the airport - we had driven 2670 miles! - and then flew back to Syracuse.

This was a wonderful holiday. There aren't enough adjectives to convey the spectacular scenery we saw: Painted Desert, Petrified Forest, Oak Creek Canyon, Sedona, the Grand Canyon, Zion, Bryce Canyon, The Arches, Mesa Verde. We often spoke about this fantastic trip in the following years.

The Canadian Northwest, Vancouver, and Alaska Cruise, 1994.

We flew to Calgary, Alberta, where we began our tour of the Canadian Rockies the following day. The bus departed at 6 a.m. for Banff, a pretty drive. In Banff, which is surrounded by the Canadian Rockies, we changed to a tour bus, which took us to Lake Louise. We got off the bus at Chateau Lake Louise, which is in a fabulous setting, beautiful flowers, snow-capped mountains behind a blue lake, to take in the view. The bus went on, through the Rockies, with an excellent tour guide explaining the various natural phenomena. In Yoho National Park we crossed the Continental Divide - saw a river flowing down, dividing, with one branch ultimately heading to the Pacific, the other to the Atlantic. Our route took us through Spiral Tunnels, Roger's Pass, where we stopped to see the giant cedars, Kicking Horse Pass, Kamloops, to Lac Le Jeune where we had dinner and stayed overnight.

The following day the bus went via the Coquihalla Highway to Minter Gardens, where we stopped for lunch and a walk in the pretty gardens. Our driver continued to provide interesting history about British Columbia. We arrived in Vancouver, a modern city with skyscrapers and a harbor, in a spectacular setting with a backdrop of mountains. We rented a car and the next day we drove to the University of British Columbia and spent three hours at their Museum of Anthropology, with its interesting collection of totem poles, Indian and African art.

We took a tour of Vancouver on a double-decker bus, went up to Elizabeth Park to admire the view of the city, and to Science World to see some of their excellent displays and watch an Omnimax movie

"The Secret of Life" about the interdependence of plants and animals. Then we drove our car onto a ferry going to Victoria Island, which took 1 1/2 hours, to beautiful Victoria.

We visited the Undersea Gardens, a very interesting display of marine life, and went to an excellent concert at Christ Church Cathedral, part of Victoria's 23rd Annual International Festival, where we heard Bach's Suite #4, Bartók's Duo for two violins, Mozart's Piano Quartet K478, and Schubert's "Death and the Maiden" Quartet.

We spent quite a lot of time at Butchard Gardens which has spectacular displays of flowers, a Japanese garden and a sunken garden, and then at Crystal Gardens, with exotic tropical plants, birds, and butterflies.

We took the ferry back to Vancouver, returned our car, took a bus to Princess Tours, and got onto our boat, the Star Princess, for our Inside Passage Tour to Alaska. We had a very nice room and chose the First Sitting for our Dinner, where our table mates were a couple from Lancashire, England, and another couple from North Dakota. The food was excellent and very plentiful.

The next morning, I got up early, went for a walk on the sundeck, booked our various tours, and played in a ping-pong tournament. We both participated in a quiz game. We sat on the deck as we went through a narrow passage with little hills on both sides. We went to learn "Line Dancing Mania". There was a formal dinner that evening, which was excellent, including caviar, followed by a lively show. Later that evening we went to the Flaming Fruit Jamboree consisting of a fantastic array of deserts, ice carvings, etc.

We spent most of next morning on deck, saw whale spouts, dolphins, and snow-capped mountains in the background. In the afternoon, we went on a glacier expedition by helicopter, six persons per helicopter. It flew over glaciers, lakes, forests and mountains and landed on a glacier, a fantastic experience. The glaciers appear bright blue, and some have formations reminiscent of Bryce Canyon. The dinner that night was typical English, roast beef and Yorkshire pudding, trifle for desert. We had docked at Juneau and after dinner we wandered into the town, saw some beautiful carvings of precious and semi-precious stones, fossilized ivory and wood, and talked with the artist, Steve Stegall.

Next morning, we were docked in Skagway. We took a little plane to Hanes, flying over lakes and mountains. There we took a bus, driven by one girl, with another girl as guide - both were Biology graduates - that went through the countryside with many flowers and birds. We saw an eagle, and salmon being counted and tagged, puffins and mergansers, and went for a walk into the rain forest. The enthusiastic guide was very good at explaining everything. The bus took us back to Hanes, where we took another small plane, seating just 4, which flew over several glaciers as well as lakes and mountains. It was a spectacular experience! The plane then took us back to Skagway and a bus took us to our boat.

After the Italian dinner that night, we went to a very good Broadway Review, and also "A Night at the Klondike", a hilarious audience-participation show. Later that evening we got a tour of the galley, followed by a sumptuous Italian supper of all sorts of cold cuts and dozens of deserts. The food on this cruise was plentiful and delicious.

Early the next morning I took a vigorous walk on deck. Our boat had gone to Margerie Glacier in Glacier Bay, then to Grand Pacific and Johns Hopkins Glaciers, where we saw large chunks of ice break off the glaciers into the water. We saw seals and various birds. The dinner that night was French, semi-formal, after which we went to a Spotlight Showtime.

The next day we were docked at Ketchikan, and went for a tour of their Indian village, with its numerous totem poles, and there was dancing, in which children participated, and we saw them carving totem poles and a canoe. The dinner was formal, after which we went to an excellent show "A Night on the Town", with Broadway hits. We also went to the "Windows to the World" bar to hear a pianist at the bar, and then to a stunning gala buffet.

We had a leisurely day the next day, then went to an amateur night show. We were instructed about disembarkation the next day, highly organized to take cognizance of passengers' airline schedules etc. The last morning, we disembarked, took a bus to the airport, picked up a rental car and had an excellent lunch at a huge Chinese restaurant "The Pink Pearl". We went to the Dr. Sun Yat Sun Chinese Garden, which was beautiful, and where we had a guide. Later we drove to Grouse Mountain in N. Vancouver, taking a beautiful drive through Stanley Park, over Lion Gate bridge. We took the tramway to the top of the mountain, where one has a superb view of the city.

On the final day of this vacation we got up very early, returned our car, then checked in at the airport for our flight to O'Hare, where we had a long walk to the gate for the Syracuse flight. In Syracuse, we were met by Karen, her husband Maurice and our dog Shaka.

Five-Year Family Reunions, 1970, 1975, 1980, 1985, 1990, 1995

My mother's and aunt's birthdays are July and August, respectively, five years apart, and so for many years from 1970 to 1995, we had family reunions to celebrate their birthdays in those years. Many family members participated. The reunions were held at different locations all over the country. The reunion in 1990 was very special as it was my mother's 90th birthday. I had rented some rooms at the Brae Loch Inn in Cazenovia for the first two days, where we all gathered. We had a gala dinner, and a concert that I had arranged, performed by five members of the Syracuse Symphony Orchestra, to which we had invited several of our Syracuse friends. On the third day, we went to our house for a luncheon.

In addition to the trips Betty and I undertook together, each of us did quite a lot of travelling relating to our own interests. Betty's trips were in connection with transcendental meditation, in Amherst, MA and South Fallsburg, NY and a week to Maharishi University in Fairfield, Iowa, with a group of Syracuse meditators. Because of her interest in African American History she joined the African Heritage Studies Association and went to New York to examine documents at the Schomburg Center for Research in Black Culture. Her fascination with, and deep interest in Ancient African, especially Egyptian civilizations, led her to join the Association for the Study of Classical African Civilizations, an organization devoted to the rescue, reconstruction and restoration of African history and culture, and to attend their meetings, held in different locations in the United States, and to go with them on three excursions -- to Egypt in 1987, West Africa in 1992, and Brazil in 1995. These trips were transformative experiences for her.

My travels were related, primarily, to my profession as an academic biochemist, including attending, and speaking at various professional meetings. These included several International Congresses of Biochemistry. The first of these I attended, in 1958, was before our marriage. The second (in Moscow in 1961) and fourth (in Tokyo in 1967) are described above, and Betty came with me. In the 1980s I initiated a collaborative research program with Margaret Adams, an X-ray crystallographer at Oxford University, to elucidate the three-dimensional structure of glucose 6-phosphate dehydrogenase (G6PD). I visited England on several occasions to discuss our research with her. She also was a visitor in my lab several times, leaning how to prepare the enzyme. Between 1994 and 1997, three of those trips involved extensive discussions about the G6PD structure.

Whenever I had occasion to travel in Europe, I always included England. Ever since I arrived in England in 1939, on a *Kindertransport*, it became the country that saved my life and I have had a deep love for it. There were many people, relatives and friends, with whom I had a strong bond, whom I visited on every possible occasion. Others were professional colleagues. There were always wonderful concerts or plays to attend, often with my friends Peter and Irene Gore, so that I had a rich cultural experience on each of my visits.

Before describing these trips, I will introduce my friends Peter and Irene Gore, who were my hosts on every visit to England.

I first met the Gores while I was on a one-year postdoctoral fellowship in London from 1958 to 59 (see Chapter 4). Irene Gore was a member of George Popják's laboratory, where I was doing research. She invited me to her house to meet her husband, Peter, and thus began a friendship that lasted well over half a century. Irene, like I, was a biochemist and Peter was a chemist.

Irene, and her twin sister Katie, were born to Russian parents who had moved from Siberia to China. Peter was born in Berlin to Jewish parents, three years before I. He moved to England with his family in 1939, the same year as I, but then moved almost immediately to Australia, where he spent the war years. Irene had also come to Australia to go to University, and it is there that she and Peter met.

After he earned his doctorate in chemistry, Peter went to England for post-doctoral research and remained there to pursue his career. He and Irene married in England and had two daughters, Janine and Rosanna. Peter's scientific credentials would have allowed him to join the faculty of most premier academic institutions in England or the

United States, but he chose deliberately to locate in London because of its unparalleled musical ambience. He was a fine organic chemist, specializing in the Friedel-Crafts reaction, but also a passionate lover of classical music, which played a decisive role in his life. The academic institutions with which he was associated in London were not in the top tier of British universities, but they matched his aspirations and allowed him to live his life the way it suited him, in a city with almost unlimited opportunities to attend musical performances.

Irene became interested in the process of aging, an interest no doubt stimulated by her remarkable mother, who had led a difficult life, had always been devoted to her daughters, and was a fiercely independent woman who achieved a great deal through her own initiative. Irene read extensively about gerontology, talked to experts in the field, then wrote an article which developed into a book, *Add Years to Your Life and Life to Your Years*, that was well received. She subsequently wrote other books on the same general topic. Peter also wrote a book outside his area of professional expertise, about Egypt. Irene also wrote a beautiful autobiographical memoir, for her daughters, which included a fascinating account of her early years in China.

After my postdoctoral year in London, I encountered the Gores again the following year in Lerici, Italy where they were on vacation and where I was traveling with my friend Howard Goldfine. In 1961, we met again in Moscow, where the Gores and I attended an International Congress of Biochemistry and where Betty accompanied me, so that she and the Gores also met. In 1972, I went to England, for a sabbatical year of research at Oxford University, accompanied by Betty and Karen, and we met the Gores several times. Thereafter, I saw Peter and Irene on several visits to England in conjunction with my research, and stayed with them on each visit. Irene and I corresponded sporadically, but then in 1996 I started corresponding with Peter via e-mail, which suited both of us well, and it was as though a faucet had been turned on, out of which poured a massive correspondence. We wrote about many common interests – music, science, politics, world affairs, books, and our families. It became clear to both of us that our correspondence was worth saving, so I bound the letters, one year's correspondence per volume. We included some photographs that we had e-mailed to each other, and Peter prepared indexes for each volume. This went on for nine years and resulted in a total of 2,270 pages of correspondence. I sought an interesting name for these tomes, and came up with E PEGORILE, E for e-mail, and then our names, viz. PEterGOreRIchardLEvy. This name, which had the added attraction that it sounded like the title of a baroque opera, appealed to Peter, who was especially fond of Handel's operas, all of which he knew. This correspondence is a well-written, rich and lively source of many facets of our lives, and many anecdotes and comments.

Peter's interest in music began when he was an adolescent growing up in Australia. His knowledge about all aspects of music was vast, and his pursuit of opportunities to hear it was boundless. In addition to his love for, and interest in music, it seemed that he was compelled to catalogue everything he ever heard. He wrote critiques of every concert he attended and bound them into volumes. He maintained this practice all his life, and the number of volumes was huge. In our E PEGORILE correspondence he frequently cited these catalogs, writing that he had heard a particular work so many times, or that the last time he heard this artist perform was in such and such a year. His father once told him that his interest in music was largely statistical, which Peter denies, though he admits that there is an element of truth in it. He loved to compare, to organize, and to catalogue.

Irene shared Peter's love of classical music and they attended many concerts together, although Peter also attended many alone. They both enjoyed chamber music and were especially fond of the Endellion Quartet, whose members they came to know personally. The Endellions published a little booklet in 2004, to commemorate their 25th anniversary, in which they mentioned that Peter and Irene were their most loyal fans, having by then attended 284 of their performances! For Peter's 80th birthday in 2006, they gave a recital at the Gore's flat, including a piece especially composed for Peter. Peter especially loved the music of Mozart and Bach, and Handel's operas, most of which he heard several times. For several years, he attended various churches in London every Sunday so that he could hear their choirs perform ecclesiastical music, and got to know several of the church's music directors.

Peter and Irene had two daughters, Janine and Rosanna. Like the rest of the family, they have special affectionate monikers that tend to change from time to time. When I first got to know her, Janine was

Poppety, and she had also been Anya. Rosanna was Tip. Irene's mother, who lived with them as long as I knew them, was Whap or Whaplik. Katie was Nyadush. Janine married, divorced, and remarried, and has lived in France for many years. She had no children. Rosanna married, had two children – Natalie and Gilbert – divorced and remarried. I was fond of Janine and Rosanna from the time I knew them, the feeling was mutual, and our friendship continued after both Peter and Irene died. Natalie had precocious artistic gifts as a young child, that later embraced music and writing as well as art. Gilbert was musically gifted.

Sadly, Irene developed Alzheimers disease in the first decade of the 21st century. Around that time, she and Peter moved to Long Buckby, the little village in the north of England where Rosanna lived, and for many years Peter was her primary caretaker, until that became too heavy a burden and she was moved to a care facility. She died in December, 2015. Peter also began to show signs of aging, and although Rosanna in England, and Janine in France devoted much time to looking after him, he was finally moved to a facility in Cambridge, where he died in January, 2017. I last saw Peter and Irene in 2009, after my visit to Leipzig, when I spent an afternoon with them in Long Buckby (see Chapter 11).

Between 1970 and 1999, I visited England ten times, and Paris once. Nine of those trips were for professional reasons, including attending conferences and consulting with my coworker, Margaret Adams, on our research project. One trip was in order to speak at a memorial service for Bernard Schlesinger and one to attend one of the ten-year reunions held by the "Hostel Children", those children whom the Schlesingers rescued, along with me, in 1939. On every trip to England, I stayed with the Gores, and every one of these featured concerts, plays, other cultural events, and good conversation. Instead of detailing each visit, I will highlight some unique aspects of each.

England and Switzerland, 1970.

The principal reason for this trip was to attend the 8th International Congress of Biochemistry in Switzerland. Before going to Switzerland, I spent a few days in England and stayed with the Schlesingers for six days. We stopped to see Mount Pleasant, the little house where we had lived during the war, and I visited my old school in Newbury. I also spent some time trying to find brasses to rub -- brass rubbing, mostly at churches, had been a passion of mine while I was in England for my post-doc 1958-9 -- but it had become more difficult since then to get permission, probably because the brasses were being worn down.

I then flew to Geneva, and, took a long bus ride to Interlaken, site of the first International Congress sessions. Facilities there were quite poor, there was considerable chaos and confusion. I stayed at Interlaken three days, attended various sessions, met some interesting scientists, but also met with Irene and Peter Gore, their children Janine and Rosanna, and Irene's mother, Whap, who happened to be travelling through this part of Switzerland on a holiday.

On my way to the next location of the Congress at Luzerne, I took the train to Jungfraujoch, the highest train station in Europe (over 11,000 ft.), a spectacular ride. At Luzerene, the meetings were much better, the town very quaint.

Konstanz, Germany, and Canterbury, England, 1973.

Both these trips took place while I was on sabbatical in England in 1973, to attend a meeting of the German Society for Biological Chemistry and a joint meeting of the British and French Biochemical Societies, respectively. One of the principal reasons I went to Konstanz was to meet with Birgit Vennesland, my Ph.D. advisor, who was spending a year in Otto Warburg's lab in Berlin. Besides attending the scientific sessions, I spent quite a lot of enjoyable time with Dr. V., as we had a lot of catching up to do.

England and Hamburg, Germany, 1976.

The purpose of this trip was to attend the 10th International Congress of Biochemistry in Hamburg, but first I spent some time in England.

I rented a car, drove to Boxford to visit Win and Bernard, and drove to Oxford to visited George Radda, with whom I had spent my sabbatical year, and talked with many individuals from his group. I went to see 321 Woodstock Rd., where we lived during my sabbatical. I called Rose Chukwukwere, with whom we were friends while on sabbatical 1972-3, and rang up Mrs. Jeffries, my landlady while I was in London for my postdoc, 1958-59. In Hamburg, the Congress sessions were at the elegant Congress Center.

England, 1981.

An important objective for this trip was to meet with Hans Krebs about our differences in interpretation of the results of experiments on G6PD regulation (see Chapter 7).

First, I visited the Schlesingers, who had aged noticeably, We went to a barbecue at a nearby barn in honor of the royal wedding. Everyone from the village was there, nice people, but many evincing the typical British supercilious attitudes that I have come to loathe, off-hand, sneering remarks about Nigerians moving to London, devaluing property, etc.

I had asthma, which got worse, and I had very little spray left. It was a panicky situation, being away from home, where I could take care of getting more medication at once. I was with two old persons in medically unfamiliar surroundings. I had a terrible night with very bad asthma, so little spray, I rationed it, but I was awake all night and was exhausted. Bernard took me to Newbury next morning, where, as a physician, he was able to get me another spray.

In Oxford, I met with Radda, and then spent about an hour talking with Krebs. I explained in detail what we had done, why our interpretation differs from his. He grasped my points at once, was very impressed with the care and methodical way we did the work, suggested that we publish at once, but later, agreed with me, that it would be better to wait until we understood the problem better, which he thought was very important.

Krebs made three interesting comments. First, he told me that conductor Bruno Walter's original surname was Schlesinger, but in Germany, such a Jewish name was an impediment, so he simply used his middle name, Walter, as his surname.

Second, when we discussed Rodriguez-Segade's experiments, he asked whether he was from Alberto Sol's department in Madrid - he was not. He said Spanish scientists were only rarely first-rate, like Sols. He told me of a book by Darlington, a history from the view point of genetics in which Darlington writes that Spain has still not recovered from its expulsion of the Jews in the 15th century.

Third, he revealed to me that Birgit Vennesland had displayed very peculiar behavior, both in Chicago and Berlin, and had been in an institution in both places for some time. This was new and disturbing news for me.

I spent some time with Steve and Mary at their house in Hertford and then with the Gores in Ealing. John Schlesinger had arranged for a special showing of his latest film, "Yanks", for me. I told him how interested Janine Gore was in an acting career and so he had invited her and Irene to come too. We found the film to be very emotional and evocative. At his flat, John, in white pants and sports shirt, met us in his living room. The flat was very opulent, full of many works of art. We had drinks and then lunch in a most elegant dining room, served by his cook-housekeeper. John spent some time giving advice to Janine. We had coffee on a patio overlooking his sculpture garden, then John showed us the rest of the house, all very opulent. Two other men, Michael and Noel live there - the relationship was not clear to me at that time. Nureyev lived opposite to John's flat, Lord Snowden around the corner.

England, 1982.

The purpose of this trip was to examine G6PD crystals by X-ray diffraction in Margaret Adams's lab, and to consult with two scientists, Gronenborn and Clore, at Mill Hill, about TRNOE experiments (see Chapter 7).

In Oxford, Margaret had arranged for me to stay at a room at her College, Somerville. We took the enzyme crystals that I had brought with me to her lab, and she found that they diffract beautifully!! We spent most of the next day writing a draft of the paper reporting on the crystallization of G6PD. I also visited George Radda again.

In London, I had lunch with Gronenborn and Clore and discussed with them TRNOE experiments I wanted to do with G6PD.

Back in London, I took in several cultural activities while I stayed with the Gores: marvelous portraits by Rembrandt, Raphael and Titian; an excellent performance of "Amadeus"; the film "12 Angry Men"; the film "Mephisto"; and an excellent Prom concert by a Belgian chamber group, La Petite Bande, playing Bach, Handel, and Rameau.

I also visited my friends Walter and Sylvia Weg, and Renate and her husband Robert, doing lots of reminiscing.

England, 1984.

I went to England in order to deliver a tribute to Bernard Schlesinger, at his memorial service. This took place at the Institute for Child Health.. Many family members and others were there to give talks or read poems. I read a tribute, for myself and the Hostel children[1]. There was beautiful music at the service, played by the Fairfield Quartet, and I thought that the whole service had the right balance of solemn, uplifting and humorous talks. I joined John and the rest of the family for drinks at his house, and then we all went out to a Siamese restaurant for dinner.

I gave a talk to a group from the Laboratory of Molecular Biophysics in Oxford. I met George Radda, who had a new endowed chair from the British Heart Association and a large group which was heavily into NMR-related studies. He told me that my sabbatical with him (1972-73) was an example of mutual contribution, which he really appreciated, contrasting it with some individuals who try to "suck him dry". I had lunch with Margaret at high table at Somerville College.

As usual, my visit to England included a number of wonderful cultural events: with Peter and Irene to hear the Medici Quartet at Wigmore Hall play Haydn, Bartok and Cesar Frank; watching John Schlesinger's latest film for TV, about John Burgess, "An Englishman Abroad"; in Bungay, East Anglia, seeing Janine perform in "No Song, No Supper", a series of vignettes from early times of theater; and, with Peter, a concert in Kintbury presented by the Chilingirian Quartet with Steven Isserlis, playing Schubert's Quartettsatz, and the C minor Quintet.

England, 1988

The reason for this trip was to participate in, and give an invited talk at the British Biochemical Society meeting in Sheffield.

On my flight to London, the woman sitting next to me spilled ginger ale all over me and my jacket. When we arrived at Gatwick, my luggage, which I had checked through to London from Syracuse, had not arrived. This was a big worry, as it had my talk plus clothes in it that I needed for my talk, plus clothes to wear until then. Fortunately, the conference was not for several days, so there was still time for the suitcase to arrive. The Gores met me and we drove to London and to their beautiful new flat. Irene washed and ironed my shirt, Peter lent me a shirt (it was, of course, much too big), and Irene went to buy some socks, underwear, a shirt, tooth brush etc. for me. It is, of course, extremely difficult to find something my size, except boys' clothes; in the States, I use special stores for short men.

Peter's latest passion was hearing pre-Bach music sung *a cappella*, performed at many churches. He talks to the choir directors and studies the architecture while he's at it -- in thorough typical Peter style!

I spent a little time at Syracuse University in London, where I took Beth Harrelson (she was in my Impact of Science on Medicine class) and Dean Carlow (an undergraduate formerly in my lab) to a pub for lunch. I also took Bryan, Betty's nephew, who is here on a study-abroad program from Notre Dane, to dinner at a very good German restaurant where I had a long, interesting conversation with him, especially about his experiences with racism and his growth from them, and about the effects of Epstein-Barr virus, which he has had for some time. He has had no help from doctors, and gets very tired and sick.

To my great relief, I finally received a call from Gatwick that they had found my suitcase at Heathrow, and we drove there get pick it up. Peter drove me to Oxford, where I met with Margaret. I drove with her to Sheffield. We heard several excellent lectures, and a superb CIBA Medal lecture by Blundell on X-ray analysis, protein structure, and design of new molecules. My talk went very well.

Back in London, I went to see Steven appearing as King Claudius in a production of Hamlet put on by a fringe company called Performance Exchange. Bar Webber was there, had come specially to see me. After the play Steve, Bar, an actress and I drove to Steve's council flat way out in the East End in Poplar. We had a very enjoyable evening with drinks. Steve fixed a chicken pie which we ate at about 1 a.m. with some wine that I had brought. I finally got to sleep at 2:30 a.m. in Steve's bed, which he let me use while he slept on the couch.

I spent some time with John Schlesinger, who told me that Herbert von Karajan has asked him to produce Verdi's "The Masked Ball" at

Salzburg. Later, John Glees, my third cousin, picked me up and we met his mother, Eva and went to an excellent Turkish restaurant for an entertaining dinner. Before returning to the States, I had the opportunity for a long heart-to-heart chat with Hilary.

Paris, 1989.

I was invited to attend a conference on steroids and enzymes, sponsored by the Institut Scientifique Roussel-UCLAF, who paid for all meals and accommodations.

I met many scientists from all over world, some I knew, including Paul Talalay, and attended some very good session at Maison de la Chimie. We were served an excellent, cold lunch with wine, and a superb desert. Paul invited me to join his group for a good dinner with excellent wine at Brasserie Lipp at St. Germain de Prés. I went to the Musée d'Orsay, which now housed most of what used to be in the Jeu de Paume. It was a railway station, most imaginatively converted into a museum. I only had time to see the Impressionist collection of paintings and sculptures, which is incredible and vast, very well arranged and lighted.

The conference was very good and the food was extraordinary.

England, 1994.

This trip was undertaken in order to discuss the G6PD structure, which Margaret's group had solved.

Things got off to shaky start - Karen was supposed to drive me to the airport but hadn't shown up in time, so I drove myself. At the airport, I found out that the flight to JFK was cancelled because of yesterday's snowstorm. I had to book a flight to Raleigh-Durham, then to JFK, then to London

Peter picked me up at Heathrow. His latest venture is visiting churches in London on Sundays to listen to their services and learn about the music. He makes notes on everything, talks to the choirmasters and often corresponds with them. He has gained a vast knowledge about Renaissance music. I also visited my old friend Walter and his wife Sylvia, and Renate and Robert joined us for a very enjoyable afternoon.

In Oxford, Margaret, had arranged a room for me again at Somerville College. I heard the great news: Paul Rowland and Margaret had just solved the structure of our *L. mesenteroides* G6PD! This was a huge advance in our research! Also, Claire Naylor has crystallized human G6PD in a form suitable for X-ray analysis. We spent most of afternoon examining our G6PD structure, looking for critical residues to mutate and rationalizing our data for those mutants we had already analyzed.

That night, I had a most unpleasant experience. I had symptoms of a thyroid problem that I had first experienced a couple of years ago when it was diagnosed as Hashimoto's, an autoimmune disease in which the immune system attacks the thyroid, leading to hypothyroidism. The symptoms included a pounding heart, hunger, frequent bowel movements and urination, and feeling anxious. I couldn't sleep. There was no telephone in my room, and if there had been, I wouldn't have known whom to call. Although the situation was potentially frightening, I remained calm and developed a plan for the morning. Clearly, I had to see a physician as soon as possible in order to continue working.

Next morning, still feeling ill, I walked to the lab to explain the situation to Margaret. She called her clinic, and I was able to get an appointment with a physician there that afternoon. Meanwhile, Margaret and I continued our examination of the G6PD structure to locate interesting residues to mutate. I walked to the clinic, where the physician examined me briefly, told me that, frankly, he didn't know anything about thyroiditis. He read about it, with me, in a medical text. He could have drawn blood and have the appropriate tests done, but the results would not have come back before I was due to leave England. I told him about my previous episode and suggested that he should give me the same medications I had before, prednisone and propranolol, to tie me over until I got back to the States. He agreed, wrote a prescription, and I began taking the medications right away, which helped to stabilize me sufficiently that I was able to continue the visit.

I visited George Radda again. He is now the head of Biochemistry, including Molecular Biophysics, with a total of 550 faculty and staff. He was able to dictate his own terms because he was pushed to take the position.

The next evening, Margaret had a party at Somerville, with champagne (cider for me, she remembered my allergy!) for her whole group to celebrate the solution of the G6PD X-ray structure. There was an excellent catered dinner.

The following days in London, staying with the Gores, were filled with meeting friends and attending concerts and plays. Although the medication was working, I still got very tired and had difficulty sleeping, due both to the thyroiditis and the many stimulating experiences.

The day I left for the States, Heathrow was closed. There had been some bomb attacks by the IRA, and they discovered more unexploded bombs. However, Terminal #3, from where I was to depart, was open, although there were delays on the approach roads. I took the tube and had no difficulties getting to my flight on time.

After one more, brief episode of Hashimoto's a year or two later, I had no further recurrences.

England, 1995.

I flew to England for discussions with Margaret Adams. First, I spent a few days with the Gores, and, as usual, my visit was most enjoyable, filled with warmth and interesting conversations.

In Oxford, Margaret and I discussed details of the G6PD structure and plans for further experiments.

I rented a car for a nostalgic journey into my past in England, and to take photographs. I stopped in Woodlands St. Mary to chat with Betty Bradley, the Schlesingers' maid, and to take a picture of Oliver's Cottage in Boxford, their last residence. I went to my old school in Newbury, which was completely shut, but I managed to get into the grounds to take some pictures. I drove to Kintbury, then looked for Mount Pleasant, the little house we lived in during the war. I knocked at the door and talked for about 45 minutes to the current owner. He built onto the original house, doubling its size, and converted the barns in the back to a little cottage called Mount Pleasant Cottage; he renamed the house Winterley House. He showed me the deed of the house and some photos from 1906. The following morning, I began a journey to the places where my mother stayed during the war, and the villages nearby, to take photos for her. In Burford, I found the office of The Countryman, where John Cripps was editor, and the Bay Tree restaurant, where my mother and I sometimes had tea. In Filkins, I took pictures of Goodfellows, the house where my mother worked for the Cripps family, and met the current owner, Mr. Morley. I saw St. Peter's House, where the Cripps family and my mother stayed after they moved out of Goodfellows. I drove back to Oxford via Faringdon.

Back in Oxford, as I got onto a bus to Heathrow, I heard someone talk about enzyme kinetics - it was Sven Lindsky from Sweden who had been in Oxford when I was on sabbatical! We sat together and chatted on the way to Heathrow.

England, 1997.

The purpose of this trip was to discuss our manuscript on the mechanism of the G6PD reaction with Margaret Adams. I took a daytime flight to London, which was much less tiring, as one arrives in time to go to bed and is fresh the next morning.

First, I visited Peter Marsh, my friend from Syracuse University who had led the Mellon Project which was such an important part of my career at Syracuse (see Chapter 6), and who was now a professor at the University of Birmingham. The day started badly as I bumped hard into a glass door at the hotel exit, splitting open the bridge of my nose, which bled profusely and swelled. The hotel staff did their best to apply first aid, an ice pack, and band-aides. I was scheduled to take the morning train to Birmingham, and had to call to say I would arrive later. Getting to Euston Station was quite exhausting as I had to carry my heavy suitcase and carry-on luggage up and down stairs at the tube stations. I took the express train to Birmingham, where Peter picked me up, and we took a cab to his delightful apartment on the 3rd floor of a converted factory in the jewelry district, an interesting area, nicely restored. Later, we walked along the canal toward Symphony Hall, stopped for a very good supper at Café Rouge, followed by a superb concert. Simon Rattle conducted the City of Birmingham Symphony Orchestra in a program featuring Walton's brief Anniversary Fanfare; Turnage's Four-Horned Fandango (written for the CBSO's astonishing horn players); Elgar's Violin Concerto, featuring Nigel Kennedy; Walton's Belshazzar's Feast with the City of Birmingham and Cleveland Orchestra Choruses and Simon Keendyside, baritone soloist. This was one of those marvelous, memorable concerts that one treasures. After each piece, there was thunderous applause. Rattle is a fabulous conductor, mesmerizing to watch. After the concert, we walked back to Peter's apartment, talked a while before going to bed.

The following day featured extended conversations; a walking tour of Birmingham, with Peter an excellent, enthusiastic guide, to explain the history of this city that he loves; excellent meals at a pub and a restaurant; and some live jazz.

In Oxford, I discussed our paper with Margaret and the other co-authors. I had a long, very contentious discussions with Margaret about one portion of the paper. Margaret, who can be very difficult, started off being very condescending and became increasingly angry with my apparent obtuseness. However, very slowly she came around to agreeing. She is very stubborn and opinionated, but she does listen to reason. She said, with one section after another: "This is where I really come to grief with you", but one after another, she quietly yielded to my very non-threatening but firm stance. We finished making the revisions to our paper.

During my stay with the Gores in London I was treated to three outstanding concerts. The first was at the Guildhall School of Music and Drama Gold Medal Final competition, to which Peter and I went. Four singers competed, a counter-tenor, soprano, tenor and baritone. For the first half, each participant sang four or five songs accompanied by piano, in the second half they did three arias with the all-student Guildhall Symphony Orchestra. It was all excellent and most interesting.

The second concert was at the Royal College of Music, where Peter, Irene and I went to hear the U.K. premiere of a concert performance of Vivaldi's "Tito Manio" (1719) by La Serinissima. The performance was preceded by a one hour talk by Prof. Michael Talbot, the performance itself lasted almost six hours (!), including a one-hour break between Acts one and two, during which we drove back for a light supper. The performance was superb! Despite the length of the opera and the convoluted plot, it was a marvelous experience. My musical experiences in England continued to be dazzling!

The third concert was at St. John's, Smith Square, an old church now used as a concert venue. We first had some lunch in a little restaurant in what was once a crypt. Then we heard the Takacs Quartet perform Haydn's op. 74 #2, and Beethoven's 2nd Razumovsky Quartet.

Peter showed a home video of a portion of his 70ᵗʰ birthday party, which included an appearance of their favorite Quartet, the Endellion, who played a "happy birthday" composition, written especially for him.

I also visited the younger Gore daughter, Tip, and her family in Long Buckby; Steve and Mary Webber and their children in Hatfield; and my childhood friend Walter Weg in Eastcote. The Webber family, including all the children, are still as full of love and warmth as ever, which is why they are my favorites among the Schlesinger relatives. Steve is still acting, mostly without pay, awaiting to be "discovered". I took Roger Schlesinger to dinner at the Abingdon. In a long talk about the family, Roger revealed that John has diabetes, that he, Roger, had a heart attack, and that Sue (who committed suicide in 1963) had had manic-depressive disease.

England, 1999.

This trip was non-professional. I went to attend the Hostel Children's 4ᵗʰ decennial reunion. As usual, I stayed with the Gores, and was treated to four excellent concerts. The first was in Cambridge, where we first had a picnic supper, and then heard a concert by the Endellion Quartet: Hugo Wolf's Italian Serenade, Britten Quartet #3, Schubert Death and the Maiden Quartet. We talked with the Quartet members afterwards. They are friends of the Gores, who are their most loyal fans, attending many of their concerts every year.

The second concert was at St. John's Smith Square, a charitable performance by the Orchestra of St. Martin in the Fields with Steven Isserlis (cello) and Julian Bream (guitar; he was friends with Sue some years ago), 23-year old Daniel Harding, conducting. Mozart, Symphony No. 28, Haydn Cello Concerto in C, Bach Suite No. 6 for unaccompanied cello transcribed for guitar, Mozart Symphony No. 29, and a poetry reading by the poet laureate, Andrew Motion. The Haydn and Mozart were great, I didn't think the Bach worked well on guitar, and the poetry was not very inspiring.

The third concert was at St. Vedast-alias-Foster, where Peter, Irene and I went to hear the all-female Sorrell Quartet give a beautiful performance of Haydn's Quartets Op. 50 No. 1 and Op. 64 No.

6. Afterwards, we walked to a Turkish Restaurant, Efas #2, on Great Portland Street for an excellent Turkish dinner.

For the fourth concert, I went with Peter, Irene and Janine's friend Philip Rham, to Christ Church Spitafields to hear a concert by the Royal Academy Soloists, Clio Gould, Director. They performed "Chant for E. Timor" by Luis Tinoco, "Polyphony for 14 String Instruments", a world premiere by Joel Erikson, and the Mendelssohn Octet. Both Tinoco and Erikson were in the audience for this excellent concert. Afterwards we went to the former, now converted Spitafields Market to have some tapas for lunch.

Another day I went with Peter to the National Gallery to see "Rembrandt by Himself", an exhibition of over 60 self-portraits. We were able to see this before the exhibition opened for the day because Irene's nephew Geoff is manager of publications at the National Gallery and could get us in.

CHAPTER 10

Religion and the Mysterious

Although I was born to Jewish parents, religion played very little role in our family Our Jewishness became a critical component of our life after Hitler came to power in 1933, when increasingly suppressive restrictions were placed on Jewish citizens. I soon became aware of the Nazis' anti-Semitism. When I was seven and eight, I went to a Jewish school because the Nazis did not allow Jewish children to go to school with Christian children. At school, among other subjects I learned Hebrew and read bible stories. I was aware of the virulent anti-Semitism around me, as evidenced by the fact that I kept a diary titled "Happenings on the Streetcar" (see Chapter 2).

The first nine years of my life, in Germany, did not provide a Jewish tradition that I could draw on later and, in fact, they did not leave me with much about being Jewish that was pleasant. This failure to connect to my Jewish heritage was further exacerbated in England. The Schlesinger family, who took me into their home, were also Jewish but gave even less evidence of that fact than did my family. They did not practice the Jewish faith and quite soon after I got there I sensed, from remarks made by one of their children, that there was some shame for them associated with being Jewish. I only learned much later about the insidious anti-Semitism that Dr. Schlesinger had to endure in his career, and the enormous efforts made by the family to draw little attention to the fact that they were Jewish (see Ian Buruma's *Their Promised Land. My Grandparents in Love and War*).

The distancing from my Jewish heritage continued at my school. I went to Newbury Grammar School, where I was one of about forty boarders. As I relate in Chapter 2, all the boarders had to attend church on Sundays, but the headmaster was sufficiently enlightened to tell the few Jewish boarders that they did not have to do so. I decided, however, that I wanted to go because I was very intent on fitting in with the other boys, who knew that I was from Germany, a country with which England was now at war, but who did not understand that a German Jew was unlike other Germans. I believe that I expended a lot of emotional energy in becoming more English than the English. I loved everything about England and perceived it to be the country that had saved my life.

It turned out that I really liked going to church. It was a beautiful, very old church with stained glass windows, the music appealed to me very much, and there was the added benefit that there were quite a lot of girls from the neighboring high school there, and we boys were starved for female interactions. I actually told my mother that I wanted to convert to Christianity because of these experiences, but she understood what was happening and suggested that I think about that again later, so, fortunately, nothing came of that youthful impulse.

By the time that I came to the United Sates, at age 16, there was little that was Jewish left in me, and there might have been none at all, had I not begun to learn about the Holocaust and its toll on our family (see Chapter 2). The Nazis had murdered my grandmother, an aunt and uncle, and numerous other family members. They brutally beat my father and imprisoned him for ten days. During the second world war my grandfather survived in Leipzig, under harrowing circumstances, presumably because his second wife was not Jewish. My mother was in very sporadic, infrequent contact with him throughout the war, and she told me about his situation. All this tragedy reconnected me with my heritage, but it did nothing to propel me to practice my religion. My aunt and uncle, with whom we lived in Red Bank, NJ, were connected to their local Jewish community. They occasionally went to temple, and they tried to get me to participate, with little success. While I attended Rutgers University I tried a few times, at my aunt's and uncle's urging, to participate in Hillel events, but I was always put off by these attempts and felt like an outcast. Because of my virtual lack of a Jewish background, I found little to connect me with the Jewish students at Hillel, and this has always been the barrier that has prevented me from becoming more involved in the Jewish life of my community. I have read about Jewish history and practices, but that has never substituted for the missing connections with Jewish traditions in my childhood. I did participate (as did Betty with me), for several years, in the Havurah group in Syracuse, which consisted of several Jewish men and women who were much more secular than religious. Although we had brief prayer services (Shabbat) at the outset, the bulk of our meetings was devoted to talks given by the members (I gave several) followed by spirited intellectual discussions. There was hardly any religion involved, but there was a strong sense of community.

The lack of any religious or spiritual involvement did not seem to bother me throughout my college and graduate school career. In 1960 Betty and I were married. Betty was not particularly religious at the time, but we decided to ask the minister at the First Unitarian Church in Chicago, Dr. Leslie Pennington, to perform the ceremony. We had attended his church a few times to learn a little about Unitarianism, we liked Pennington very much, and he graciously agreed to marry us. When we moved to Syracuse in 1963, and especially after we adopted Karen in 1966, we looked at some churches that might appeal to both of us, and that might be good for Karen, but neither May Memorial Unitarian Church nor the Unity Church appealed to us at that time (we did not know about the First Unitarian and Universalist Society then), and so we did nothing about that. For me, it did not matter. I never tried to join a temple because, just like my experiences at Hillel, my lack of Jewish tradition made me very uncomfortable at a temple. Not only do I not celebrate Jewish holidays today, I am barely aware of them. This is not surprising, because I never celebrated them as a child, so I have no tradition to fall back on, unlike many Jews. Much later, I did participate in the annual Holocaust (Yom Hashoah) Memorial commemorations that were held at various temples in Syracuse. By that time, I had begun to give talks about my experiences in Germany and with the *Kindertransport*.

So, why and how do I identify myself as a Jew?

In his book, *God Was Not in the Fire, The Search for a Spiritual Judaism*, Daniel Gordis poses the question "Why be Jewish?" and provides three possible answers: 1. to avenge the Shoah; 2. because of

Jewish supposed intellectual and ethical superiority; and 3. to maintain the continuity of Judaism. He argues that none of these answers
are satisfactory because none explain how Judaism can enhance our
spiritual lives, especially because the rituals associated with Judaism,
many of which seem archaic and incongruous in our modern lives,
fail to fulfill this need. I agree with this last point. Whenever I have
attended a synagogue, for a funeral, or in commemoration of the
Holocaust, the rituals and prayers have not "spoken" to me.

Another book that deals with this problem is Robert H. Mnookin's
The Jewish American Paradox. Mnookin asks: "Why is being Jewish
meaningful to you, especially, if you are nonreligious?" His own
answer is three-fold, relating to the Jewish head, the Jewish heart, and
the Jewish heritage. The first refers to the fact that the Jewish people
have always been committed to education and the life of the mind. The
second concerns the Jewish people's commitment to social justice, to
tikkun olam. By Jewish heritage Mnookin refers to the remarkable
story of the Jews' three-thousand-year history. Reflecting on these,
I realized that all three explain my reasons, also, for identifying as a
Jew.

My grandfather did not practice his religion. As a Jew who survived
the horrors of life in Nazi Germany (see Chapter 2), he had concluded,
I now believe, that being identifiably Jewish will always be dangerous.
When he joined us in America after the war, he suggested to me that
I should change my surname from Levy to one that was not identifi-
able as Jewish. My unhesitating response was that I would never do
so. The lives of my ancestors, until the late nineteenths century, were
inextricably tied to their Jewishness, and even – especially -- those of
my grandfather and mother were profoundly tied to their Jewishness,
necessitated by the actions of the Nazi regime. My identification as a
Jew stems primarily from my strong desire to remain connected to
my antecedents, a desire that was enhanced as I worked on writing
the genealogical survey of our family (see Chapter 12). Jewishness is
an essential part of my heritage, and despite the fact that the Jewish
religion means little or nothing to me, and even though I have sought
spiritual fulfilment in Christian churches at various times in my life, I
am unable and unwilling to discard it. Being a Holocaust Survivor is
an integral, ineradicable part of who I am, and I have given numerous
talks about this and attended annual Yom Hashoah services for the

last several years. Among these talks, one was about Jewish scientists who were expelled by the Nazi regime, and one about Sephardic and Ashkenazi Jews. Regarding this topic, I recall my mother telling me that our ancestors were Sephardic Jews, but discovering later that they were actually primarily, if not entirely Ashkenazi. When I was a child, my mother spoke disparagingly about "Eastern Jews". I was shocked, because this stance was not in character with my mother. But her desire to identify with Sephardim came, I'm sure, from the fact that as a group, Sephardic Jews were more cultural and enlightened than Ashkenazi (Eastern) Jews. Interestingly, one of our ancestors, the renowned rabbi and scholar Moses Isserles (1525 or 1530 - 1572), wrote the "Mappah", which sought to reconcile differences between the religious practices of Ashkenazi and Sephardic Jews by creating a legal code acceptable to both groups.

I have also practiced *tikkun olam* and a commitment to social justice during my adult life. One example of this is my strong involvement in the civil rights movement, which resulted in my being arrested and put in jail during the demonstrations in Syracuse in the 1960s (see Chapter 5). Another is my annual giving to various agencies and the charitable legacy document I have prepared for the disposal of a portion of my assets when I die. After Betty's death, I created a Betty Levy Memorial Fund that is devoted to funding various initiatives directed toward social justice for African Americans.

I am also proud to be a member of a group that has, throughout its history, been disproportionately represented among the intellectual and artistic leaders world-wide. When Hitler forced Jews to leave Germany, before initiating his campaign of genocide, the cultural and scientific impact on the two countries that absorbed the bulk of those scholars and intellectuals, Great Britain and the United States, was enormous. Hundreds of musicians, architects, choreographers, film makers, historians, philosophers, writers and scientists emigrated to these two countries. Two books that document the extraordinary contributions that these individuals made on their new adopted countries are *Hitler's Gift. The True Story of the Scientists Expelled by the Nazi Regime* by Jean Medawar and David Pyke, and *The Hitler Emigres. The Cultural Impact on Britain of Refugees from Nazism* by Daniel Snowman. A disproportionate proportion of Nobel Prizes in science and medicine after 1933, for example, went to refugees from Nazism who had emigrated to Britain or the United States.

Those of us, like I, who fled Nazi Germany as children, have also been extraordinarily successful as a group. This was documented by Gerhard Sonnert and Gerald Holton in their book: *What Happened to the Children Who Fled Nazi Persecution*, which is about the second wave of immigrants from Nazi Germany and Central Europe. The book is based on a five-year study of more than eighteen hundred individuals who fled Nazi persecution in Germany and some Central European countries as children, and came to the United States (including some 200 who, like I, first fled to England) to build their lives here. I was among those interviewed. As stated in the book's jacket:

> Despite arriving under disadvantageous and traumatic circumstances, without means, language skills, often without parents, and haunted by harrowing memories, this resilient group of young refugees became extraordinarily successful in the United States and made significant contributions to their new country.

The various criteria of success enumerated by the authors include the following comparisons with the general American population at large. Almost three times as many became professionals. Their representation in the various Marquis *Who's Who* volumes far exceeds those in the general American population: 8.4-fold in education, 10.3-fold in business and industry, 14.4-fold in the arts, 20.8-fold in the humanities, and 28.2-fold in science, engineering and architecture. The percentage of individuals whose educational attainment was greater than four years of higher education, was far greater among this group than among those born in America.

These, and numerous other comparisons, analyzed in great detail with careful statistical comparisons, document the success of this group of individuals. The authors also discuss the possible reasons for this success, including strong values in education, family expectations, values inculcated early during upbringing, superior early schooling, and the strengthened reverence for *Kultur* by their parents, immunizing them to some extent from the surrounding popular culture. In addition, success appeared to come to some extent *because* of adversity: the desire to emulate the resilience of their parents, and the responsibility to make the most of their lives because they recognized that their survival was a rare and unlikely gift. Factors that contributed to my own success, stemming from my departure from Germany and my growing up in England, included the superior schooling in England; the values and expectations that my parents and the Schlesingers transmitted to me; and my strong desire to make my mother and the Schlesingers proud of me.

There are two other matters related to my Jewishness that I wish to mention. First, is the fact that as a young boy in England I was troubled by the idea that we did not leave Germany during the early years of the Nazi regime, when Hitler's attacks on the Jews became increasingly threatening. Why did the vast majority of Jews not leave in the early 1930s? My mother told me that she recognized early on, that the Jews would come under increasing attack and argued for our leaving. But she was persuaded by my father and grandfather that, without connections or prospects for a livelihood abroad this would be foolish. My father's cousin, Heinz Joske, was one of the very few of our relatives who took the risk of leaving, moving with his family to France in 1933. They survived there during the war and came to the United States in the late 1940s.

Much later, I read a book that was especially revealing and meaningful for me in this regard: Amos Elon's *The Pity of It All. A History of Jews in Germany 1743-1933*. Elon explores the rise of the Jewish Enlightenment in the eighteenth century, in which Moses Mendelssohn played a major role, and which led to the Jews playing increasingly prominent roles in German culture and business, becoming deeply integrated into German life, despite the lingering presence of anti-Semitism. It has been said that the German Jews were more German than the Germans, and Elon masterfully depicts their bewilderment and disbelief when Hitler rose to power and launched his murderous campaign against them. It was exceedingly difficult for German Jews, assimilated for so long, many who served in World War I, and many who had risen to prominence in their professions, to comprehend Hitler's intentions. The majority thought that this was just an aberration that would soon blow over. For many, their realization of the bitter truth came too late.

The other matter concerns my attitude toward the state of Israel.

Few Jews in the diaspora lack strong opinions about Israel. Like many of us, my initial reaction when Israel became a state in 1948 was one of elation. During the early years of Israel's existence, I was thrilled by their progress in agriculture and science, their ability to "make the desert bloom", the kibbutzim with their socialist and egalitarian principles, and also by their military successes against their Arab neighbors who attacked them in several wars. But with time, as the Palestinians sought their statehood, and as I learned more about how the Israelis, as occupiers, degraded and demeaned the lives of Palestinians, and as the Israeli settlements continued to expand, I became disenchanted. I am aware of the failures of Palestinian leadership, of their refusal to recognize the existence of the State of Israel, and of the brutal intifadas, but this must be viewed, I believe, in the context of the vast disparity in power between the occupiers and the occupied. I am deeply disappointed in the responses of the Israelis. I am the only member of my family who has never visited Israel. Some years ago, I wrote a letter to Moshe Moscovic, husband of my now deceased cousin Ora (née Lotte Kanstein, my father's niece), in which I sought to contrast our attitudes about Israel.[1]

For some time, I subscribed to Tikkun, the liberal Jewish magazine founded by Rabbi Michael Lerner, devoted to *tikkun olam*, healing the world. The views about Israel expressed in *Tikkun* concurred with mine, and some of the spiritually-oriented articles appealed to me. Upon its founding in 2007, I became a member of J Street, the liberal Jewish advocacy group that promotes a two-state solution for Israel and opposes Jewish settlement expansion. It stands in stark contrast to the strident, conservative American Israel Public Affairs Committee (AIPAC) whose policies I oppose.

Although I am not religious, I have been attracted to certain religious individuals, especially some liberal Catholics whom we met in Syracuse, including members of the Berrigan family. A deep serenity seemed to emanate from these individuals that appealed to me very much. Betty began to have experiences that awakened her spirituality and to practice transcendental meditation, which she found very beneficial, and which I also tried, with only limited success. Through Betty, I was exposed to various spiritually oriented books and found that they struck a chord inside me. I have continued to seek out and read such books as well as books about religion.

I participated in a couple of events that had a powerful effect on me. One was a conference held over a long weekend at the Omega Institute in Rhinebeck, NY, sometime in the 1980s, at which Deepak Chopra gave a series of presentations, before he became world-famous. Both Betty and I were inspired by his presentations. Another was a transcendental meditation conference in Washington, D.C., also in the 1980s, to which I accompanied Betty. That had a powerful effect on me. I remember how open and vulnerable I felt on the drive home from Washington.

Despite these positive effects, I had an approach-avoidance attitude that always limited the extent to which I became involved. My logical, scientific mind seemed to prevent me from accepting fully many of the ideas I was exposed to. Certainly, none of them propelled me to become involved in any organized religious activity. Then a series of events occurred that changed this, at least for a few years. Betty had looked for a church to attend and found that she now liked the Unity Church and Spiritual Center, where Daniel Douglas was minister, and she began attending sometime in the early 1990s. Because of her progressive neuromuscular condition, after a while she had some difficulty driving herself to the church, and with getting to the sanctuary from the parking lot, so I accompanied her. Because the church is some distance from our house, I stayed for the services. After church, we would go to a restaurant for a Sunday luncheon and the whole outing became an enjoyable event that we could share. Despite the fact that the principles of Unity were too Christian for me to swallow, there was such a palpable spirit of love and community at that church that it captivated me. In addition, the minister at that time, Daniel Douglas, was a spiritual, inspirational man, and so I continued to accompany Betty every Sunday.

After a while, Rev. Douglas left Unity Church, and for some time there was no minister. This worked quite well because there were church members who did a good job of running the services, especially Cybie Mauro, and there were often very interesting pre-service discussions that we enjoyed. But then another minister was hired who was much more fundamentally Christian and I could no longer bear being there. At the same time, friends of ours, who also attended Unity, left and found that the minister and the services at the First Unitarian and Universalist Church were very much to their liking and urged us to come to see for ourselves. Betty declined to change, but I decided to try. The minister at First UU, David Blanchard, was a remarkable man whose services at First UU were outstanding. He had been married and had two daughters, but went through the painful process of discovering that he was gay, a journey that contributed to his deep spirituality and sensitivity.

The principles of Unitarian Universalist congregations are as follows:

1. The inherent worth and dignity of every person
2. Justice, equity and compassion in human relations
3. Acceptance of one another and encouragement to spiritual growth in our congregations
4. A free and responsible search for truth and meaning;
5. The right of conscience and the use of the democratic process within our congregations and in society at large
6. The goal of world community with peace, liberty, and justice for all
7. Respect for the interdependent web of all existence of which we are a part.

These principles appealed to me very much and resonated with my own beliefs. I decided to leave Unity and began to attend First UU on a regular basis. (Betty was quite upset with me for doing so, and it was a bone of contention between us for some time.) I found the services to be meaningful and they caused me to become more engaged with my spirituality. There were many interesting individuals in the congregation, including several Jews. The ambience was more intellectual and less religious than it had been at Unity; on the other hand, there was less spontaneous love and warmth at First UU than at Unity. I became involved in several of the activities at the church, especially in a book discussion group that was very stimulating, and I served on several committees and enjoyed the fellowship of the community. I participated in the church choir, including the annual concerts.

After I had been at First UU for a couple of years, David Blanchard was forced to resign following escalating concern within the congregation about his management style. This grew into a painful struggle that divided the congregation into irreconcilable factions, pro- and anti-David. Arbitrators had to be brought in to resolve the situation, but eventually David was forced out. It was a major event at the church which took a long time to heal, and resulted in some members leaving permanently. An interim minister was hired while a search was conducted for a permanent replacement. This was quite disruptive, and the ambience that I first encountered when I began attending First UU was never fully regained. I continued to attend, however, until I returned from my visit to Leipzig in 2009, which was a life-changing event for me (see Chapter 11), and which connected me more firmly to my Jewish roots. I realized when I returned that I could no longer remain a member of a church congregation. Nothing had changed, of course, with the principles of Unitarianism-Universalism, which remained as attractive for me as before, but it felt to me as though I would betray my Jewish ancestors, and especially those who had been murdered by the Nazis, if I were to continue attending. (Several years later, when I was a resident at The Nottingham, ecumenical services were held there weekly in which individuals from First UU played a prominent role. I attended and benefited from these services). My visit to Leipzig was very emotional, and powerfully reconnected me to my past, and to my ancestors. I thought about trying to join a synagogue, but knew that the barriers that had precluded it before would still exist. I read books about Judaism and the Jewish faith, but my reactions were the same as they had always been: however interesting these books were, they did not strengthen my desire to become a practicing Jew. I sought advice from some friends. I then heard about a man in Syracuse, Jim Brule, who provided spiritual guidance and mentoring for Jewish individuals. He was a *maggid*, one who draws people to a deeper spirituality, closer to God. One way he does so is through spiritual storytelling. It also happened that he was the son of a couple who had belonged to our Book Group many years ago. It seemed that he would be an ideal person for me to interact with to try to reconnect me more firmly with my Jewish heritage. We met and I told him about my problem and he thought that he might be able to help me. We had just begun to have a dialogue when his career took him to Chicago, so nothing came of it. Jim recommended a book that he thought would help me to deal with the role of the Jewish religion in my spiritual quest, *God Was Not in the Fire. The Search for a*

Spiritual Judaism by Daniel Gordis. It was the first of several books that I read subsequently, and that deal with the struggle that many contemporary American Jews have connecting with Judaism, and the reasons for that difficulty. I began reading it just as I was writing about my difficulty connecting with my Jewish roots. Finding this book just at this moment was an example of answers coming mysteriously just as you need them, an example of synchronicity.

Synchronicity

Synchronicity is a concept first introduced by the analytical psychologist Carl Jung. It holds that events are "meaningful coincidences" if they occur with no causal relationship yet seem to be meaningfully related. Jung also attributed numinosity to such events, i.e. arousing spiritual or religious emotion, being mysterious or awe-inspiring. We all probably experience events that seem to fit that designation, but usually they are quite insignificant and we may not notice them, or soon forget them. Sometimes such events are very compelling and they cause us to reflect about their meaning.

My grandfather experienced several instances when he dreamed about, or sensed someone's death, only to discover shortly afterwards that that person had just died. My mother had a powerful sensation about her mother's being in extreme danger, to discover several weeks later that at that precise time she was being murdered in a concentration camp. I have experienced several synchronicities. As a scientist, I tend to think that they are just coincidences, but something within me makes me wonder, almost hope, that there is more to it than just coincidence. An intriguing book titled *The Tao of Psychology. Synchronicity and the Self* by Jean Shinnoda Bolen, explores synchronicities.

Here I will describe two examples of synchronicities that I experienced, one that happened to a friend, and one that occurred to my mother.

1. The hand
My nephew David is the oldest son of my sister Liz. He was born in 1965 and when he was a little over 5 months old, Liz and her husband Ron visited us in Syracuse with their little son. We had a guest book,

in which we asked visitors to write a few words when they leave, which Liz and Ron did in 1965. Liz also took David's little hand, placed it on a page in the visitors' book, and drew an outline of it.

David visited us again on several occasions. In 2004, he brought his then wife, Aimie, and their newborn son Spencer, who was then a little over 5 months old. So, when he wrote into our visitors' book he did the same with Spencer's hand as Liz had done with his hand, drawing an outline in the book.

I thought that David, who is quite a sentimental person, might enjoy having those two outlines of his and his son's hands framed, so some time later I made copies of them and was going to go to a frame shop to have this done. Before doing so, I happened to go down to our basement to look for a document, totally unrelated to the outlines of these little hands, which was in a suitcase down there, and as I was searching for that document I came across a piece of paper which I didn't recall ever seeing before. It was the outline of my sister Liz's hand, made in 1938 when she was a little over 5 months old, and which my mother had made for her father's birthday as a greeting from his new granddaughter.

Seeing that literally took my breath away! I now had the outlines of David's, his mother's and his son's hands, all made when each of them was a little over 5 months old, over a 66-year span. I took all three and had them framed for David who was thrilled with this unique gift. Thinking back on this powerful synchronicity episode still gives me the chills.

2. Communing with the departed

The second episode I will describe involved one of Betty's friends, Elizabeth Williams. Elizabeth, like Betty, was a very spiritual person and she claimed that she could contact a beloved departed and report back from them. She received compensation for this service. If you wished to have a session with her to try to contact a departed person, you first told her a few things about that person and then meet with her for a session. Betty had done this after her mother died in 2000.

One morning in 2006 or 2007 I was having breakfast with Betty and we happened to talk about Elizabeth, whom we had not seen for several years, and had probably not ever talked about since then.

My mother died in 2002, and Betty mentioned that I should contact Elizabeth and set up a session like the one she had. I was not particularly interested in doing that as I didn't really believe it was possible to contact someone who is dead. For lunch that day we decided to go to an Indian restaurant some miles from our house, and when we were seated there, in walked Elizabeth Williams! She didn't see us, and she and her friend sat down at a table nearby. I was quite shaken by this "coincidence", enough so that I went over to speak with Elizabeth. Subsequently, moved by the power of the synchronicity of encountering Elizabeth, I set up a session with her to try to contact my mother, though I was very skeptical that this was possible.

As it happened, the "contact" with my mother was not very dramatic or meaningful, but Elizabeth asked me whether there was a "Philip" who had died recently, and who wanted to contact me. My friend Arthur Phillips, a professor at Syracuse University, had died a few weeks ago. During his last years, he lived at a rehabilitation facility in Syracuse and I visited him regularly, brought him the NY Times, and sometimes did errands for him. He eventually asked me and another person to be his power of attorney, and then, when he died, co-executors of his estate. According to Elizabeth, Arthur had several messages for me, all of which seemed reasonable.

I am still skeptical about this event. Meeting Elizabeth under the circumstances that I described was mind-blowing, and propelled me into doing something I would not otherwise have done. The "contact" with my deceased mother was not very compelling, but with Arthur Phillips it was! In retrospect (and taking a cynical view), Elizabeth might have gleaned enough facts about Arthur from speaking with me during the session to make her comments about Arthur's message to me plausible. This does not detract, however, from the powerful synchronicity of meeting Elizabeth at the Indian restaurant.

3. The house

The third incident occurred to my friend Valarie Vought, who came into my life in 1993 when I hired her to be the technician in my lab at Syracuse University (see Chapter 8). I had just been named the Biology Department's chairman, and needed someone reliable to carry out experiments and run my lab at a time when I would be consumed with a great deal of work. Valarie turned out to be exceptionally good and we have been friends ever since. She is a very spiritual person, about 40 years younger than I.

For some time, Valarie had been looking to purchase a house. One day she was on her morning walk, and she often prayed as she walked. That day she happened to walk past a house in a very pleasant street and was immediately very taken by it. She just knew she wanted that house, and prayed that she would get it. There was no "For Sale" sign on the house. When she got home that evening, after work, she had an e-mail form her real estate agent, informing her that a house had just come up for sale – *that* house! She told her agent to immediately put in an offer, and to prepare an offer $3,000 above the asking price. Her agent said: "You haven't even seen it yet!", but Valarie told the agent that she knew she wanted it, and explained what had happened that morning. The house was going to be available for inspection that Saturday, and Valarie told the agent to bring the offer, and to try to arrange to get the first appointment.

The agent did prepare an offer, but noting that there were no other offers yet, omitted to add the extra $3,000. They went to the house on Saturday and put in the offer. The owner, a woman accepted it, even though subsequently someone put in an offer $11,000 above the asking price, because she wanted to honor Valarie's offer. Valarie moved in and loved the house. She told me: "Never underestimate the power of prayer!"

4. The passport

This event happened to my mother during the tumultuous months following *Kristallnacht*, in November 1938, and after my parents had sent me to safety in England on a *Kindertransport*, in March 1939, and after my father died five weeks later. My mother had to start the emigration process all over again, as my parents' first plan was based on my father's working abroad. By that time, Jews no longer could retain their own money; the Nazis had confiscated it from them, and they got an allowance for subsistence. They had to apply every time they needed money for anything else, with all the proper forms filled out, typical for pedantic German thoroughness. Also, a Nazi-condoned packer had to supervise packing their belongings. To get such a packer one needed one's passport. The Nazis had confiscated my mother's.

On numerous visits to the passport office, she was told it wasn't there, but my mother saw it, as it had a noticeable ink smudge on it. She was in despair whether she would ever get it back, when she remembered my father telling her about a man at our factory who was a homosexual and who, he thought, might prove to be useful at some point because he could be bribed. My mother had never in her life bribed anyone, but she was desperate, and so she took the courageous step to ask him if he could retrieve her passport. He agreed, and told her the price. But how could she get the money for him under the strict Nazi monetary policies? It happened through an extraordinary twist of fate. My mother had to sort through the family belongings in preparation to pack them, a task she found extremely difficult. Just at that time, an old friend, Fritz Weg (the father of my friends Walter and Renate), stopped by to return some furniture my parents had lent him, and he offered to help, as he had just gone through the same task with his family's belongings. At one point my mother came across several of my father's wallets. Mr. Weg told her that she had better look inside them. To her horror, she discovered 700 marks in one of them, which was a lot of money. Possessing this money was an extremely serious offense that might have cost her her life had it been discovered by the Nazis. At first, she couldn't imagine how my father had left so much money in a wallet, but then she remembered that shortly after his last business trip abroad, he had to have major surgery, and while he was being anesthetized he mumbled something about money in a wallet. My mother paid no attention, thinking he was muttering some nonsense because he was half conscious. She now realized that he must have had this money left over after his business trip, and had forgotten to hand it over to the authorities. This was the money, then, that she used to pay the bribe. She was able, a few weeks later, to leave Leipzig with my little sister, to emigrate to England. Before that, however, she visited her aunt in Holland. After a few days in Holland, it became clear that war was about to break out, so she and my sister flew to England on what turned out to be the last KLM plane to leave Holland before the war began. I was one of the very few, among the ten thousand *Kindertransport* children, to be reunited with at least one parent.

The actual synchronicity in each of these examples is what is so striking, so breathtaking, and it can be isolated and distinguished from any outcome that ensued. The actual outcomes in these four examples of synchronicity are very different. The first two examples did not lead to any important outcomes. The third example did lead to an important result: Valarie bought the house she had encountered on her walk and knew she wanted. The fourth example is the most extraordinary, as it literally saved my mother's life. But, regardless of the different outcomes, each is a vivid example of synchronicity, each seemed like a miracle, and each evoked a powerful sense of astonishment.

The Mysterious

Synchronicity is but one example of various phenomena that appear to be mysterious, inexplicable rationally. Communicating with the dead is another. As a scientist, for much of my life I dismissed such things, or ascribed them to coincidence. As I became more attuned to my spirituality, my views broadened. I began to realize that rationality is not the only mode of viewing events around us. Love cannot be understood rationally, and there are many other experiences we have that should not be dismissed as being invalid because we can't explain them. I have become much more open to such experiences, indeed welcoming some because they enrich me.

Synchronicities come unexpectedly, and they can take one's breath away. I savor them, even though I can't explain them – I don't have to explain them. Other occurrences leave me more skeptical, e.g. communicating with the dead, but even those I no longer dismiss entirely. Being open to non-rational explanations has expanded my consciousness and enhanced my ability to experience wonder and awe.

An experience that Betty had is one such mysterious event that cannot be explained rationally, and that many would dismiss as being irrational or absurd, but that was certainly real for Betty and that I accept without understanding it. Betty had been very ill for about ten weeks, suffering a great deal of pain, unable to sleep in her bed, having difficulty with her balance, and being generally quite depressed. Her primary care physician had prescribed three different medications. The first two did not help, the third one helped a little. Then, one day, I noticed that she seemed to be better, and mentioned it to her. She agreed, and told me that her hairdresser, whom she had just visited, said the same thing. It was only after I told her about Valarie's experience that she told me what had happened to her the previous day. She was meditating and praying to the Holy Spirit, as she usually did every morning, when suddenly her head made uncontrollable, jerky movements, as though she was "possessed". Betty decided to let whatever was happening proceed without trying to control or stop it. When it was over, she felt noticeably better and continued to feel better subsequently. She attributed it to the Holy Spirit, and to her it was not all that extraordinary because – like Valarie – she was a practicing, deeply spiritual woman.

A few years since I wrote this section of my autobiography - in June, 2021 - a similar, powerful event occurred to me. For several months, I had experienced pain in my left hip during the night. It got increasingly bad, awakening me as I tossed in my bed, trying to find a comfortable position to go back to sleep toward morning. Finally, I concluded that the pain was due to osteoarthritis, and began taking Tylenol. Although that moderated the pain, it did not relieve it sufficiently. On June 7, I asked my physician if he had any suggestions what else I could do, and whether I should come in for an X-ray. I hadn't heard back from him yet when the following occurred. On June 11, the second anniversary of Betty's death, I spent some time at her grave and I "talked" to her for quite a while. It was a soul-wrenching conversation in which I apologized for some of my actions and insensitivity. I had reflected on these increasingly in the past months. That night I had no pain, and had none for many more months. The scientist in me says that my conversation with Betty and the disappearance of the pain were not related, that it was a coincidence. But I know, in fact, that the disappearance of the pain was a direct result of talking to Betty. I don't believe that this was a "communication with the dead", as Elizabeth Williams describes them. Betty did not heal my arthritis, but I believe my arthritis was an example of the internalization of my concern about some interactions with Betty, and that by talking about them at Betty's grave I relieved them.

God

Do I believe in God? What is God? These are questions that have occurred throughout my life, but that I have not dwelt on often. I write in the opening sentence of this book, that when I was a little boy, I wrote on a piece of paper "I don't believe you exist, God" and threw it out of the window, but soon afterwards wrote another to cancel the first note. This ambiguous attitude about God remained with me for many years, but eventually I became a non-believer.

When I went to boarding school in England, Win Schlesinger gave me a bible. I copied into it the first few lines of a poem that must have deeply impressed me:

> And I said to the man who stood at the gate of the year:
> "Give me a light that I may tread safely into the unknown."
> And he replied: "Go out into the darkness and put thine hand into the hand of God.
> That shall be better than light, and safer than a known way."

I now know that this poem, titled "God Knows", was written by Minnie Louise Haskins in 1908. King George VI quoted it in his Christmas broadcast to the British Empire in 1939, and perhaps I heard it then. I think that, as a young boy experiencing the turmoil of Nazi Germany, and then being transplanted to England, I yearned for something safe and certain to believe in and to sustain me, but this is speculation from a very distant time point. As I describe above, I loved going to church. At that time, in England, I also said my prayers at night, so there was something meaningful for me connected with the idea of God.

Now, in my old age, I certainly do not believe in the biblical God. I cannot believe that such a God would have let the Holocaust happen, and so many other cruel events in history, like slavery in the United States and the events that followed. I do not believe that he is there to listen to our prayers. I believe that when we pray, we open ourselves up to communion with our better selves. But I do believe that there is something bigger than us that connects us, and that we can tap into: the grandeur of the universe, the souls of our fellow human beings, that brings deep meaning to our lives.

CHAPTER 11

A Journey Back in Memory and Time

Leipzig, 2009

How it started

On July 28, 2009, I received a telephone call from Joel Ettinger, the husband of a distant relative who lives in Connecticut, and with whom I had been in correspondence for some time about the family genealogy. Like I, Joel was engaged in assembling a family genealogy. Unlike I, Joel posted his genealogical research on the Internet. He had received the following e-mail message, which he forwarded to me:

From: *"Oehls, Nadine"*
To: *ettinger*
Sent: *Monday, July 27, 2009 7:14 AM*
Subject: *search for HANS RICHARD LEVY*

Dear Joel,

I am searching for Hans Richard LEVY, born 1928 [sic] in Germany, possibly still living in the United States. Hans is the son of Berthold Levy (ID I5473) and Charlotte Frank (ID I5470).

I found his genealogy on your site and wonder if you could help me finding him [1418] or living relatives.

This is in relation to a television series about genealogy called "Die Spur der Ahnen" (traces of the ancestors). People write to us and ask for assistance in verifying the stories or legends that are told in their families.

A very decent German woman who was once very close with one Levy family in pre-war times has asked our help to find out the destiny of Hans-Richard Levy - who was able to flee the Nazi-terror just in time and immigrated to the US. It is her greatest wish to get an answer to this question.

I would be very grateful if you got back to me soon. Please get in touch with me in any case.

Thank you so much and kind regards from Leipzig/Germany,

Nadine Oehls

Freelancer

MITTELDEUTSCHER RUNDFUNK
Programming Culture/Science
Die Spur der Ahnen
04360 Leipzig
Germany

Tel: +49 341. 3005712
Fax: +49 341. 3005713

nadine.oehls@mdr.de
www.mdr.de

I immediately sent the following message to Ms. Oehls:

Dear Ms. Oehls:

I have just received an e-mail message from Joel Ettinger, attaching your message to him. I am the Hans Richard Levy about whom "a

very decent German woman" contacted you. I would be most inter-
ested to hear who she is.

Sincerely,

H. Richard Levy

Ms. Oehls responded at once, as follows:

Dear Mr. Levy,

*Thank you so much for your e-mail - I'm glad to hear from you. (In
fact we were all jumping off our seats in the office this morning!)*

*The Very Decent German Woman we are doing research for is
living in Berlin. We are holding close contact with her. She will only
hear about your being up and happy when we are actually producing the film - so that we can witness with the camera. :) Just so
much: She is descending
of the Frank branch of your family.*

*After the production, of course we will reveal her identity and con-
tact details to you. According to our planning, the production will
take place sometime in September/ October, 2009.*

*I do not want to push you, but can you provide us with a telephone
number? What time zone do you live in (not to wake you up)?
Maybe I can answer some of your questions over the phone, and, of
course, we have a lot of questions regarding your live story - if you
like to share that with us.*

Kind Regards from Leipzig,

Nadine Oehls

A few days later Ms. Oehls called me to break the news that the
television program, *Die Spur der Ahnen* (Traces of Ancestors), with
which she is associated at the Mitteldeutscher Rundfunk (MDR,

Mid-German Broadcasting Network) wanted to create an episode involving me and my relative, and asked whether I would be willing to come to Leipzig for the filming. They would take me to various places that were of significance during my life in Leipzig, and also to my father's grave. They would cover all my expenses. The "very decent German woman" turned out to be Marianne Wintgen, who was born after I left Germany, and who is my third cousin.

My first concern was whether we could find someone to stay with my wife, Betty. That problem was quickly solved when Betty called our good friend Rhoda Linton in nearby Ithaca, who said she could come, but not until early October. I then called our daughter Karen, who was thrilled and immediately said that she wanted to come with me to participate in this unique opportunity to see something about the environment in which I spent the first nine years of my life. I decided to go, and wrote to Ms. Oehls, telling her that I would come, and that my daughter would probably accompany me. Within the next weeks all the arrangements were made via numerous e-mails and telephone calls between me, and several MDR employees. The MDR offered to cover Karen's expenses also.

Marianne Wintgen

When my mother was a child and young adult, she was very close to Robert Wintgen, who was a sort of confidant for her when she needed advice. He was a Christian man, a professor of physical chemistry at the University of Cologne, whose second marriage was with my maternal grandmother's cousin, Helene Frank. (It is interesting that he was a professor of physical chemistry, and I was a professor of biochemistry). One of his sons, Georg (Göre), married Madeleine; Marianne was one of their children and she is, thus, my third cousin. As a half-Jew in Nazi Germany, Göre was unable to study mathematics in his native Bonn, but was able to gain admission to Leipzig University. While in Leipzig, Göre and Madeleine were often guests at my grandfather Richard's home. Our family thus saw a lot of him, and a close friendship developed. I even remember him dimly as he came to our house and taught me a little mathematics.

Marianne was born in 1942, after my mother, sister and I left Germany, and so none of us met her. But my mother maintained contact with her parents, especially during the difficult time following the end of the war, when they lived in the Russian zone of Berlin and experienced many shortages. She sent them packages, some of which included clothes that my sister (who was born 3 years before Marianne) had outgrown, and which Marianne wore.

My family was a focus of considerable interest in the Wintgen family, but although I knew about my mother's close relationship with her parents and grandfather, I had not had any special relationship with them. The genealogy that I assembled included little about that branch of the family. Marianne had also delved into her family's genealogy, which extended into my family. She had attempted, for several years to establish whether I was still alive, searching for "Hans Levy", or "Hans Richard Levy". The fact that she was unsuccessful is undoubtedly due to the fact that, when I emigrated to the United States in 1946, I stopped using my first name (because, in England, no one seemed able to pronounce it correctly), and since then have used "H. Richard Levy" professionally and otherwise. In April, 2009, Marianne sent an inquiry about me and my family to a website "leipzig-gedenkt" ("Leipzig remembered"). It was this inquiry that was, eventually, picked up by the MDR program *Die Spur der Ahnen*, and which prompted Nadine Oehl's inquiry cited above.

My departure from Leipzig, 1939

In Chapter 1, I describe the events that led up to *Kristallnacht* in 1938, and to my departure from Leipzig on the *Kindertramnsport* in 1939, bound for London, where I would spend the next seven years with Win and Bernard Schlesinger's family.

My return to Leipzig, 2009

During the weeks before I returned to Leipzig, many thoughts crowded my mind. I had not been back to my hometown since I left in 1939. I had no desire, since that day, to return to Germany, and had only been there briefly twice: once, in 1959, when my friend Howard Goldfine and I drove through Germany on our way from France to Switzerland, staying overnight in Munich (see Chapter 9); and in 1976, when I attended an International Congress of Biochemistry in

Hamburg. In 1959 I felt the anti-Semitism, but less so in 1976. During the first years after fleeing Germany I did not want to interact with Germans because the question always arose in my mind whether they, or their relatives, had been Nazis. In England, as a young boy, I did everything possible to "become" English. It was a matter of survival in my boarding school, during the war with Germany, where the boys would not understand that I was a Jew, and that this was different then from being a German. I did not want to speak German, and so I forgot my native language almost entirely until, when I was about 13, I realized that this was foolish. So, I asked my mother to speak and write to me in German and, in that way, relearned the language, though my usage is not very sophisticated. Another reason for wishing to relearn German is that hearing my mother speak to me in the language I had always heard as a child, restored to me my mother as she used to be, which was somehow reassuring. On this journey to Leipzig, my German proved to be very useful.

Someone at MDR made all the travel arrangements for Karen and me (business class for me, economy for Karen, but I upgraded her to business class), and on the evening of October 3 we departed from Washington D.C. to Frankfurt. Karen had taken the red-eye from Los Angeles the previous evening, and I had come from Syracuse that afternoon. The flight was smooth and comfortable, the food excellent. (But we arrived almost 3 hours late because the first airplane we had boarded had a problem and we had to get onto another one). We were met at the airport by Nadine Oehls, the lady who originally contacted me, and who did all the research on me and my family for the program. Nadine is a charming, young lady who speaks English well. We got into a company Audi, driven by a company driver, and took off for Leipzig. It was a drive of almost 4 hours on the Autobahn (long stretches without any speed limit), with mostly cloudy and rainy weather, through beautiful countryside. It was striking to see the hundreds of wind turbines, the first of many signs that Germany is very committed to being "green". We made a couple of stops on the way, and Nadine had brought refreshments for us. As we got closer to Leipzig, I recognized many of the names of the towns on the signs along the road. Once in Leipzig we went, at my request, to the Thomaskirche (St. Thomas Church) so I could take photos of J.S. Bach's and Felix Mendelssohn's statues. Mendelssohn is a very distant family relative, the 8th cousin of my great-great-grandmother Rosalie Blachstein. Although Felix Mendelssohn was born into a prominent Jewish family - his grandfather, Moses Mendelssohn was a renowned philosopher and the leading figure in the Jewish Enlightenment - he was baptized as a Lutheran. Nevertheless, the Nazis forbade the performance of his music and in 1936 they removed the monument that had been erected in 1892. It was rebuilt and dedicated in 2008. We were then driven to the very fine Linder Hotel, where there were reservations for Karen and me. That evening we had dinner at the hotel with Peter Dreckman, the director or producer of *Spur der Ahnen* (and other programs), a most interesting man. He was currently involved in making a film about orphan elephants in Kenya.

Leipzig: the first day

Karen and I had breakfast at the hotel, a very large buffet selection of all kinds of food, from cereals and fruit to sausages, cold cuts, meat and cheese, to croissants and various breads, and juices, coffee, etc. Nadine picked us up and drove us to the large train station, the *Leipziger Hauptbahnhof*, which I recognized. There I was to meet Marianne in a filmed encounter. Marianne was told the previous night that I was in Leipzig; before that she learned that they were looking through archives to locate me, but she became suspicious and was pretty sure I would be there. I was to walk down the platform as though I had just arrived on a train, and Marianne was to look for me. I was fitted with a microphone and transmitter (used for all the filming both days). In fact, she recognized me because I resemble my grandfather and her great-grandfather, Max Frank. We embraced warmly and immediately started a non-stop conversation, in German as she speaks no English. Here I also met Anett Friedrich, with whom I had corresponded by telephone and e-mail during the last couple of months. She is the one who is directing the film, and who would interview me throughout.

From the station, we took a streetcar toward our former apartment building. First, we stopped at a very nice, old café, Grundmann, where we all had lunch together. Anett had asked me to bring some photographs, representing various stages of my life, and after lunch I placed them onto a table. I was then asked to pick some of them up and discuss them with Marianne, which was filmed. When that was finished, in one of the many moving moments during these two days, Anett gave me the following documents that the MDR had procured for me: a copy of my father's death certificate; a copy of a page from the police blotter from November 10, 1938, noting my father's arrest after *Kristallnacht*; a series of documents concerning the "arianization" of our factory, including the legal document that was prepared for the Nazis' takeover of the factory, which included not only statistics about the value of the various machines, the building, the land, etc., but also a brief history of the factory, and which documented for me a claim that my mother had always made about the knitted goods made there, namely that they were of the highest quality in Europe; it also included correspondence from the Bank of Dresden, which was to undertake the factory's sale, and which ends with the usual salutation then, "Heil Hitler!"; and a copy of a notice, dated September 24, 1941, to auction a large lot of books by the secret police, that originated "with the Jewess Charlotte Sara Levy" (the name Sara was added by the Nazis to all female Jews, and the name Israel to all male Jews) which also ended with the Heil Hitler salutation. Also, Marianne gave me some copies of letters from my grandfather to her parents. (The following day she gave me a copy of *Erinnerungen und Zeugnisse* (Remembrances and Testimonies), her extensive genealogical research about her branch of our family).

We then went to our former apartment building at Brandvorwerkstrasse 80, a still modern-looking structure, which I vaguely remembered, with a rose-brown and cream-colored exterior, on a cobblestone street, all quite upscale-looking. They filmed Marianne and I walking down the street, pointing out the building, and then we went inside. We had lived on the first floor, up a few steps. The apartment, which was currently used as a center for abused and disturbed children, was made accessible to us, and we went inside. Although I didn't clearly recognize any details, the overall layout, the size of the rooms, etc., were familiar to me: the living room, dining room, my room. I remembered that there was a balcony in the back, and that it overlooked a lawn that led out to a forest. At the back, right corner was a sandbox in which Werner (now Pierre) Joske and I used to play and make *Beppermumpe*. We went back, and indeed, that was true, though the sandbox was no longer there and a large apartment building (recently built) partly blocked the view to the forest. While we were in the apartment, Anett interviewed me, and Marianne showed me two silver napkin rings, embossed with the names Berthold and Lotte, which my mother had given to Marianne's parents when she left Germany, and now Marianne gave me the one with my father's name.

I remembered that there was a butcher shop at the next corner. It is now another shop, but a lady in the apartment told us her family had run a butcher's shop a half block further down, so I thought I might have been mistaken. However, Walter and Renate confirmed for me, later in the week, that I was correct.

Karen, Marianne and I were asked whether we would like to have dinner with Anett and Nadine, but I was exhausted and so too, it turned out, was Marianne, so we declined. Karen and I ate at the hotel, I called Betty, and then went to bed.

Leipzig: the second day

After we ate an excellent breakfast at the hotel, Karen and I were picked up by Nadine, who then picked up Marianne and we drove over to Fregestrasse. When we were evicted from our apartment at Brandvorwerkstrasse my mother had to find another place that would accept us. She did finally find a small apartment at Fregestrasse 7 to which we moved early in 1939 (see Chapter 1). The MDR film crew wanted to do some filming there. We did not go into the apartment, but Marianne and I were filmed walking down the street to the building, and then in the yard in the back, where Anett interviewed me about Kristallnacht and the move to Fregestrasse.

We then drove to the factory at Berlinerstrasse 65, Gebrüder Frank, which was owned by my father and grandfather. It was partly in ruins, partly being rebuilt, but I remembered it a bit, especially the yellowish brick building. High up on the façade on one side one can still see the inscription *Strickwaren Fabrik* (Knitted Goods Factory), but the sign *Gebrüder Frank*, was no longer evident. My cousin Reinhard Frank, ironically, saw this sign as he was being transported to Theresienstadt concentration camp as a fifteen-year-old boy, while the train stopped briefly in Leipzig. Anett interviewed me about my memories of the factory.

Nadine took Karen, Marianne and me to lunch at a nice little restaurant, and then we all met at the Old Jewish Cemetery, where my father is buried. I had seen pictures of the grave but, of course, had never seen the actual grave. The entrance to the cemetery is very inconspicuous and shabby, in part, perhaps, so that it could not readily be located, as there has been desecration in it (apparently, the entrance to the New Jewish Cemetery is quite different). This cemetery was not well maintained. Marianne and I were given a map, showing the location of the various graves and family plots, and were filmed using it to locate ours. The MDR film crew was most respectful, keeping their distance. Several scenes were set up in the cemetery, including, finally, one of me, at my father's grave and looking at the gravestones in our family plot. Seeing my father's grave was a moving experience, and I spent several minutes communing with him. Karen told me that for her, this was a very moving, difficult scene. At the wall behind the plot is a large plaque stating that this is the plot of families Selmar and Wilhelm Frank, who were brothers. Others who are buried here include Selmar; Wilhelm; Richard (my maternal grandfather) and his Christian, second wife, Amanda; Rosa née Löwenbaum (my grandfather's mother); Auguste Frank (Wilhelm's wife); and Käthe Kantstein, my father's sister. (Amanda is probably the only Christian buried here). I was surprised that my grandfather Richard was buried there, as he died in New Jersey, but apparently, he was cremated and his ashes flown to Leipzig. Another surprise was Käthe's grave, as she was murdered by the Nazis, in the Ravensbrück concentration camp; perhaps this was merely a marker. The family plot and the plaque on the wall were very overgrown with ivy and other plants, which Karen and I removed. Next to our family plot is one of the Family Benjamin Schachian. The large plaque on the wall had been desecrated with words such as *Juden Schweine* (Jew pigs), and one could see that there had been attempts to clean it up that were only minimally successful.

Anett interviewed me in the cemetery about my feelings at seeing all this. I mentioned that it had taken me a long time to be able to talk to Germans without thinking about whether they, or their relatives, were Nazis who had murdered some of my family members and other Jews, but that I had eventually shed that feeling. She later told me that she still wonders whether any of her family were involved in the atrocities.

We then went to the Jewish Cultural and Meeting Center (*Kultur- und Degegnungszentrum Ariowitsch-Haus*) at Hinrichsenstrasse 14, right around the corner from Funkenburgstrasse, where my grandfather used to live. Anett had written to me, asking whether I would be willing to be interviewed by some reporters and also by some children after the MDR filming was complete, and I had agreed. The interviews were to take place here. While waiting, we saw some exhibits, and Marianne spotted photos on the wall, including some of my grandfather, who became president of the Jewish Community after the war, when only 16 of the 16,000 Jews who had lived in Leipzig remained. Some photos were taken of me standing under those pictures. In Chapter 1, I describe my grandfather's second marriage to a Christian woman in 1926. It was, presumably, for this reason that he was not deported into a concentration camp or murdered, although being married to a non-Jew did not prevent other Jews in Germany from befalling such a fate. His harrowing years in Leipzig during the war were chronicled in letters to my mother and to Marianne's parents.

First, I was interviewed by two reporters: Thomas Mayer, the chief reporter of the *Leipziger Volkszeitung* (Leipzig Folknewspaper), and a reporter from the radio division of the MDR, for a public broadcasting program. They asked about my feelings about being back in Leipzig, why I hadn't come previously, and various other questions. Mr. Mayer subsequently sent me a copy of the paper with the interview. Then came one of the most moving events of the two days in Leipzig. Two boys, Julius Völkner and Paul Moritz, about 17 years old, interviewed me. They had worked for the past months on a school project about me and my family. They conducted the interview in English and asked some excellent questions, including quite probing ones about my feelings during my first months in England. Their teacher, who actually performed the research, also asked a few questions. They then presented me with a beautiful, bound book containing the results of the research, with all the documentation, and pictures, and also a CD of it. They also gave a copy to Marianne. They gave us both a bouquet of flowers (which we gave to the film crew), and gave me a very large, framed document: a receipt dated December 9, 1902, for some socks with a *Gebrüder Frank* logo showing a picture of the factory. It was very beautiful, but too big for me to take, so the MDR crew shipped it to me. This was a most remarkable event, and one that inspires hope for the future of the German youth.

There were two events that had been planned but did not materialize. First, we were originally scheduled to visit my former Jewish school, which the Nazis closed in 1938. I don't know why this didn't happen, but probably because of lack of time. Second, a filming had been scheduled of the installation and dedication of a *Stolperstein* (literally a stumblestone) in my father's honor outside our former apartment on Brandvorwerkstrasse. I describe these Stolpersteine in Chapter 1. The artist Gunter Demnig, who creates and installs the *Stolpersteine* was so overwhelmed with requests for these stones that he was behind schedule in delivering them, and the one for my father was not due to arrive in Leipzig until around January (see below). In Leipzig, the cost of installation was being born by *Die Rote Hilfe* (The Red Help), a left-wing organization that supports victims of oppression, as well as by a school group.

We then said our farewells to the MDR crew, with whom we had developed a strong bond during this brief, intense time together. Marianne, Karen and I and our belongings were transferred into one of the MDR Audis to drive us to Berlin. Before leaving Leipzig, we did a little shopping at the mall at the station. The trip to Berlin on the Autobahn was amazing, reaching speeds of 230 Km./hr. (140 mph)! We got to Berlin about 10 p.m. Karen and I stayed at the Grand Westin Hotel; Marianne was driven home, and we agreed to meet the next morning at our hotel so she could show us some of the sights in the city. Karen and I had dinner at the hotel and called Betty. There were some anxious moments at the hotel when I thought someone had stolen my wallet with $280, and Karen couldn't print out her boarding pass. All turned out well in the end, but we didn't get to bed until about 1:30 a.m. Trying to sort all this out the next morning also delayed starting our Berlin tour.

Berlin

We stayed in Berlin, a city neither of us had ever visited, for only one day, so it was important to make the best use of our limited time. I told Marianne that I wanted to see the Jewish Museum, look at the Memorial to the Murdered Jews of Europe, and anything else she recommended. She and her partner, Lydia came to pick us up at the hotel. We began with the Jewish Museum, designed by Daniel Libeskind. Although we only saw a few sections of it, we were both deeply impressed. It deliberately conveys a disturbing sense of disorientation because of the tilting floors and the angles at which the walls meet. Numerous displays concerning the fate of individuals or families, letters, or descriptions are extremely moving because one can relate to the individual experiences, and Karen and I were very moved. The two thousand years of German-Jewish history is explored in numerous exhibits, and there is much more that we didn't see. I found a poster with a picture of Moses Isserles, our famous ancestor (~1525-1572); Karen took a photo of me standing in front of it. It was somewhat jarring to be brought back so vividly to the horrors of the Nazi era after a much more healing time in Leipzig. We ate lunch at the museum restaurant, and then went to see the Memorial to the Murdered Jews of Europe, which was also very interesting in its concept of over 2,700 concrete slabs of various heights, but which did not move me as much as the museum. We then did a lot of walking to see the Brandenburg Gate, Reichstag, Tiergarten (a park, not a zoo!). We were Marianne's and Lydia's guests for all these excursions, and they were very helpful in explaining things. Karen spent one more night at the hotel before taking off early next morning for Frankfurt and then Los Angeles; I took a British Airways flight to London.

England

I arrived at Heathrow about 9 p.m. and by the time I got my luggage, took the Heathrow Express to Paddington, and a taxi to the Park Inn, Russell Square, it was nearly 11 p.m. This hotel is certainly sufficient for me, but not of the same class as the hotels we stayed at in Germany! (I have always noticed that the British don't do things in as convenient and practical a way as we do in the States, and saw several examples of that at this hotel: there is no outlet in the bathroom; the hairdryer is hidden in the desk drawer, where one only discovers it by chance; there is no telephone book in the room; the towel rack in the bathroom is made so that when you put your wet towel on it, it covers the dry ones, underneath). I found my wallet with the money, that I thought I had lost in Berlin, when I unpacked!

Next morning after breakfast in the hotel I called Tip (Rosanna Gore), then walked to Euston Station, and took the express to Rugby. Peter and Irene Gore have been very good friends since my postdoc year in England in 1958; they have two daughters, Anya and Rosanna (see Chapter 9). The train was very comfortable and very fast. Tip met me at the platform and Peter was waiting downstairs. We took the half-hour drive to Long Buckby through lovely countryside. Peter had not changed much, but seemed slower especially his speech, after his recent stroke. At their new home I met Anya, who had come over from France to see me, and Irene. Irene was not as changed as much as I had feared after her diagnosis of Alzheimer's. She held a perfectly normal conversation, but Tip and Peter said that she was extremely forgetful and difficult with them. The home is lovely, very sunny, very *gemütlich*, with a little garden. Anya fixed an excellent lunch and Tip's husband David joined us. We had a very enjoyable time talking, I told them about my experiences in Germany. Peter was obviously uncomfortable with my emotionalism. I was there from about 11:30 to 4. Tip and Peter took me back to the station, and I took train back to London and had a dreadful dinner at the hotel.

Friday morning, I spent a couple of hours at the nearby British Museum, then took the tube to Cockfosters to Renate's (Daus, née Weg) house, where Walter and Sylvia soon joined us. Sylvia had M.S. and walked, though with great difficulty, to their great delight, because for months previously she was confined to a wheelchair. We spent a delightful afternoon, after an excellent lunch prepared by Renate, reminiscing about Leipzig and my telling them about my experiences. Their memories were far superior to mine, and they remembered details about our apartment on Brandvorwerkstrasse that I had forgotten, as well as numerous details about Leipzig. I very much enjoyed this warm encounter with my very old-time friends. I stayed a few days with their parents in early 1939 while my parents moved from Brandvorwerkstrasse to Fregestrasse (see Chapter 1) and after Walter and Renate had already gone to England.

I was able to tell Walter and Renate a story about their father, Fritz, a synchronistic event which they had not heard before, and which I recount in Chapter 10. Fritz Weg was helpful again at another occasion a few weeks later, when the man came to pack my mother's belongings. He was a very large man with a reputation for trying to get his way with women. At my mother's request, Fritz Weg stayed with her during the packing.

I took the tube to Bayswater to meet Hilary Schlesinger for dinner at the Royal China restaurant. Hilary was the sole survivor of that family who took me into their home when I arrived on the *Kindertransport*, and with whom I stayed for seven years (see Chapter 2). I had been in frequent touch with the family ever since, but had not seen in Hilary in ten years. It so happened that yesterday was her 80th birthday, and in two weeks it would be my 80th, so I suggested this dinner to celebrate. Hilary wanted to hear about my trip, and I asked her to tell me some details about her conversion to Catholicism and joining Opus Dei. Her spiritual journey was a very long one, but the seeds for it were sown when she was at Badminton School, where the headmistress was a left-wing Quaker. Her parents were always totally supportive of what she did. I learned several interesting things about Susan, John, and the parents that I had not known before. Hilary was one of those people who radiate a serenity born of deep faith, and she seems to be without ego. It was a lovely meeting that lasted about 3 hours, and the meal was superb.

The next morning John Glees came over for breakfast and to drive me to Heathrow. John and I are second cousins, and his relationship to Marianne is exactly the same as mine. His mother, Eva, was the daughter of Agnes, who was a sister of my maternal grandmother Elise, Richard Frank's first wife. John was as joyous and excitable as ever, and was visibly moved by my story of the events in Germany. He asked lots of questions and told many interesting stories. I spoke by phone with his sister Helga in Norway, and with his partner.

The flight back to the States

On the flight from London to Washington I sat next to a man named Kevin Nichols with whom I had an interesting conversation. We chatted about where each of us had been, and he was very interested in my story. He then told me a bit about his background. His maternal grandparents were German Jews who left at the same time as we did. His paternal grandparents were German Catholics, and he was quite sure their forbears were Nazis. His specialty was international law, but currently he worked to install web sites at major companies worldwide. He was also involved in pro bono work to help individuals and institutions gain restitution for war-related crimes. This interest arose after he served in the U.S. army in Bosnia and saw the horrors there. This encounter seemed like a fitting conclusion to my journey.

Some final thoughts

This journey was an extraordinary event in my life, something I never anticipated, something that came unsought, and that profoundly affected me. It was as though all those connections to the past lay dormant inside me, and although I spoke about many of them with my mother and others, I never relived them, and in doing so I felt that some healing had taken place, healing I didn't even know I needed.

Three things contributed to the fact that this was such a positive experience. First, the fact that Karen accompanied me meant a great deal to me, much more than I anticipated. She was very supportive, she helped to take care of many little details, and she kept me grounded. It was evident that she was moved by our experiences in Leipzig and Berlin and was very involved in the whole venture, and that the MDR crew and Marianne greatly enjoyed being with her. Having her with me was a wonderful, unique father-daughter experience.

The second thing that was so positive was the MDR crew. Every one of them was kind and thoughtful, they were very sensitive to the tenor of the whole event, very respectful of my feelings, and they behaved in a truly loving way toward both Karen and me. We bonded during the interviews, and they were drawn into the story that unfolded. Anett Friedrich, the director of the film, the one who interviewed me throughout, was so moved that she cried openly on several occasions. All this facilitated my openness with them and contributed, I believe, to the fact that the event was so powerful. Carsten Waldbauer, the camera operator, showed his friendship and sensitivity throughout. He told me that he did not want to take any close-up shots in the cemetery as he felt this was an invasion of my privacy, which he could not overcome. This was why they had another photographer from MDR there. Nadine Oehls, the lady who conducted all the research, was our driver and guide throughout. She picked us up and delivered us at the hotel, took us to lunch, and always had refreshments for us in the car. She also picked us up when we arrived in Frankfurt. Her English was the best of the crew, which was very helpful. She was a very attractive, charming young lady who made us feel very welcome. Incidentally, I have remained in contact with her ever since. Thomas, the camera assistant, was very amusing and made my use of the microphone effortless.

The third positive thing was that I got to know a member of my family whom I had never met, Marianne Wintgen. Our meeting developed into a close relationship and to frequent correspondence after my return home. This continuing friendship between the two families is something that our parents and grandparents would have relished.

A couple of things were very noticeable throughout our visit. One was that the Germans seemed to be very involved in going green. One testament was the hundreds of wind turbines we saw en route from Frankfurt to Leipzig. Another was the signs everywhere, e.g. those in our hotel rooms asking us to reuse the towels if possible, to save energy used for washing them. Another very striking thing, which was especially noticeable in Berlin, were the constant reminders of Germany's role in the Holocaust. In the book the boys gave me there is a section that deals with the upcoming events in Leipzig to remember *Kristallnacht*, and there were others on the web. In Berlin, we saw very many classes of schoolchildren being taken to the Jewish Museum and the Memorial to the Murdered Jews in Europe. Marianne told us that all schoolchildren in East Germany had to take excursions to the concentration camps, and Rosanna Gore told me in England that her daughter Natalie went on such a trip to Germany also. This all seemed to me to be of huge importance, and it made me think that we, in the United States, have nothing comparable to deal with the horror of slavery and the post-slavery period in American history, and that were we to do so, it would help greatly to deal with our continuing problem with race.

Standing at my father's grave was a very moving event. It caused me to think about the importance of having a location where members of future generations can come to pay their respect, and to reflect about the person buried there. I had always said, somewhat glibly, that I want to be cremated, but had not thought about what to do with my ashes. Betty had not answered to herself whether she wants to be buried or cremated. My mother asked to be cremated, and to have her ashes scattered in a beautiful location near some water, and I did so, at Chittenango State Park near Syracuse. But now, there is nowhere for us, and future members of our family to commune with her should they want to do so. Betty's father is buried, and her mother and sister were cremated, but their ashes are in urns at a cemetery in Chicago, and we have been there. I need to rethink this matter. (I did rethink this later. Betty was cremated, her remains were buried at Oakwood Cemetery in Syracuse, and after I am cremated, my remains will be buried beside hers.)

I must reiterate that this trip was a very important event for me, especially what transpired in Leipzig. Seeing the Jewish Museum in Berlin, although much too briefly, was another powerful experience. Visiting my old friends the Gores was most enjoyable. Reminiscing about Leipzig with Walter and Renate was very important. The dinner with Hilary Schlesinger was another reconnecting experience that had great meaning for both of us. Reconnecting with John Glees was more meaningful than I had anticipated. Even the discussion with the man on the flight home was a sort of improbable coda to the whole experience. I can easily imagine revisiting Germany, a possibility I could not have conceived of before this trip. Finally, reliving some of my experiences from seven decades ago reinforced the fact that, despite everything, I was extremely fortunate. I am eternally grateful to my parents, to the Schlesingers, and to the British government who saved my life and laid the groundwork for my future happiness.

The film

The film, entitled "The Little Boy and the Nazis", was shown on German television on November 25, 2009 as an episode of *Die Spur der Ahnen*. I was provided a web site link to view it before it aired. It was a skillful mix of Marianne's search for me; our visit to various locations in Leipzig, which served as backdrops to the interviews of me; scenes from my childhood, recreated by actors depicting my parents and me; family photographs; and historical footage of *Kristallnacht*, the *Kindertransport*; and Leipzig during the 1930s, including the anti-Semitic signs that were displayed around the city. I participated in a chat room with viewers after the film. I had never been in a chat room before, let alone one conducted in German on such an emotional subject. Dozens of viewers participated in the one-hour chat. I was astonished at their reaction. Many viewers were deeply moved. They asked about my feelings at returning to Germany, and many expressed their admiration that I did so. The father of the child actor who played me as a boy wrote that this was a great honor for him. Perhaps my statement, in the cemetery about the necessity of letting go of anger and bitterness struck a chord. Obviously, my experiences were not exceptional, and they were trivial compared to those of countless other children, most of whom never lived to tell their tale. My story had a happy outcome, which may have made it easier for people to relate to. Marianne thought that the film made a statement against prejudice of all kinds. If so, I am most gratified. MDR sent me a DVD of the film, and upon my request, created and sent me four copies with English subtitles. I have shown the film several times.

The book

The book that Julius Völkner and Paul Moritz gave me in Leipzig was called *Kindertransport nach England! Er war doch nur ein neunjähriger Junge!* (Kindertransport to England! He was still only a nine-year-old boy!). It was written by Torsten Schleip, the boys' teacher at the *Immanuel-Kant-Gymnasium* and chairman of the Leipzig Peace Center, and Richard Gauch, who was associated with several left-wing and pacifist organizations in Leipzig, and was project director of the group *Gedenkmarsch* (Remembrance March). Subsequently, Mr. Gauch asked me to review and correct this version of the book, which I did. In 2011, the book was published under the slightly different title *Er war doch nur ein neunjähriger Junge: Hans Richard Levy. Kindertransporte nach England 1938/1939* (He was still only a nine-year-old boy: Hans Richard Levy. Kindertransports to England 1938/1939) by Richard Gauch and Torsten Schleip. Publication was supported by the Rosa-Luxemburg Organization, and the book was scheduled to be used by all schools in Saxony beginning in September.

Dedication of the *Stolperstein*

The installation and dedication of a *Stolperstein* in memory of my father had been planned to occur while I was in Leipzig but had been delayed. This event took place on June 10, 2011. I was unable to be there, but Marianne and Lydia participated and sent me written and audio files recording the event, and many photographs. As of this date there were already 135 *Stolpersteine* in 67 locations in Leipzig; on June 10 eight more were installed, including one dedicated to my father. The Cologne sculptor Gunter Demnig creates these brass plaques and installs each one himself. The ceremony began with the laying of flowers at my father's grave in the Old Jewish Cemetery, witnessed by a group of about a dozen individuals, including Marianne and Lydia. Then some 30-40 people gathered outside our former apartment building at Brandvorwerkstrass 80, including representatives from various organizations, from the Saxony parliament, and including Julius, Paul, Marianne and Lydia. Several individuals spoke: Torsten Schleip, a representative from an organization *Rote Hilfe* (Red Help), and Marianne, and someone read remarks I had prepared and sent to Mr. Gauch. Mr. Demning installed the *Stolperstein* and some flowers were laid next to it. A lady who lived in one of the apartments said that she would look after the *Stolperstein* and keep it clean. At the conclusion, a musician played a beautiful saxophone solo.

CHAPTER 12

Life After Retirement

I retired from Syracuse University as a Professor Emeritus in July 2000. Jack Bryan, my long-time friend and colleague, who was also my associate chair while I was department chair from 1993 to 1999, arranged a reception in my honor at the department. He gave a talk and presented me with some gifts from the department – a house plant, a little desk on wheels with an adjustable top. Cathy Newton, Dean of the College of Arts & Sciences and a friend, gave me a book.

Something I remember about Jack's talk had a big effect on me. He was citing my accomplishments and I anticipated that he would focus on my publications. Instead, he talked about my excellence as a teacher, including the fact that I had won the William Wasserstrom Award for Excellence in Graduate Teaching. I was disappointed that he had not emphasized my publications, and it was only afterwards, over time, that I came to realize that he was right: my influence on my students was the greater accomplishment. I was so enmeshed in the "publish or perish" culture of academia that I had minimized my role as teacher, though I had always enjoyed teaching, found it very rewarding, and had throughout the years received compliments from my students.

As my retirement approached, Betty was concerned about what I would do. She knew how deeply involved I had been in my work throughout my career and didn't think there would be anything to take its place. As it turned out, she need not have worried. I took my cue from Bernard Schlesinger, my "adoptive father" during my years in England, who was a prominent pediatrician but who, when he retired, decided to do something entirely different: he became involved in the Citizens Advisory Bureau of Newbury. I knew that I had many interests that I could pursue and I did, indeed, become involved in several activities that were rewarding and enjoyable. Among these, music and writing played major roles.

Music in my Life

Music played a major role in my life, and in the lives of my forebears. Although none of my ancestors were professional musicians, many enjoyed music as an avocation. When my maternal great-grandfather returned from the opera, he played the arias on the piano to his wife's delight. My maternal grandfather played the flute and the piano, and he and my grandmother frequently played fourhanded transcriptions of Haydn and Beethoven symphonies and other works, as was the custom among upper middleclass Jews in Germany at that time. My grandmother also sang. My grandfather was a great admirer of Wagner's music, which was modern and controversial during his youth. My mother sang with the Leipzig Gewandhaus choir for a while, including a performance of Beethoven's 9th Symphony under Furtwängler's direction. My sister also played the flute, and my father played the flute in a local orchestra in Leipzig, and in some amateur chamber music groups, which occasionally gathered at our apartment. One such gathering had been planned for the evening of November 10, 1938, but was canceled when it was learned that a German diplomat, Ernst vom Rath, was killed by a Jew in the French embassy the previous evening, the pretext that led to *Kristallnacht*. My life-long love for classical music probably began in our apartment, listening to those chamber music concerts. The first piece that I remember liking was Mozart's *Eine kleine Nachtmusik*. I don't recall ever going to a public concert in Germany, probably because Jews were no longer allowed to attend such public events. But only two days after I arrived in England, Win Schlesinger took me to a concert for children by the London Symphony Orchestra, a memorable event. I sent the program to my parents, annotating it with my preferences. The conductor was Malcolm Sargent, and the program consisted of Beethoven's

Coriolan Overture; the first movement of Elgar's Violin Concerto in B minor; "Song Before Sunrise" by Delius; Handel's Concerto No. 3 in G minor for Oboe and Strings; and the Overture to The Meistersingers of Nuremberg by Wagner. I liked the Handel best, and the Beethoven least.

The Schlesingers were a very musical family; both parents and all five children played musical instruments. I attended many concerts as a young boy in England and received private piano lessons at my school. In Chapter 2, I describe how this turned into a missed opportunity that I regretted later in life. There were additional occasions to learn about music in my school. Every morning at assembly, there were prayers and announcements, preceded by a brief piece played on the piano by the music teacher, Mr. G.H. Keene. Several of us boarders at the school had a serious interest in classical music. One of us had a small gramophone, and some of us had records, so we would gather somewhere to listen together. I kept a little book of music sheets on which I wrote down the tunes from pieces I especially liked, and displayed this at our annual hobbies exhibition. In my last year at the school I played the part of Ko-Ko in our production of Gilbert and Sullivan's "The Mikado", which was a great success.

I didn't participate in any musical activities at Rutgers University, but as a graduate student at the University of Chicago I sang with a glee club. I also attended many concerts in Chicago, symphony, chamber music, and operas. I heard the Russian pianist Sviatoslav Richter, violinist David Oistrakh, and cellist Mstislav Rostropovich appear with the Chicago Symphony Orchestra during the great cultural thaw in the 1950s and 1960s. I was an avid listener to WFMT, the local classical music station, where I heard numerous concerts and educational programs, including a memorable series on Beethoven's string quartets. One of the graduate students with whom I shared an apartment was Martin Picker, a music student from whom I learned quite a lot, especially about modern music. Martin later became a professor of music at Rutgers University.

In Syracuse, Betty and I frequently attended concerts, chamber music, choral, symphony and opera. During summers, we occasionally drove to the world-renowned Glimmerglass Opera in Cooperstown to hear first-rate performances. When we first came to Syracuse in 1963 the Syracuse Symphony orchestra was not very good, and they didn't have a good venue. But over the years that changed. The orchestra improved greatly and was directed by some outstanding conductors, and a fine venue was built at the Civic Center downtown for its performances.

Both Betty and I joined the Syracuse University Oratorio Society (SUOS), where we sang for more than three decades. Participating in SUOS required passing an audition (which was not hard), and re-auditioning every three years. The director when I joined was Rhonda Fleming, who left after a couple of years and for many years thereafter the director was G. Burton Harbison. In 2003 Elisa Dekaney took the directorship. She was a young, energetic and very personable woman from Brazil whom most of us liked very much. In my last year, 2011, John Warren became the director; Betty retired from the Oratorio Society in 2005.

The SUOS presented three or four concerts per year, primarily with the Syracuse Symphony Orchestra (SSO), but also with other groups. Learning and performing this repertoire of music was an enriching musical experience. Many times, a work that seemed obtuse, or difficult to sing, became clear and beautiful to our ears once we rehearsed it several times. A prime example was portions of Philip Glass's *Satyagraha*, which was written in special musical notation, and which seemed utterly strange, but which we came to love. There is no doubt that performing music is the best way to appreciate it. We performed many works from the standard repertoire, and sang under numerous conductors and with many soloists. Highlights from those performances included Sir Michael Tippett's *A Child of Our Time*, conducted by the composer, and Janacek's Glagolithic Mass, which we performed in 1978 in Carnegie Hall, New York, conducted by Christopher Keene. This was a very difficult work musically and linguistically. Among my favorite works that we sang with the SSO were Handel's *Messiah*, which we performed often (but I never tired of singing it), Brahms's *German Requiem*, Verdi's *Requiem*, J.S. Bach's *Magnificat*, Mozart's *Ave Verum* Corpus, and Mahler's Symphony No. 2. Favorite works that we sang with smaller ensembles included Rachmaninoff's *Vespers*, Thomas Tallis's 40-part motet *Spem in Alium*, and Morten Lauridsen's *O Magnum Mysterium*.

An annual musical tradition that Betty and I enjoyed very much was a tasty and musical feast that was held on the evening after Christmas

(Boxing Day) at the home of our friends John and Carol Oberbrunner. John was the principal flautist with the SSO for many years, and his wife, Carol, a philosophy professor at Hobart and William Smith College in nearby Geneva, was a member of Oratorio Society. Some thirty to fifty guests brought food and wine. We began by singing Christmas carols for an hour or so, then stopped to eat and drink, and then returned for a complete performance of Handel's *Messiah*. Someone conducted (often it was Syracuse University philosophy professor Stuart Thau) and someone provided the piano accompaniment. It was always an exhilarating evening.

I was also active in two musical organizations. From 1983 to 1987, I served on the board of Syracuse Camerata, a small orchestra that performed locally, and I was its general manager from 1984 to 1987. In 2003, I was invited to become a board member of Civic Morning Musicals (CMM) and remained on the board for thirteen years. CMM was a musical organization that served various functions throughout its long history. Founded in 1890 by ladies who performed music for each other monthly, it later expanded membership to include men and began inviting outside artists and groups to perform. For seven decades, it became the impresario that brought leading musicians, chamber groups, orchestras, opera companies and ballet companies to perform before Syracuse audiences. This function was superseded when musical organizations, such as the SSO, Syracuse Friends of Chamber Music and the Syracuse Opera Company were founded. Another major focus for CMM was mentoring talented, young local musicians through scholarships, establishing a school for underprivileged children to learn musical instruments, and sponsoring various competitions. The latter included the Concerto Competition and Vocal Competition. The Concerto Competition was undertaken in collaboration with the SSO and provided the opportunity for the annual winners to play a movement of a concerto with the SSO at one of their concerts. Also, CMM mounted a series of weekly lunchtime concerts, free to the public, from September through May, as well as several paid-admission Sunday concerts every season. The performers in these concerts were usually local musicians or those having some connection with Central New York.

For the 2015-16 season, in celebration of CMM's 125th anniversary, we organized a series of special concerts. I proposed that these

concerts should feature former Concerto and Vocal Competition winners who had become established musicians, and agreed to head a
committee to arrange them. To locate former competition winners
required a good deal of research and much correspondence which
took me the better part of a year, but it had a very successful outcome. We mounted seven concerts, including one in collaboration
with Symphoria (the successor to SSO, which had gone bankrupt in
2011), featuring 14 former competition winners. I also wrote a book on
CMM's history titled *Civic Morning Musicals, 1890-2015. 125 Years*,
in collaboration with Beth Sotherden who did the artistic work. I spent
a year doing research for the book, my principal sources being CMM's
own archives and the extensive archive collection at the Onondaga
Historical Association. For this work, CMM honored me in 2015 with
their Lifetime Achievement Award.

Listening to, and especially performing music has been an important part of my life. Music can stir me to my innermost depths, and
move me as nothing else can. Often, as we were on stage performing
some of the great choral works composed over the past centuries, I felt
thrilled by the experience of re-creating what was written long ago and
performed innumerable times since then across the world.

On my visit to England in 1982, Anya Gore showed me this lovely
quote from *Duet for One* by Tom Kempinski: "Music, Dr. Feldman, is
the purest expression of humanity that there is. Because, you see, it's
magic, true mystery, not trickery. You can say it is sound, as speech is
sound, but it isn't. It's itself. A piece of music which expresses pain or
sorrow, or loneliness, it sounds nothing like what a lonely man says or
does, but it expresses it, and even better than the person does. Magic.
You see, there's no God, you know, Mr. Feldman, but I know where
they got the idea; they got it from music. It is a kind of heaven. It's
unearthly. It lifts you out of life to another place."

Another activity that I engaged in after retiring that related to my
love of music, was as a volunteer announcer for the local classical
music station, WCNY. I heard that they used volunteers to supplement
their paid announcers, and made some inquiries. I was interviewed by
the principal announcer who was impressed with my pronunciation
of German (!) and French and my knowledge of music. After several
more interviews and practice sessions I was hired in October 2001
and remained there for three years. Usually, I went twice a week for a

couple of hours each time. Most of the programs that I announced were selected by one of the regular announcers, but there was always extra time, and for that I could select what I wanted from their large collection. I usually made a few comments about each selection I played, mostly garnered from the record jacket, but also from my own knowledge. I also had to read advertisements, public service announcements, weather forecasts, and brief news items that I could select from the wire services. I enjoyed this very much, and was gratified how many favorable comments I received from friends and acquaintances who listened to WCNY. When this "job" came to an end, many people, for a long time afterwards, would ask me why I was no longer doing so. The real reason WCNY stopped asking me (and another volunteer) to come in was never made clear, but the word was that they wanted a more "homogeneous" sound from their announcers, an unlikely reason as they all sounded different and unique. Several years later I was asked if I would like to come back as a paid announcer. The time slot was for Sundays from 6 a.m. to noon, which did not appeal to me.

My principal activity for the years following my retirement involved writing, which I enjoy very much. During the first five years of my retirement I continued my frequent and lengthy e-mail correspondence with my friend Peter Gore, and to assemble our messages in annual volumes of E PEGORILE, a total of nine volumes comprising 2270 pages (see Chapter 2). I also continued something I had begun shortly before retiring, assembling our family genealogy. I wrote a book on the history of the Department of Biology at Syracuse University that was published by Syracuse University press, and I wrote a book about the history of Civic Morning Musicals for its 125th anniversary in 2015 (see above). I began writing my autobiography. I also published several essays and contributed articles to publications from the NY Civil Liberties Union and Peace Action of Central New York. Around the same time, I was asked to join the board of the Central New York chapter of the American Civil Liberties Union (ACLU), which I did for two or three years. I had been an ACLU supporter for many years and found it interesting to see what goes on behind the scenes. Gradually, and increasingly after about 2013, much of my life was devoted to being the principal caretaker for Betty, whose medical condition continued to deteriorate. These ventures are described below.

The Genealogy

My maternal grandfather, Richard Frank, who was born in 1870, began researching his family's ancestors at the beginning of the 20th century. He was joined in this effort by his cousin Alfred Frank. After my grandfather's marriage in 1898 to Elise Frank (no relation), his research encompassed her ancestors also, and when his daughters married, he researched the ancestors of his new sons-in-law. Richard and Alfred pursued these studies into the 1930s and their extensive notes came into my mother's possession, who passed them on to me. The notes were mostly handwritten in the old German script, but some were typed, and there were also booklets and genealogical charts. The initial task I set for myself was to organize this information on my computer, and to supplement it by contacting relatives for their input. This took a couple of years before it acquired shape and became organized into a book with many chapters, each one dealing with one family. A problem that I encountered was deciphering my grandfather's hand-written notes in the old German script. I had some help from a friend living in Syracuse, Edith Schmitz, originally from Austria.

Initially, I noted the vital statistics for each individual – date and place of birth and death, date of marriage, children, etc. – but as I acquired more information I also included what I could glean about their lives and included photographs when these were available. A substantial amount of all this came through correspondence, but I also did some research on the Internet, especially in order to push the timeline further back.

Eventually, a book materialized that I titled *A Genealogical Survey of Two German, Jewish Families Named Frank, Joined by Marriage in 1898*, which I produced on my computer and had bound. There are 27 chapters, each dealing with one portion of the genealogy, often one large family. The individuals are presented in chronological order, each one assigned with a number corresponding to his or her place in the chapter (the last two digits) and the chapter number (preceding digits). For example, Richard Frank is #704, the 4th, person in chapter 7, and Ruth Plaut is #1237, the 37th person in chapter 12. Over 1800 individuals are included in the book, listed alphabetically in an index. The genealogy goes back to the year 1040, but the information prior to the 16th century is much less reliable than that for more recent individuals, and this is discussed in a chapter on reliability. There are other chapters on organization and usage and other ancillary material. The book contains more than 100 photographs, some dating back to the 19th century, and each chapter is followed by one or more charts, depicting the relationships among the individuals comprising that chapter. Many of the photographs came from my mother and grandfather and others came through correspondence with numerous family members throughout the world.

Working on this genealogy had several interesting consequences. In 2008, I was contacted by Ivan Greenhut from South Carolina. He had heard about my genealogy project through Joel Ettinger. Joel was the husband of a relative who was also assembling a genealogy. We initiated a correspondence that provided additional, useful information. Joel was also the source of my subsequent connection with Nadine Oehls, which led to my visit to Germany in 2009 (see Chapter 11). Another very interesting consequence was my interactions with Robert Weinberg. In October 2010 I received an email from him that read: "Dear Prof. Levy, out of curiosity, are you the son of Berthold Levy and Lotte Frank?" I learned that this Robert Weinberg was a professor at M.I.T., a scientist, well-known for his discovery of the human oncogene, who received numerous awards, including the prestigious Wolf Prize in Medicine in 2004. Weinberg, who is a refugee from Nazi Germany, has been interested in his family's genealogy since he was an adolescent boy. It turns out we have a common ancestor eight generations back, Aron Heinemann Levi (a grandfather of Michael Feibes, listed in my genealogy).

Weinberg and I have been in occasional contact since 2008, and at his request, I sent him a copy of my genealogy. I have learned some interesting things from him about some of our common relatives. One such fact is that Walter Loeb, who was an electrochemist, performed an important experiment published in 1913 concerning the possible origin of life, for which he never received proper credit. Stanley Miller conducted a similar experiment in the 1950s, without acknowledging (or, presumably, knowing about) Loeb's experiment. Miller's work received wide coverage and served to ignite modern interest in the origin of life. Miller and I were graduate students at the University of

Chicago at the same time and I was actually in the audience when he announced his discovery, which generated a lot of controversy at the time.

I was also contacted by Hellmuth Salamon, who later used the name Ernest Sanders. He heard that I had a copy of a memoir by my great-aunt Hedwig Ems, about her survival in the concentration camp Thersienstadt. In this memoir, she mentions Hellmuth's aunt Franziska Salomon, and Hellmuth wondered whether I had any more information about her. I subsequently corresponded with him and learned more details about his family that I incorporated into my genealogy.

In 2018, I was contacted by Jill Rosenheim in England, who heard about my genealogy from her second cousin, Rob Frank, in Sydney, Australia. It turned out that we were related: her mother and I are third cousins. We have corresponded several times since, and I sent her a copy of my genealogy.

In 2021, I was accepted into a longevity study, after providing the research group with some data from my genealogy book relating to the life spans in my father's and mother's families. My father died at the age of forty. Both his parents died in their forties, as did his paternal grandmother and maternal great-grandfather. Also, his nephew died at age 42, and his niece at 50. My sister was also only 49 when she died. In stark contrast, numerous individuals on my mother's side of our family lived into their nineties, or became centenarians. My mother and her sister both reached the age of 102. Their father and paternal grandmother were 90 and 91, respectively, when they died, their grandfather's sister was 89, their maternal great-great-grandfather was 102, and their paternal great-great-great-grandmother and -grandfather died at 103 and 108, respectively. The latter was, according to an obituary in the local newspaper, "…in possession of all his faculties, lively and spritely up to his last hour."

It was startling to see the differences in these life spans, and it seemed clear that they must have a genetic component. In 2021, when I was 92 years old, I sent this information to the Longenity/Longevity Studies at the Albert Einstein College of Medicine in the Bronx, NY, inquiring whether they would be interested in having me participate in one of their longevity studies. They contacted me, interviewed me on the telephone, and accepted me into a study of longevity among

Ashkenazi Jews (my ancestors were Ashkenazi Jews). Since then I have submitted a blood sample to them, plus numerous forms, and have had some cognitive tests performed over the telephone. This interaction will continue annually. Participants in this study usually come in personally for testing once or twice per year, but because I live outside of the city, they will continue to test me by telephone or Zoom. I am very pleased still to be able to make a contribution to science.

It took about ten years to complete the genealogy. I sent copies to interested family members. Inevitably, typographical errors and wrong dates appeared which were corrected in subsequent revisions. Marianne Wintgen (see Chapter 11) especially, was very helpful in this regard. I also sent copies of the book to the Jewish Museum in Berlin, and to the Leo Baeck Institute in New York, which is dedicated to the history and culture of German-speaking Jews.

Here I will describe a few facts from the genealogy. The record on my father's side is quite sparse. Because my father's parents died when he was so young, he knew little about his ancestors. What information we have is due to the research conducted by my grandfather and mother. One branch of the family was traced back to Ichel ben Löb, born in 1768, who lived in Jessnitz, and whose father was named David Löb. Ichel was married to Albichele Levy Löwenheim who died in 1847. They were the progenitors of my father's grandfather, Louis Löwenheim (1819 – 1899), who was married to Johanna Märker, who also died in 1899. Johanna Märker's paternal grandparents were Meyer Marcur, (died in 1814) and Henrajette Wolff, who were merchants and owned a small-scale farming enterprise. All these individuals lived in Germany.

On my mother's side of the family there is a rich record. Levi Wolf-Frank was the first member of her family to use the surname Frank. He was born in Oberstreu in 1772, then moved to Harzgerode, where he received a letter of protection (*Schutzbrief*) in 1797 (a valuable document for Jews in those days) and where his 11 children were born. The first man named Frank in Elise Frank's family was Emmanuel Frank, born 1729, probably in Bedburg, where his son and grandchildren were born. These ancestors also lived in Germany.

In 1898, Levi Wolf-Frank's great-grandson Richard Frank (1870 – 1960) married Emmanuel Frank's great-great-granddaughter Elise Frank (b. 1874, murdered by the Nazis in 1942), thus joining these two Frank families. I am the grandson of Richard and Elise.

Richard Frank started collecting information about these families in the late 1890s and continued into the early 1930s, when he and his cousin Alfred Frank began a collaborative exploration of the family history. They pursued this project until the difficulties brought about by the Nazi regime impeded their progress and turned their attention to more pressing problems. They both lived in Germany, like most of their ancestors had for seven centuries before them, Richard in Leipzig and Alfred in Charlottenburg, Berlin.

In addition to updating the material I inherited from my grandfather, I was able to expand the time line back to the year 1040. This was possible through a fortuitous event, unrelated to my genealogical endeavors. In 2005, I gave a talk about Ashkenazi and Sephardi Jews at a meeting of a Havurah group to which my wife and I belonged,. In researching this topic, I recognized the name of one of our ancestors, Moses Isserles (more about him below). My grandfather was, evidently, unaware of Isserles's prominence. In researching Isserles further, I was able to trace our lineage back to Solomon ben Isaac, known as Rashi, born in 1040, who was a renowned scholar of the Bible and Talmud, born in France (see below). Among Rashi's descendants are many members of the extensive Luria and Treves families, including Jochanan Treves Ashkenas, born in 1265. According to one account, Ashkenas settled in Germany after being driven out of Spain in 1306, but another account claims that he came to Germany from France, where he was born. The name Ashkenas derives from Ashkenaz, a man described in the bible, whose kingdom eventually located to Germany. The Jews living in this region of Germany, on the banks of the Rhine River, called themselves Ashkenazi Jews. They settled in Eastern Europe in the 15th and 16th centuries.

It is not entirely clear why my ancestors adopted the surname Frank. Earlier, many Jews did not have surnames, eventually doing so when it became necessary or acceptable. Perhaps the name Frank comes from the city Frankfurt, where some of our ancestors lived. Perhaps there is some link to the Franks, a German tribe known since the third century A.D., who occupied territory on the banks of the Rhine. In the 10th century this became the duchy of Franconia, also known as Franken. My mother writes that Levi Wolf-Frank (see above) added Frank to his name Wolf because he came from Franken.

The documentation of the information in my genealogical survey for Richard Frank's ancestors is reliable back to Nathan Grünhut, who died in 1684. His son Leiser Grünhut (1657 – 1731) was born in Prague, then moved to Halberstadt. He was reputed to be a pious, learned and modest man. Elise Frank's ancestors were traced to David Frank's father Emmanuel Frank, born in 1729. My genealogical survey includes information on Nathan Grünhut's ancestors, which includes some prominent individuals noted below, but which is less reliable. I have detailed the assumptions I made in tracing these connections in my genealogical survey, and provided strong supporting evidence.

Marcus Herz (Katzenstein) and his wife Esther Feile were Richard Frank's maternal great-great-grandparents. Marcus (1745 - 1854) and Esther (1742 - 1845) lived to the astonishing ages of 108 and 103, respectively! The following obituary notice appeared in the *Westfalische Zeitung* (Westphalian Newspaper) on Saturday, March 11, 1854 (my translation):

> Steinheim (Höxter District) March 5
> Today the citizen Marcus Herz, born in August 1745, gently expired after a brief illness. He reached the rare age of 108 years and seven months. His only child, a married daughter, preceded him on the same day, in the same hour, in her 64th year 3 years ago. The deceased was in possession of all his faculties, lively and spritely up to his last hour, and is survived by 13 grandchildren, 38 great-grandchildren, and one great-great-grandchild.

Apparently, Herz was a scholar. In 1782, at the request of the great German Jewish philosopher, Moses Mendelssohn (who wrote an introduction), he translated *Vindiciae Judaeorum* (1656) by Menasseh b. Israel. This book was aimed at refuting the attacks against the readmission of the Jews to England, from where they had been expelled in 1290 under an edict issued by King Edward I. After a proposition to Oliver Cromwell by Menasseh b. Israel in the late 1650s, the Jews were readmitted to England

Marcus and Esther were not the only centenarians in our family. On my maternal grandmother's side of the family, her great-grandfather, Emmanuel Frank (1729-1831) lived to be 101. My mother, Charlotte

(Frank) Levy (1900 – 2002) and her sister, my aunt Martha (Frank) Heyman (1905 – 2007) both lived to be 102. They were the first individuals whose genes came from both Frank families. Both their father, Richard Frank (1870 – 1960) and his mother, Rosa (Löwenbaum) Frank (1838 – 1929) died when they were 90 years old, and there are others on my mother's side of the family who lived into their nineties or late eighties. This is in sharp contrast to my father's side of the family. My father, Berthold Levy (1899-1939) died when he was only 40. His parents, Bernhard Levy (1859 – 1908) and Clara (Löwenheim) Levy (1860 – 1905) also died in their 40s, as did my sister (Clara) Elisabeth (Levy) Aronica (1938 – 1987). Others in my father's side of the family also died at an early age.

Marcus and Esther Herz's daughter Johanna married Lippmann Levi (or Cohen) Lilienthal (1777 – 1851). At the age of 32, he became one of the two deputies from the Kingdom of Westphalia to the *Grand Sanhedrin*, set up in Paris by Napoleon as a Jewish high court. It was based on the original *Sanhedrin*, which was the main judicial and legislative body of the Jewish people in classical and late antiquity (Wikipedia).

One of Marcus Herz and Esther Feile's granddaughters was Rosette Lilienthal (1806 or 1807 – 1862) who married Calman Löwenbaum (1792 or 1793 – 1871). Rosette was an ardent democrat who followed the meetings of the national assembly in Frankfurt a/M with great interest. She especially admired Gabriel Riesser from Hamburg and Johann Jakobi from Königsberg (whose picture she had hanging in her room), both pioneers of Jewish emancipation, who were relentlessly militant for Jewish rights. (Amos Elon writes about Riesser and Jakobi in *The Pity of It All*). Calman was a prosperous businessman, pious and very charitable, whose wealth was enhanced when he became the sole heir to his father's estate. Unfortunately, he was constantly the victim of the inheritance laws of Westphalia. As a consequence, he designated his oldest son, Cäsar, as his sole heir, stipulating that he should administer the estate for the rest of the family. Cäsar married at an advanced age and then died after a brief, childless marriage. According to the inheritance laws of Westphalia, his widow was designated as the sole heir, and thus the majority of Calman's wealth was lost to the family.

The progenitor of the large Frank family, which included my maternal grandfather Richard Frank, was Karl Frank (1809 – 1882), who married Rosalie Blachstein (1808 – 1894), a direct descendant of Nathan Grünhut. They had nine children, four boys and five girls. He had a manufacturing business and a wholesale wine business in Harzgerode, Germany. He was a small man, quite a bit shorter than his wife, who placed great stock on his appearance. His business required him to visit neighboring towns, for which he used a decorated horse carriage, which he drove himself, wearing a black suit, stiff hat and white leather gloves.

Karl and Rosalie's oldest child was my maternal great-grandfather Selmar Frank (1837 – 1908). He married Rosa Löwenbaum (mentioned above). Selmar was a businessman who had an imposing figure as a grown man, but like his father, he was small, and had to stand on a stool behind the counter when he served his customers. (I was interested to learn that my own, short stature, derives not only from my parents, but from other ancestors). In 1865, he moved from Harzgerode to Halle and, that year, founded the firm *Gebrüder Frank*, together with his brother Wilhelm Frank (1842 – 1910), initially a wholesale knitwear business, with production outsourced, that did not flourish. In 1875, he and his wife moved to Leipzig, taking *Gebrüder Frank* with him, where it thrived and by 1893 production began in-house. In Leipzig, Selmar was a councilman from 1886 to ca. 1898, and for several decades he played a prominent role in the Jewish community and Jewish charities, and had various honorary positions. He was also a Freemason.

After Selmar's death, his son Richard (my grandfather) took his place as co-owner of *Gebrüder Frank*, and within two years, after Wilhelm died, his son Hermann Frank replaced him. Hermann died in 1932, and at that time, my father, Berthold Levy became a co-owner, along with Hermann's wife Hilde.

On my grandmother, Elise Frank's side of the family, the progenitors were Emmanuel Frank's son David Frank, born 1769 and his wife Esther Abraham (1780 – 1853), both born in Bedburg. David was a horse dealer with business extending into Holland. In 1790, the French came into the land and took his horses. David and Esther had 13 children, but only five reached adulthood. One of David's grandsons, also named David Frank (1840 – 1915), married Bertha Ems (1841 – 1919). He began a business in silk scarves, wool rugs, etc. in Paris when he was only 16. Later he had a similar business in Cologne, with two brothers, called Herzbach & Frank. His nickname was "King David" because of his reputed wisdom. David and Bertha were my mother's living grandparents and she writes glowingly of her childhood visits to them in Cologne.

There are a number of prominent individuals who are members of our larger family – both contemporary and from several centuries ago. Among the former are the following.

Franz Rosenzweig (1886 – 1929) was the great-grandson of the above-mentioned Rosette Lilienthal and Calman Löwenbaum, and thus my mother's second cousin. He was one of the leading German philosophers of the 20th century whose seminal work, *The Star of Redemption*, concerns his philosophical answer to life. He had struggled with converting to Christianity but eventually chose not to. He founded *Das Freie Jüdische Lehrhaus* (the Free Jewish House of Learning) in Frankfurt, dedicated to Jewish studies of the highest intellectual standing, and featuring novel methods of teaching. One of his teachers was Martin Buber, with whom he translated the entire Hebrew bible into German. In 1922, he became ill with amytrophic lateral sclerosis (Lou Gehrig's Disease), a progressive, debilitating form of paralysis which resulted in his losing all movement and speech. He continued writing, with his wife's help, until his death.

John Schlesinger (1926 – 2003) was the son of Bernard and Win Schlesinger, the family that took me into their home after I left Germany on the *Kindertransport* (see Chapter 2). Win and my mother were second cousins. John became a world-renowned film director with films such as "A Kind of Loving","Billy Liar", "Darling", "Sunday, Bloody Sunday", "Marathon Man", and "Midnight Cowboy", which garnered three Oscar Awards in 1970, including Best Director for John. He also directed plays, including at the National Theater in London, where he was an associate director, and operas at the Royal Opera House Covent Garden, Salzburg Festival, La Scala, Milan, and the Los Angeles Opera.

Ian Buruma (b. 1951) is the son of John Schlesinger's sister, Wendy and her Dutch husband Leo Buruma. He is a writer, editor and historian living in the United States, who was for a brief time editor of

The New York Review of Books, and from 2003 to 2017 a Professor at Bard College. His many books include *The Wages of Guilt: Memories of War in Germany and Japan, Inventing Japan: From Empire to Economic Miracle, Murder in Amsterdam: The Death of Theo VanGogh and the Limits of Tolerance, Year Zero: A History of 1945,* and *Their Promised Land: My Grandparents in Love and War.*

There are also ancestors, whom my grandfather and I have traced back several centuries, who rose to prominence and worldwide renown. As I have explained in my genealogical survey, tracing back our family that far requires making certain assumptions, for which I provide what I believe to be compelling evidence. With these reservations in mind, the following are two of the most prominent ancestors. My comments are taken from my genealogical survey.

Solomon ben Isaac, known as Rashi was born in 1040 and died in 1105 in Troyes, France. Rashi is the acronym for Rabbi Solomon ben Isaac. He was reputedly descended from the royal house of King David. Rashi was a leading commentator on the Bible and Talmud. Although a vintner by trade, his reputation rests on his scholarship pursued in his spare time. He founded a school ca 1070 which became very important and attracted many pupils. A distinguishing characteristic of his biblical commentary is a compromise between the literal and the *midrashic* interpretations. His commentaries are characterized by great clarity and thoroughness, and are among the most inclusive and authoritative in Jewish exegesis. He wrote the first comprehensive commentary on almost the entire Talmud. In his book *Jews, God and History*, Max Dimont writes about Rashi: "His great contribution to Jewish life was his reinterpretation of all relevant passages into the vernacular of the day, in such clear, lucid language, with such warmth and humanity, with such rare skill and scholarship, that his commentaries became revered as scripture and loved as literature". Rashi's commentary on the Pentateuch (printed in 1475) was the first dated Hebrew book published.

Moses (Moshe) ben Israel Isserles (1525 or 1530 - 1572 in Cracow, Poland). His full name was Isserel-Lazarus, shortened to Isserles, and he is referred to as "the Rema" (acronym of Rabbi Moses Isserles). He was a Polish rabbi, codifier, a great authority on *halakha* (Jewish law), well versed in Talmud and *Kabbalah* who also studied philosophy, astronomy, and history. He was a renowned scholar. In his youth, in 1550 he was a member of the Cracow *bet din* (panel of 3 rabbis who decide on legal matters in Jewish communities), and later he became chief rabbi of Cracow. He gained a worldwide reputation as a *posek* (arbiter) who was consulted by all the great scholars of the day. His contemporaries considered him to be the "Maimonides of Polish Jewry", resembling the latter in his universal outlook, his attachment to both Talmud and secular knowledge, his homiletics and his science. He was one of the forerunners of the Jewish enlightenment and he played an important role in bridging the differences between the religious practices of Ashkenazi and Sephardi Jews.

The same assumptions mentioned above link our family – albeit very distantly -- to the Mendelssohn family – Moses Mendelssohn (1729 – 1786), the great philosopher and leader of the Jewish Emancipation, and his grandson, the composer Felix Mendelssohn (1809 – 1847) and his sister, also a composer, Fanny Mendelssohn (1805 – 1847). Felix and Fanny were 8th cousins of my great-great grandmother Rosalie Blachstein.

The History of the Department of Biology

While I was chairman of the Department of Biology I initiated an annual newsletter titled *BIO@SU* that was sent to several thousand departmental alumni. It was edited and produced by Jack Bryan, the associate chair, and proved to be a great success. It kept us in touch with our alumni, who turned out to be very interested in the department; it helped to generate financial contributions to the department; and it led to the creation of an alumni advisory board that proved to be very helpful for the department, especially during the time when we were trying to expand departmental facilities; it was influential in persuading the university's administration to approve the construction of a new building for the department. It was because of my association with *BIO@SU*, as well as the fact that I had been on the faculty since the early 1960s and thus knew more about the department than most other faculty members, that chairman John Russell and associate chair Larry Wolf suggested that I might be persuaded to write a history of the department. The hope was that this could be completed in time for the projected opening of the new Life Sciences Complex in

2008. My first reaction to this suggestion was an emphatic "no", but Betty talked with me about it, pointing out how much I had enjoyed working on the genealogy and on editing *BIO@SU*, and so I reconsidered and decided to do it. Once I delved into this project, it became clear that it would not be ready in time for the 2008 opening of the new building, but I prepared a very brief summary of the history for that occasion.

I spent five years writing the book, and many hours in the University's Archives, locating various relevant items and numerous photographs. I contacted many faculty and former faculty, as well as former students. I asked John Russell, Larry Wolf, and Ernie Hemphill, a faculty member who had taken over editing *BIO@SU* and who was very familiar with the department's history as well as with the history of biology, to be my editorial review committee, and asked them to read sections of the book as it developed. What eventually resulted from all these efforts was a book consisting of six chapters, five of which dealt with five successive time-periods, plus one chapter consisting of reminiscences from several faculty members and alumni about their experiences in our department. There were also six appendices dealing with various documents, a listing of all the faculty, brief biographies of selected alumni, and a listing of students who had received awards from the department or University. Syracuse University Press agreed to publish it, but recognizing that it would only have a limited readership did so, provided we could solicit funds to cover a portion of the cost of publication. We had no difficulty in finding alumni and friends who contributed to this effort, and the book was published in 2012 with the title *Biology at Syracuse University 1872-2010*. I found this to be a very interesting and rewarding project. Sales of the book were modest, but it was also used by the Department and the College of Arts & Sciences as gifts for selected individuals.

The History of Civic Morning Musicals

I describe Civic Morning Musicals, and the genesis of the book I wrote on the occasion of CMM's 125th anniversary, above.

Autobiography

A few years after I retired, I began writing my autobiography. It started after my return from Germany in 2009, with an essay about that trip. Several people who read this essay urged me to write more. I realized that a major impediment to my doing this was the vast gaps in my recollections about my life. I did have numerous letters, some diaries, and other items to draw on to try to remedy this, so I began slowly to assemble my thoughts over the next ten years. It has been an enjoyable experience, and has served to close some of those memory gaps. Importantly, it has allowed me to reflect about many events in my life. Time for reflection was sparse while I worked, but has been plentiful after I moved into a retirement community (see below).

Caregiver

During the years following my retirement, I gradually became Betty's principal caregiver. Since the early 90's, Betty began to experience pain and weakness that, increasingly, impacted her life. The house we lived in since 1978 consisted of three stories, with the bedrooms on the top floor, the kitchen and living and dining rooms on the main floor, and the laundry in the basement. This meant Betty had to use the stairs daily, which became increasingly difficult for her. In January 2000, we moved to another house, on Scott Avenue, which had everything Betty needed on one floor. It did have a finished basement, with a bathroom and kitchen, and a large, storage area, but Betty did not need to go there. It became our facility for guests.

When we first moved to Scott Avenue, Betty was still mobile. She drove a car and still did much of the cooking. But I soon began to help with the cooking, and within a year or two was doing it all. Betty's condition deteriorated, she stopped being able to drive, and our life styles changed gradually.

The progression of Betty's illness was intertwined with her deep suspicion of the medical profession. Her experiences with three physicians, all white males, made her exceedingly distrustful of doctors. The first experience occurred when she was in her late thirties or early forties. She needed to have a hysterectomy and her gynecologist decided to also remove her ovaries at the same time, because there was some problem, I believe some cysts. He did this without notifying her until after the fact. Betty was, justifiably, very angry that he had performed this life-changing operation without her consent.

The second incident occurred in about 1987. Betty noticed a lump in her breast and consulted a physician who handled such matters, one of the leading surgeons in Syracuse. I went with her for the consultation. After he examined her (and, she told me, tried to grope her) he said that the lump needed to be removed quickly, and scheduled the surgery. Betty told him that she first wanted to seek a second opinion. At this he got angry and told her that if she did so, she need not bother to come back. We both walked out immediately. Betty did, indeed, go to another physician who said, right away, that it looked like a cyst to him and proceeded to insert a needle. Indeed, it was a cyst, which he drained and sent the fluid to a lab to test for cancerous cells. There were none.

The third experience was with her general physician for many years, who was also my physician and, indeed, the physician of several of our friends. He had a reputation, unknown to us, of interacting very well with his male patients, but not at all well with his female patients. Betty found that he did not seem to take her complaints seriously, telling her that what she experienced was "in her head". She was exasperated by this and finally left him.

Being a black woman who was keenly attuned to racial prejudice, and who was also a feminist, these interactions with three white, male doctors galled her and forever left her deeply distrustful of physicians. She had no primary physician for some time, and then heard about an African-American female doctor, who had set up her practice in a predominantly poor African-American section of Syracuse. Betty was excited about this and went to see her to discuss her medical issues. This physician's treatments, which involved no drugs, were quite unorthodox, which very much appealed to Betty, and she put Betty on various diets to try to help her. She also surmised that Betty's principal problem was due to an infestation with parasites, though I don't recall her ever actually demonstrating the presence of parasites. She prescribed some sort of natural supplement to get rid of the parasites, something that was not available in the United States, but could be obtained, with a physician's prescription, in Canada. I had a friend in Kingston, Ontario, who was a collaborator on one of my research projects, and through him we were able to get an appointment with a physician willing to get this material for Betty. So, one day we drove there and Betty met with this physician who provided her with a prescription. There were problems, subsequently, with getting the material through customs, and Betty never got it. My recollection is that there was no further discussion of parasites.

Betty then went to a female primary care physician, whom we also knew socially, and who respected Betty's predilection for natural remedies and her desire to use drugs as little as possible. She was very tolerant of Betty's views, which appealed to her, and tried to manage her illnesses with minimal interventions. So, the relationship between them was very good, but I'm not sure whether it was entirely beneficial for Betty's health as this physician largely let Betty dictate what treatments to use. In 2015, she had to retire prematurely from her career because, like Betty, she suffered from peripheral neuropathy, which eventually made it impossible for her to treat patients. By this time, she had joined a family practice, and after she left, another female physician in the same group practice took over as Betty's primary care physician. She was more rigid than her previous physician, but, for the most part, Betty tolerated her.

In addition to these physicians, Betty consulted several neurologists, pain specialists and other specialists, to try to deal with her symptoms. These symptoms included severe pain on the left side of her body, especially in her left leg; a modest scoliosis; peripheral neuropathy; wounds at the back of her left leg; increasing weakness of her body; and high blood pressure. It proved difficult to clearly diagnose the pain and weakness, in part because Betty did not tolerate MRIs, but a diagnosis of spinal stenosis seemed to account for much of her pain.

This pain was, at times, excruciating. Betty referred to these attacks as "barracudas". A variety of medications and treatment were used over the years to deal with these, and often a particular treatment (e.g. TENS stimulation, or lidocaine patches) would help for a while, but then become ineffective. Eventually, despite her aversion to drugs, Betty had to resort to powerful pain killers such as gabapentin, tramadol and hydrocodone, and these had deleterious side effects, making her very sleepy and affecting her memory. During the last year of her life she was able to get a prescription for medical marijuana, which she used with mixed success, but did not like the way it made her feel.

Betty also used many supplements, tried numerous relaxation procedures, had a number of physical therapists who came to the house when she could no longer easily go to them, and tried various exercises, most of which she found too strenuous. She consulted several chiropractors, had massages, and consulted specialists at the Spine and Wellness Center.

All this occurred over a period of years, and during this time her strength slowly declined. We had to make various provisions to compensate for the faculties she was losing, and she resisted having to use each one of them. For a while, she tried using a cane to help her walk, and then began using a walker. Later, she was unable to navigate with the walker and we had to provide a wheelchair (transport chair). Because the pain flared up at night, and also because she found lying down very uncomfortable, she tried using a hospital bed, and a recliner, sometimes favoring one, sometimes the other, but she was never happy with either one, or with different kinds of mattresses. The aides who eventually stayed overnight with her, tried all sorts of strategies using pillows, folded blankets, wedge pillows, etc., to make her comfortable, but it was an ongoing struggle.

We also had to make a number of modifications in the house to try to accommodate her needs. First, when she could no longer climb into the bathtub where the shower was located, we removed the bathtub, so she could walk into the shower. Then we installed a seat in the shower, and later, used a shower bench for her to sit on. During the last few years we had one or more aides who would help her in her shower, and help her to get dressed, and also dress her wound. In her final two years, We had essentially 24-hour care, including someone to stay with her at night. When she could no longer manage to walk up or down the steps leading from the garage to the back door, we installed a ramp, and, later, when it became difficult for me to push her up and down the ramp in her wheel chair, we installed a stair lift in the garage.

These changes occurred gradually, over a period of about ten years. Although we started having various individuals come to the house to help, beginning in 2013, including someone to manage her care and to provide physical therapy, and numerous aides, I was the principal caregiver. I coordinated everything, did all the cooking, shopping, laundry, took Betty to her doctors' appointments (until we began using a transport service in 2016), purchase medical supplies, and managed the house. I supervised her medications and made sure she took them. I took her blood pressure daily and kept a record. I accompanied her to all her doctors' appointments and helped her go to the bathrooms at the doctors' offices. This necessitated giving up many of my outside activities, including my long-time involvement with Civic Morning Musicals, all but a few concerts, and most lunch appointments with friends. After my trip to Germany in 2009 (when our friend Rhoda stayed with her), I did not travel outside Syracuse except for a one-day trip to Boston in 2011, to attend Reinhard Frank's funeral, and a brief visit to nearby Utica in 2014, to give a talk at their Jewish Community Center.

This all took a toll on me, exacerbated by the fact that Betty was, understandably, very unhappy with what was happening to her, especially with her increasing dependence on others. She was always a very independent woman, and losing her independence was exceedingly difficult for her. She took out her frustration and anger on those around her, most notably me, not infrequently accusing me of being careless and uncaring. I understood and tried to make allowance for the fact that she was hurting much more than I, and made a great effort to be extremely patient, something that did not come easily to me but that I learned to master.

During her final weeks, she lost interest in life, spent most of her time sleeping or dozing. She could no longer concentrate on reading. She had difficulty writing her name, or cutting her food, or brushing her teeth. She appeared to be exhausted with living. She mentioned several times that life was no longer worth living, and that she wanted to join her brother Jimmy, who had died a couple of years earlier.

The End

On May 24, shortly after the caretaker for the morning shift arrived, she tried to get Betty out of bed but had great difficulty moving her. She asked me to help her, and when we got her onto the wheel chair, the aide noticed that Betty's face looked crooked. As a nurses' aide, she recognized Betty's affect as indicative of a stroke. I called an ambulance and they took her to the emergency room, where they confirmed that she had a stroke.

For the next two weeks, Betty was in Crouse Hospital. Karen took off from her job at Cornell University and spent nights with her, I was there during the days. The stroke left her paralyzed on her right, formerly strong side, and virtually unable to speak. She tried to talk with me, but I was unable to understand her. It was agonizing not being able to connect with her and I have been haunted by not being able to know her final thoughts or wishes. She was fed through a nasal-gastric tube, but that proved very irritating, causing her to bring up lots of phlegm and making breathing very difficult. It was terrible to see and hear her excruciating struggle. After a few days, the tube was removed, and also the physician told us that, realistically, there was little hope for her recovery, or even for rehabilitation. She was declining rapidly. They suggested a couple of places where she could go for hospice care, and Karen and I went, on June 6 to look at two. The first, Francis House, had an outstanding reputation, but was difficult to get into. It was founded by the Sisters of St. Francis, was staffed by over 400 volunteers, and the medical care was administered by Hospice. We were extremely impressed. It is a beautiful facility, consisting of two houses, each with eight beautifully furnished rooms, situated on a quiet street, surrounded by lovely gardens. When one enters, the love and serenity arc palpable. The sister who gave us a tour told us, as we left, "If God wants Betty here, she will be". We then went to another facility, which was much more commercial, nowhere near as nice. I went back to the hospital to tell the woman who was arranging Betty's transfer, that we very much would like Betty to go to Francis House, but before I could even get the words out, she told me that Francis House had just called to accept Betty! It was meant to be!

On June 8, Betty was transferred to Francis House. She was taken off all food and drink, and kept comfortable. The following 4 days were the most peaceful that Betty had experienced in many months, if not years. The care was amazing, so lovingly provided. She was able to have visitors any time of day or night. June 10 was her birthday, and she had many cards, flowers, and visitors. Betty was in and out of consciousness, and I don't know how much she actually knew about what was happening. She was still unable to speak, but I brought music for her to listen to, some of her favorites, and I could tell that she heard and liked the music by her reactions, and this was very moving for me. Karen was encouraging her to "let go", that all would be well.

In the afternoon on June 11, Karen and I went to get a bite to eat in the evening. A friend from Unity Church who was also a physician, came just after we left. When we returned, he told us she had just died, peacefully, a few minutes previously. After the terrible two weeks in the hospital, and the difficult months preceding her stroke, it was a great relief to us that her end was so peaceful, and that she was no longer suffering.

The Aftermath

Following Betty's death, I was left with many conflicting feelings: sadness at her passing, happiness that she was no longer suffering after so many years of struggling, relief that a big burden had been lifted from my shoulders. My biggest problem was how to get past the anger and frustration and loneliness that I had felt for the past several years when she was so harsh with me just as I was helping her the most. I wanted to get beyond those feelings and to recall those times when we had been in love, and those times during our long marriage when we had done so many things together.

I did three things to try to help. First, I went to a grief counsellor. Hospice of Central New York provides free grief counselling for 13 months to those who have lost family members. Karen, who reacted to Betty's death perhaps more profoundly than I, also went. She found it helpful, I was less impressed.

Second, I went through photographs from the past sixty years to try to reconnect, and also because I wanted to assemble some to take to the service to commemorate her life, which was scheduled for July 27 at Unity Church.

Third -- and I felt as though I was guided to do this -- I read through her numerous note books that she had kept for several decades while she was studying ancient Egyptian and other African civilizations as well as African-American history. For many years, she gave lectures about her findings and planned to write a book, which I encouraged her to do. I had never seen her notebooks, which were remarkable, and which provided the principal theme of the remarks I prepared for the service to celebrate her life. This, more than anything else, helped me, and it deepened my connection to her as the woman I loved and admired. Many who were at the service commented to me about how much they learned about Betty and how much they admired her. I believe she would have been happy with the service, and proud about what I said.

Subsequently, I thought about the possibility of preserving Betty's large collection of books in a manner where they would inspire others. I wrote to George Langford, then Distinguished Professor of Neuroscience, Professor Emeritus of Biology, and Dean Emeritus of the College of Arts and Sciences at Syracuse University, an African American man who, I thought, would probably have the right connections to help me. I knew George, as our appointments in Biology at Syracuse University overlapped briefly. I sent George a copy of my remarks at Betty's service of remembrance, as a means of introducing her to him. He suggested that I contact Angela Williams, the librarian at the Martin Luther King Library in the Department of African American Studies at the University. I sent Angela a list of about 200 of Betty's books dealing with ancient African, especially Egyptian civilizations, and African American history and culture. These were the books she had used in her research, and from which she drew so much inspiration.

Angela wrote that she was very interested. She invited me to meet with her, to show me the MLK Library, and she took me to lunch at the Faculty Center. Our interaction was very positive. I was very impressed with the library which, although small, is very interesting and quite beautiful, with art work and documents of African Americans displayed throughout. She agreed to take most of Betty's books as a donation to the library and to insert name plates in them in Betty's memory. I was very gratified with this outcome, as I am sure that Betty would have been very happy about it. It allows her passion to be continued by inspiring others.

Similarly, I donated Betty's large collection of books dealing with spirituality to Unity Church where she had been a member, where we held her service of remembrance, and which she continued to support until the end of her life. I was helped with this by a long-time friend, a leading member of Unity who led the service for Betty in July.

None of this, however, connected me back to actual memories of Betty. Looking at a photograph of her in Rocky Mountain National Park, or at Cape Cod, or in Tobago reminded me of our visits to these places, but it did not conjure up any specific incidents, or interactions with her. It is no different when I look at other photos from the past, involving other individuals; they don't bring up any scenarios that I can play in my mind to reconnect me with those places or people either, so this is a general failing on my part, not specific to my interactions with Betty. I have always had a really bad memory. There are large portions of my life that I cannot recall at all, which has always plagued me and is one of the reasons that I wrote this autobiography, to try to recapture some of what seems to have been lost. Many of those sympathy cards I received noted that I would be comforted by all the memories of our married life, but there were all too few of them. It is, perhaps, no accident that the three works which I wrote after my retirement, the Genealogy, the History of the Biology Department, and the History of Civic Morning Musicals, all deal with memories, reminiscences. A fourth work, which I have been immersed in for a couple of years, illustrates this even more clearly: it is this autobiography, in which I try to recapture my own past.

The change from being "on task" and very busy all the time, to having lots of time to myself, was dramatic and took some getting used to. It felt as though I had my life back, and that was good. I could go to plays and concerts, to dinner with friends, out to eat whenever I wanted to, go to bed and get up on my own schedule, all this was good. But I was also quite lonely, alone in my big house, and looked forward to moving to a retirement community when the time came.

We held a beautiful service at Unity on July 27 to celebrate Betty's life. I selected all the music, Cybie Mauro and Leland Jackson delivered remarks, there were numerous reflections and readings, including mine[1]. About 80 people attended, including family members and friends from out of town. A reception downstairs at Unity followed, and that evening, Karen and I hosted a dinner for about 40 of those who had attended the service at a restaurant, The Chop House, allowing for further interaction and fellowship.

My Move to a Retirement Community

After Betty died in June, family, friends, and others all showed extraordinary kindness. Cybie and Leland worked with me to create a beautiful memorial service at Unity at the end of July. Karen helped me create a wonderful dinner at The Chop House on Waring Road for those, mostly from outside Syracuse, who had attended, and the restaurant's owner and staff made it a memorable occasion.

The final months of Betty's long illness became increasingly stressful for me. Karen was concerned that this stress might prove too much. But, from then on, I began to live in an extraordinary state of grace that remained with me for about nine months. I wasn't aware of it at first, it just settled on me. But, later, when I became ill, at the Nottingham, I recognize that it was true. The calm after the months of stress was palpable. Sometimes I spent hours just sitting quietly, or reading, or listening to music. It was like balm to my soul.

About two years earlier, after Karen moved back east to be closer and to help with Betty, she planted the seed in our minds that this would be a good time to sell the house and move to a community where we could be cared for. Surprisingly, considering how much we loved our house, we both thought this change would be beneficial. We went over to The Nottingham, a large retirement community about two miles from our home, where we already knew some of the residents, to look at an apartment in their Independent Living section and to find out more about life there. We were both impressed, and I filled out an application and put down a deposit. At the Nottingham, there are three living levels for residents, depending on their health: Independent Living, Assisted Living, and Nursing Care. Residents can move from one level to another as the need arises. Our respective health conditions would have enabled me to live in Independent Living, but Betty would have to be in Nursing Care. However, alternatively, we could share an apartment in Independent Living and continue to employ the aides who had been providing round-the-clock care for Betty.

The more we thought about it, this solution did not appear workable. Furthermore, Betty's condition started to deteriorate more rapidly, making a move too difficult for her, and so we abandoned the idea. After Betty died, however, I did not want to live in our house by myself, and relished the idea of moving to the Nottingham. I learned that a new wing for Independent Living, The Glens, was under construction, and it seemed that moving there might be ideal for me. Karen came over to help me consider whether this would be a good move, and we were both very impressed. As I had already applied earlier, it was a simple matter to change the application for myself for the Glens. I wanted to get an apartment with a bed room, bath room, kitchen-dining-living area, and office. There was one of these left at the Glens and so I signed a contract for it.

The problem that then arose was that completion of the construction of the Glens kept being postponed. At first, I was told I could move in October, then November, then February. This created a potential problem for selling my house.

My real estate agent, worked with me to deal with this uncertainty. Before listing the house for sale, he brought over two ladies who, he believed would be interested in it. The second one, Nancy Leopold, loved the house, as did her husband. They put in an offer, and told me that they were in no hurry to move; once there was a date certain for my move, they would sell their current house and arrange for the closing on my house. A potential difficulty was averted effortlessly.

Meanwhile, Karen helped me prepare the house for sale. I was connected to a man who specializes in moving people into retirement homes and he did an excellent job of moving me. Again, Karen helped to prepare for, and to actually help with the move.

All this proceeded effortlessly and smoothly. I moved on February 6, with Karen's help, and arranged everything in my new apartment during the next week or two. It turned out I had made good decisions about what to take, and the apartment turned out to be beautiful and cozy, so that I was very happy with my move. My painter fixed the holes in my house left by moving items attached to the walls, and the Maids did a final clean-up after the estate sale, which was from 10 a.m. to 2 p.m. on February 23. By 10 a.m. 97 people had already assembled and had to be admitted in small groups. The sale was a great success. The closing for the house sale was on February 28.

My first weeks at the Nottingham were wonderful. I met a lot of interesting residents, participated in numerous group activities, heard lectures and listened to performances by visiting musicians. The food was excellent, the atmosphere very congenial, and the feeling of living in a state of grace continued. But then, slowly at first, but accelerating and becoming unremitting, the response to the corona virus pandemic unfolded and changed the Nottingham to an institution under siege. At first, visiting artists, lecturers, and physical therapy instructors were cancelled. Meals were held in two sessions to enhance social distancing, and then communal dining was cancelled altogether; food was brought to our individual apartments. All activities involving gatherings, such as lectures or films, were cancelled. All visitors were barred. All staff wore masks, and were examined before beginning work. Access to the Nottingham was strictly regulated at the front desk. Grocery deliveries were first sanitized before being delivered to residents. Residents were barred from visiting each other or their relatives and friends, and strongly discouraged from going anywhere, e.g. shopping. In all this, the administration complied with guidelines from the Center for Disease Control (CDC) and Department of Health. The Executive Director held weekly town hall meetings to keep the residents informed, and these were quickly moved to the in-house TV, as were exercise classes.

As sad and difficult as this was for residents, it was absolutely essential and I strongly applauded it. The residents at the Nottingham constituted the most vulnerable population to the corona virus and only by strict enforcement of preventive measures was there any hope of keeping the virus out. In fact, a small number of residents did contract the virus. They were immediately removed from the Nottingham, and not permitted to return until they were symptom- and virus-free.

Only a few months before, I looked forward to going somewhere where I would be safe. Now I was at a vulnerable site. However, in view of what was about to unfold, I was extremely fortunate that I moved when I did. I would not have been able to navigate my oncoming illness alone at my old house.

Early during the series of changes taking place at the Nottingham in response to the virus, I developed a dry cough and slight fever. As these were typical symptoms for corona virus, I reported it at once and was immediately placed in isolation in my apartment. Meals were delivered to me in the evening. My symptoms did not improve, and soon I was quite ill, unable to eat, and I lost quite a bit of weight. I was tested for corona virus and Influenza A and B, all of which were negative. But as I did not get better, and my doctor (who was unable to actually see me) did not know what was going on, I was taken to the Emergency Room by ambulance, where it was quickly established that I had pneumonia. I was admitted to the hospital, treated there for four days, and then released back to my apartment. As unpleasant as my hospital stay was, it was absolutely essential.

Already in the weeks prior to going to the hospital, Karen went into action to do what she could to look after me from Los Angeles. I sent a message to my relatives and friends after I returned from the hospital, outlining her extraordinary efforts to help me, and trying to convey who my remarkable daughter is[2].

(Almost two years later, Karen now has her own business, counselling, life coaching, and providing various healing modalities.)

After I got back to my apartment, my aides were essential. They came in for two four-hour shifts per day, helping me with food, laundry, showering etc. I was able to manage the nights without them. My condition improved slowly, so that after a couple of weeks I was able to get along without them. The slow recovery tested my patience, but gradually I began taking short walks outside, going a little further each day. My appetite returned and I began, slowly, to regain the 12 lbs. I had lost. Slowest to heal was my breathing, as the pneumonia started to clear, and I also experienced night sweats, which were a big nuisance. But the overall improvement was unmistakable, and it put me in awe of the incredible healing power of the body, something we tend to take for granted, but which is truly remarkable. Four weeks after my return from hospital, I walked outside for a half hour once or twice a day, I had a good appetite, and I regained half the weight I lost. I had some X-rays taken on May 18, which showed that the pneumonia has been resolved. Subsequently, I regained all the weight I lost and recovered completely.

One Year Later

Two events have occurred since Betty died, which have changed this country - indeed the whole world - enormously. One has been the world-wide corona virus pandemic, which has ravaged this country especially hard, with over two million people infected and over 100,000 deaths so far. I cannot imagine how we could have handled the restrictions imposed by the virus were Betty still alive and were we still living on Scott Avenue. Would our aides have been able to come to the house? Would Betty have been able to get to the Wound Care Clinic or to her doctor? Would I have been able to continue to shop safely? Each of these questions would have posed serious difficulties.

The other event is the murder of George Floyd, that was captured on TV in a gruesome video of an officer kneeling on his neck for almost nine minutes, until he died. The demonstrations that this horrendous act set off, in the United States and world-wide, were an indication that this time, at last, the conscience of the whole nation, and others beyond, has been aroused. This time it felt different, and already actions began to address the long-standing injustices in our criminal justice system. Betty would have been absolutely devastated at seeing the video, but I think she would have found some hope in seeing that so many white people participated in the demonstrations and in their aftermath, and that some changes have already been made.

In August, 2021, the police officer who knelt on George Floyd's neck, murdering him, was found guilty of second-degree murder. It was a landmark trial and decision. Yet there had been surprisingly few real changes in the justice system, and cases of police brutality continued unabated. Clearly, the long-standing institutional racism in America will not disappear quickly.

The gradual improvement of the pandemic situation during the summer of 2020 led to further easing of the restrictions imposed earlier at the Nottingham. Communal eating in the dining room was resumed, with two persons sitting 6 ft. apart at an assigned table (to allow contact tracing if necessary); numerous activities were re-instated, including various exercise classes and social activities, all necessitating wearing masks and social distancing. I participated in several of these activities, and also went twice a week to the Fitness Room to use several exercise machines, and I continued walking outdoors, usually twice a day for a couple of miles.

A welcome event was the announcement, early in the summer, that we would each be allowed to have a designated visitor in our apartment. Most residents had a family member, but as none of my family lived nearby, I asked our long-time friend, Estelle Hahn, to be my designated visitor. Designated visitors had to be checked at the front desk for each visit. Initially, visitors were allowed for half of the month, followed by a two-week pause to assess whether this was safe. When this proved to be the case, the pauses were discontinued. Estelle came to visit me approximately a couple of times per month, but because the weather was so good, we usually met for about two hours outdoors. We always had a lot to discuss, and one beneficial outcome was that I learned a lot about opera from Estelle, who has been a life-long opera enthusiast, whereas I was much more involved with orchestral and chamber music. I listened to, and enjoyed, numerous operas on line, presented daily by the Metropolitan Opera.

I was also appointed treasurer of the Resident Forum, which runs various resident programs, such as the library, a little store, and the Holiday Fund. The latter is a means for residents to express their gratitude by awarding an annual cash gift to all the employees, since tipping is not allowed. I helped by creating and putting up posters to remind the residents to make their donations, and in collecting and depositing these funds. Generally, the residents are very generous: the median amount donated by the largest number of residents in 2020 was $1,000, and several donated up to $5,000. We collected enough this year to be able to give a check of $600 to each of the 244 employees. The Resident Forum also provides for communication between residents and the administration to discuss problems and make suggestions.

By the end of 2020, we were in the midst of a two-week pause in communal dining, many activities, and visits from our designated visitors. This was done to monitor any possible outbreak of Covid cases following the Thanksgiving holiday, when some residents travelled. Our dinners were delivered to our apartments every night, as they were at the height of the pandemic in May and June. Although these were inconveniences, I was very thankful that the Nottingham administration strictly adheres to guidelines from the CDC. Their success in limiting outbreaks of Covid to very few residents stood in contrast to what happened at some other senior residential communities and nursing homes nation-wide.

Two Years Later

The year 2021 led, at first, to gradual improvements in the pandemic situation. We were all vaccinated and, later, given booster shots.

Communal dining was reinstituted, as were visits from designated visitors and, eventually, others. I continued to enjoy many activities including various exercise classes, social activities and games, and the excellent food. My friend Howard invited me to visit him and his wife at their summer home in South West Harbor, Maine. I flew to Bangor, my first flight in some time, and even though I only had to make one change (at JFK), it was a hassle, not something I'd like to do often. Howard and Norah picked me up, and we drove to their home, which is on Mount Desert Island. My visit was very enjoyable, relaxing, with lots of reminiscing and some good hikes in Acadia National Park.

When the omicron variant of the corona virus began spreading rapidly, some restrictions were re-imposed, but, as of this writing (January 2022) most activities and communal dining are continuing. My move to the Nottingham was a wise decision and I continue to enjoy living here.

My Stature

There are two definitions of the word stature: 1. a person's natural height; 2. a person's importance or reputation gained by ability or achievement. Reflecting about my life, I discovered that my stature, in both senses, probably played an unduly large role.

I inherited my height from both my parents: my mother was about 4'10", my father about 5'4". I believe that I might have achieved my father's height, had my adolescence occurred in the United States instead of England, with war-time food rationing, and at a boarding school with bad food, sometimes leaving me sufficiently hungry to eat a whole loaf of bread.

My short size led to a lot of teasing, but I don't recall that it affected me unduly while I lived in Germany and England. During my first years in the United States, however, where everyone seemed to be taller than they were in Europe, it had a profound effect on my self-esteem, especially with respect to my interactions with girls. All girls my age seemed to be taller than I. One evening, when I was at a resort in the Catskills with my cousins Frank and Pierre, I asked a girl to dance with me. She brushed me off, telling me I was too short. I was crushed; the fact that I still remember this event 75 years later attests to its impact.

My aunt, TaMa, understood better than my mother, how important it would be for me to feel comfortable interacting with girls. Already as an adolescent, she was gregarious and outgoing, whereas my mother was very shy and didn't have a normal adolescence. TaMa, who loved to dance and was very good at it, arranged for me to take dancing lessons. Unfortunately, because I was so sensitive about my size, I did not benefit from those lessons. Even being married to Betty, who loved dancing, did not propel me to learn. My self-consciousness plagued me for a long time.

Another incident related to my size occurred while I was dating a girl named Carol Wertheimer. I met Carol during my first year in college through my friend David Ostrolenk and was very fond of her. One evening, as we were walking along the boardwalk in Asbury Park, Carol tried to hold hands with me and I rebuffed her. A few days later she wrote to me explaining that this had hurt her feelings. Although she understood my sensitivity about my size, she pointed out that my attitude completely distorted the importance of our relationship versus whatever strangers on the boardwalk might think. Her letter displayed remarkable wisdom for a sixteen-year-old. It taught me a lesson, but it took a while to sink in.

There were other, similar incidents throughout my adolescence, but as I became more confident, this self-consciousness vanished. My wife, Betty, was about two inches taller than I, but by the time we met, that no longer mattered. I was sometimes surprised, seeing photos of the two of us together, that she was taller than I, clear evidence that my self-image was no longer impacted by my stature. Obviously, others noticed my small size, but I no longer did. I once overheard my friend, Peter Gore, telling someone on the telephone, that I was a very large man in a small body. I do think that my competitiveness derives from the need to prove that I can achieve big things despite being small.

The impact of the second definition of stature, reputation, became evident not long after I came to the United States at the age of 16. My strong motivation to succeed was accompanied by a need for recognition and acclaim; I don't recall ever feeling this need in England. It manifested itself in several ways. I think that my need to excel was normal, but this need was probably exhibited to an exceptional degree, as it was by all those of us who fled Nazi Germany as children. I point out in Chapter 10 that this phenomenon was analyzed by Sonnert and

Holten in their book *What Happened to the Children Who Fled Nazi Persecution*. However, my need for recognition and acclaim was, I think, distorted into a primary goal.

One manifestation of this need was something I did whenever I was on a train or bus, travelling between home and Rutgers University. I was so small and looked so young, that I thought people wouldn't take me seriously. So, I displayed on my lap a chemistry or physics or math text book, hoping that those sitting next to me would notice that I was studying something complex. I'm sure that it never worked. No one ever asking me what I was reading, or why. Probably no one ever noticed.

A second manifestation, while I was in college, was the desire for recognition by Phi Beta Kappa, the academic honor society. To be elected into Phi Beta Kappa at Rutgers required having a specific, high grade point average. I yearned to be elected, but my G.P.A. was just slightly too low, so I missed out. I was dejected. I even pleaded with the chairman of the selection committee, who was a professor in the German Department, an act of groveling, especially as I was repelled by anything German. Of course, he never replied, which added to my humiliation. It took me a long time to get over my disappointment at not making it into Phi Beta Kappa. Because I craved recognition, a grade point average replaced what was really important, i.e. learning.

I have come to think that this need for recognition might even have played a role in my decision to marry Betty. When we married in 1960, inter-racial marriages were still very rare (and illegal in about half the states), so marrying a Black woman was considered, by some, to be courageous, something worthy of acclaim. This would be, of course, utterly demeaning to Betty, and I don't think that I could ever have let this racist thought surface into my consciousness.

And here I am, a nonagenarian living at the Nottingham with over 200 other elderly retirees, and the need for acclaim still surfaces occasionally. I try to excel at all the games and exercise classes I attend. I agreed to become treasurer of the Nottingham Forum, knowing I would do a good job. I volunteered to give a talk to the residents about my experiences in Nazi Germany and my trip back to Leipzig in 2009, which garnered a lot of commentary and praise. How much of this is natural, and how much is due to my obsession with being acclaimed, and if the latter, is that a character fault? My education and enculturation in England taught me to be self-effacing and modest, so I hide my enjoyment at receiving acclaim. I sometimes wondered whether this obsession with my stature detracted from my successes, but I think, instead, it fueled my competitiveness to succeed in my career and other endeavors.

Notes

Chapter 4

[1]My letter for Birgit Vennesland's 80th birthday

Dear Birgit:

I am, delighted to join the many members of "The Vennesland Group" in honoring you on your 80th birthday. It seems just a few years ago that we were celebrating your 65th in Atlanta, yet how much science and the world have changed since then! In 1978, it was still possible to do enzymology without having cloned the gene for your enzyme, and to assure students in the biochemistry course that all enzymes are proteins. Medicine had triumphed, we thought, over infectious diseases, and when we spoke of Russia we meant The Soviet Union.

Although it has been a very long time since I was your student, those years in Chicago were of such immense significance that they still shape my life. Not only did I learn how to do, and think about science, I saw that it was possible to do so and retain one's humanity. There was never any question about the importance of science, or the need to do it extremely well in your laboratory. Those factors were true in many other laboratories in the Biochemistry Department at the University of Chicago. But you managed to convey these attributes without diminishing the value of humaneness, concern, and respect for all your students. That was far rarer in Chicago, and, as I found later, it is rarer elsewhere too. Hans Krebs, in his Third Hopkins Memorial Lecture pays tribute to the group of biochemists whom he encountered when he came to Cambridge from Germany: "I saw them argue without quarreling, quarrel without suspecting, suspect without abusing, criticize without vilifying or ridiculing, and praise without flattering." This atmosphere prevailed in your laboratory in Chicago, because you set the tone for it, and it is an atmosphere that I have tried to maintain in my group ever since. It is absolutely essential for the development of students who, as I did in the 1950s, lack confidence but not ability.

Besides being involved in serious (see the photograph) and important science in your laboratory, I also remember many lighter moments. I recall the "literature meetings" at your apartment, where your mother always greeted us enthusiastically when we arrived. (And I was reminded, recently, of your mother's fierce loyalty to Truman as I was reading David McCullough's magnificent biography). I remember the endless cups of coffee you consumed. For a time, I was housed in the same laboratory as Mendel Mazelis and Stanley Mandeles. They provided continuous entertainment. I recall with special fondness their plans to prepare borschtsicles by encasing sour cream in lyophilized beet soup. I also remember how often I strained Frank Loewus's patience beyond the breaking point with my obtuseness in learning how to prepare the deuterated samples. I believe he eventually gave up. Harvey Fisher tended to take most matters less seriously than Frank, thus providing a sense of perspective. We all coped quite well with Tchen's renditions of various operatic tenor arias, in part because his hours in the lab didn't seriously overlap with the rest of the group. (George Catravas, from Herbert Anker's lab, was more considerate: he played his violin in the animal room, with no one knows what effects on the resident rats).

I have also retained the excitement about enzymes that I first encountered in your laboratory. I was part of the stereospecificity group, and much of my subsequent professional life has involved working with dehydrogenases. I even had the opportunity, many years later, to answer a question we were unable to resolve satisfactorily in 1957: Why do some dehydrogenases (A-stereospecific) transfer the *pro-R* hydrogen to and from NADH or NADPH, while others (B-stereospecific) transfer the *pro-S* hydrogen? (In those days, of course, we spoke of the a and b sides of DPNH and TPNH). This 1983 finding was totally serendipitous. I was (and still am) working with various glucose 6-phosphate dehydrogenases, including one from the bacterium *Leuconostoc mesenteroides*, which is one of the few dehydrogenases that utilizes either NAD+ or NADP+ *in vivo*. Both nicotinamide coenzymes appear to bind to the same site on the enzyme. The principal questions we have been pursuing are: how does this enzyme "decide" whether to utilize NAD+ or NADP+? (we think we've figured that out); and: what structural features on the protein ensure that both coenzymes can bind to the same site, since most dehydrogenases have evolved efficient strategies to distinguish between the two. In the early 1980s I read about the use of the transferred nuclear Overhauser enhancement technique to ascertain the conformation of small molecules attached to macromolecules, and decided to see if this could be used to establish whether NAD+ and NADP+ bound differently to *L. mesenteroides* G6PD. The technique had already been used to examine the conformation of NAD+ to the alcohol dehydrogenases from yeast and liver, and that of NADP+ bound to dihydrofolate reductase. Together with some NMR-sophisticated colleagues in our Chemistry Department (including one named Levy, no relative) we performed the appropriate experiments. These provided an answer to the question we posed, but what puzzled me was that the pattern of the NOE transfers was quite different from those seen with the other dehydrogenases. Suddenly, in one of those exhilarating insights that we experience all too rarely, I realized that the alcohol dehydrogenases and dihydrofolate reductase are A-stereospecific, whereas G6PD is B-stereospecific. X-ray structural studies on three A-stereospecific and one B-stereospecific dehydrogenases had suggested that the orientation of the nicotinamide-ribose bond is *anti* for the former, and *syn* for the latter. We had stumbled on a rapid method of establishing this in solution, and we quickly demonstrated that the pattern prevailed for other A- and B-stereospecific dehydrogenases, thus generalizing the finding. I enclose a reprint of the paper reporting this work.

I am still trying to understand G6PDs. We have crystallized the *L. mesenteroides* G6PD and a colleague of mine at Oxford, Margaret Adams, is trying to solve the structure. We also cloned the gene, and are now using site-directed mutagenesis to try to see how it binds

NAD⁺ and NADP⁺. Currently I have a grant, but it gets more difficult to get support, and good students, every year. I try to resist the
temptation to conclude that students aren't what they used to be,
because I remember so clearly that the post-docs in Chicago felt the
same about us. As they were clearly wrong, I suspect I must be too. I
still enjoy teaching, of which I do a fair amount, both at the graduate
and the undergraduate level. At present I am chairman of our department, which does not explain why I am smiling on the recent photograph. These are very difficult time to chair a department. Syracuse
University, like so many others, is faced with diminishing resources
and enrollments. Our department's enrollments, by contrast, are
increasing, but our resources, of course, reflect those of the university. How we will resolve this discrepancy, is the major problem I now
confront. Serendipity, which favored me ten years ago, will not, I fear,
help me in this instance.

I wish you happiness and good health for years to come. I am sorry
that we can't get together to celebrate your birthday. One of the most
enjoyable things about the annual Federation Meetings in 50s and 60s
was the "Vennesland dinners". It would have been fun to have another
one (but not in Atlantic City). I hope that you will come to the main-
land again some time and visit me in Syracuse; or, perhaps, I might get
a chance to see you in Hawaii.

[2]Excerpts from my letter for Paul Talalay's 80th birthday

Science, and especially scientific research, is taught most effectively
by the process of apprenticeship; its success depends on the apprentice, the mentor, and the relationship between them. My apprenticeship with you was such a success for me primarily because of your
qualities as a scientist and as a man, but also because it occurred in the
Ben May Laboratory for Cancer Research at the University of Chicago,
all of which contributed to the opportunity to experience science at
the highest level... I was swept up by the heady ambience in your lab,
which was reinforced by what I saw throughout the Ben May, with its
motto "Discovery is our Business", but which really meant "Science is
our Passion".

Working in your lab was exhilarating, but it was not always easy.
For example, you tended to push your ideas on me. At first this

angered me, until I recognized that it would stop if I came up with my own! It took time, but it had the desired effect of promoting my self-confidence, independence, and an increased ability to think critically... Some in the lab felt that they were being driven unreasonably. I never did because I realized that in pushing me you were not just promoting your goals but also trying to further my growth as a scientist. Undergirding this conviction was your genuine friendship, showing that you cared for my development as well as the achievement of your goals.

You took time to talk to me about science and life as a scientist. You emphasized that to succeed, I had to make science the top priority in my life. It was very clear that you practiced what you preached. Slowly, in Chicago and later in Syracuse, I came to accept my limitations as well as my strengths, and how these differed from yours. Eventually, I also became a mentor with my own apprentices. As our friendship matured I recognized my debt to you more clearly. Your great gift to me was to help me to develop those qualities that enabled me to succeed on my own terms. Your laboratory in the basement of Goldblatt was my laboratory for forging a career.

Chapter 5

[1]Excerpts from my letter to my mother during the civil rights demonstrations.

Sep. 22, 1963

Most of our activity has been devoted to the increasingly important and dramatic CORE situation here, in which we have become deeply involved. The crux of the current, vigorous CORE drive (which has now been joined by the other organizations such as NAACP) concerns housing.

Last June CORE met with the mayor and urged him to do something about the situation. The point was that the city was going ahead with razing the old houses in the ghetto and relocating families in areas where they would soon have to move again, rather than first finding a more permanent solution to the problem along the lines discussed with him. Unless he acted, he was told, CORE would act to stop urban renewal. In essence, the mayor paid no attention.

In the middle of August, they met again, and CORE, noting that the mayor had done nothing at all, gave the mayor a week to halt urban renewal. He shoved them out of the door.

A nine-point proposal was set up by CORE (always George Wiley was and is the principal force behind all this). In short, the mayor refused to do any acting – preferring to appoint more committees (of which there were plenty already, and which had produced little so far). On Thursday, Sep. 12, picketing in front of the construction sites began, and since then we have picketed Monday - Friday every week, and have had members arrested for going onto construction sites.

This has woken up the whole community. The front page of the paper has had the stories every day. Meetings (nightly) first attended by 10 to 30 people are now held in large churches and attended by 300 to over 500 persons. Vicious editorials have appeared – one especially, last Sunday, directed against George personally, which helped us a great deal, I think, by drawing much more support to our side. The people on the picket line increased steadily from 10 or 20 to over 200. They included many ministers and faculty members, students, and other town people.

We first picketed last Friday Sep. 13, 7 a.m. – 9 a.m. It was a new experience for both of us. Since then one or both of us has been down there every day for a few hours. So far over 80 have been arrested, including about 15 faculty members, some of them prominent, others, including me, less so.

I know you will be shocked that I let myself be arrested, but you must believe me when I tell you that I did it with the very deepest conviction and in the full knowledge of all the consequences which may result. Let me say very quickly that I am quite sure none will, but I am prepared to face them if they do.

The arrests are conducted in a completely organized manner. Those who wish to be arrested volunteer to do so at the meeting the night before and are fully instructed. We have a lawyer, who volunteers her services. For those unable to pay bail, funds are collected daily (Friday, within ½ hr., two faculty members collected $2300 from members of the physics and engineering departments alone!). The 2 ladies in Cazenovia*, have put up thousands of dollars in bail

---

* The two ladies, Jane Anderson and Elizabeth Allen, were affectionately known as "The Old Ladies". They were both social workers who lived in a beautiful home on Lake Cazenovia, in Cazenovia. They were very lively, and were involved in progressive organizations, and used to have people out to their house for Fourth of July

money (they called me and offered to bail me out, but I declined), others have put up houses as real property in lieu of bail money.

I volunteered last Thursday night to be arrested Friday afternoon. There were 19 of us, including nine faculty members that day. We (along with about 200 others) picketed the site, with signs, from 12 (I got there at 2) until 4. We got ourselves arrested at about 3:30. We simply marched onto the construction site, where some 15 policemen were waiting. They put us into a police car and drove us to the jail. This is the same procedure used over the last few days. There is absolutely no violence (except that when George got arrested last week they purposely hurt him). Several of us, including me, elected to stay in jail overnight. It's a horrible place, but we didn't have a bad time of it. We were in individual cells, with just a wooden board for a bed. We were arraigned in court the following day at about noon. Betty visited me to bring me an overcoat at night. She was also in court, of course. Our lawyer was there with us, and we all pled not guilty on her advice – all of us so far have pleaded the same way. The trial is going to be next Friday Sep. 27. By then there will be well over 100 persons. I paid my own $26 to the bail bondsman – bail was set at $500 for each of us.

We are charged specifically, with trespassing. Everyone is confident of the outcome of the trial. Public opinion is coming more and more to our side as more clergy and faculty members, especially, are involved. It was this which was one of the factors which convinced me I ought to let myself be arrested.

The effect on the mayor so far has been rather good. He has agreed to major concessions. However, last week all negotiations broke off when he deliberately gave out a press release in the middle of negotiations despite an agreement with our side not to. There was a political motive involved here – he had hoped (and succeeded) in gaining support from an arbitrating committee on race and religion, who were conducting the negotiations, and who had come more and more

parties. I don't recall how we came to be invited to these gatherings, but we went on several occasions. Among others who were at these gatherings, as I recall, were the Guisbonds, the Felds, and Gordon and Phyllis Kent. Gordon was a professor at the College of Engineering at Syracuse University. He was the son of the well-known American artist Rockwell Kent. Their son, David, was an excellent skier at a very young age.

around to our side. The whole thing is much too intricate to explain in a letter, but the fact is that the avenues of negotiation seem, for the moment, to have been closed.

As far as I am concerned, my mind and conscience is clear. I have the greatest respect for the law, but law alone is not enough: justice is the ultimate concept to which I put my allegiance. In Germany, there were lots of laws, and the Germans – including many Jews – adhered to them marvelously. Would that an effective movement could have sprung up in Germany in which civil disobedience had been practiced. Only this way could the conscience of the country have been aroused sufficiently to end the unjust laws.

I believe in this movement with all my soul. I have said so all along. To say so is not enough. Inaction is as bad as – no, it is worse than -- overt antagonism to the goals of the movement. I cannot sleep at night if I know that I should do more, but don't. The life of comfort and luxury which Betty and I lead is in jeopardy if this movement fails. To turn our back on it is to betray the very essence of what our marriage means.

Mother, I know that you are worried about all this, and I am sorry to cause you this worry. But you must understand that I am an intelligent adult, able to take my own life into my own hands, willing to face the consequences of my own deeds. I simply cannot merely pay lip-service to an ideal. If my actions lead me into trouble, then I know it is in a just cause and I know that my inaction would have caused me greater mental anguish. I am not trying to be melodramatic, I hope you realize. For years, I have been haunted by the thought of the inaction which led to so much horror and tragedy in Germany, and which continues to create terrible tragedy all over the world. All I can do is to be sure that I have no part in it, because I feel a personal sense of guilt if I do.

I will keep you informed of all that happens. The chancellor of the university issued quite a good statement on this situation. The numbers of faculty, and eminence of some of these, makes it highly unlikely that any penalty will be involved. Not only in Syracuse, but all over the country professors are joining in the fight. It is this very pressure which ensures victory in the end. If there is defeat, then our lives are going to be extremely difficult whatever we do, or don't do.

Naturally, until the trial is over, I can no longer participate in any civil disobedience. I have not found it an enjoyable experience, as you can imagine, but I am truly happy I did it. I can assure you that it will not be necessary for me to do something this drastic again in the near future...

Please don't be dismayed. I know what I'm doing, and why. That's what life is all about!!

Sep. 26, 1963

Times are really changing. We are truly in the midst of a revolution – so momentous, we haven't yet grasped its impact. There is no turning it back. Those involved in it will one day be considered as ordinary as most people are now. The change is so vast that you can no longer judge its consequences in the old ways.

Tomorrow at the trial there will, apparently, be a postponement. We have heard that there has been such enormous pressure on the University & the mayor that the District Attorney wants to drop all charges – but he probably can't do that all at once.

Betty's name is being proposed as one, by CORE, to be on the committee to settle these problems with the mayor – the Mayor's Commission on Human Rights. It is most unlikely he'll accept her name, but it's quite an honor from CORE, who hope to get a substantial number accepted by the mayor for his 16-member commission.

Oct. 6, 1963

Tuesday CORE demonstrations started again and this time Betty got arrested. She was in good company – Roy Doi, two psychiatrists, an elected city official, another U. of S. instructor, Wretha Wiley, and others, including one of the Rabbi's daughters. Betty did not stay overnight. The demonstrations have now been halted, at least temporarily. The mayor has gone to Europe for two weeks. Before he left, he appointed a 16-man Commission on Human Rights – a gesture without much hope for us, though some. Our state senator spoke the other night on campus, and said he could see the need for our demonstrations! Incidentally, Sen. Case from N.J. gave an excellent talk here also – unfortunately I couldn't go to either talk.

Certainly, our demonstrations have really woken up the community, and already much good has come from them.

I completely disagree that our participation will hamper our effectiveness in other areas. Also, your fears about long congressional hearings are without grounds. Can you imagine any hearing involving the tens of thousands who have been arrested all over the country?! This is the only reason Kennedy moved, and the only reason that a strong civil rights measure is up for debate. I am committed to this 100%. But you needn't worry – I'm also committed 100% to my job. The two are not mutually exclusive!

Chapter 6

[1]Remarks by Dean Robert Jensen on presenting me with the William Wasserstrom Award.

One of the pleasures I have as the Dean of Arts and Sciences is the opportunity to present the University's premier graduate teaching award at the Doctoral Dinner each year -- The William Wasserstrom Award for Excellence in Graduate Teaching.

Bill Wasserstrom, Professor of English at Syracuse University from 1960 to 1985, was a brilliant scholar. He authored nine books and many scholarly articles, and in 1982 received the Chancellor's Award for Exceptional Academic Achievement. Professor Wasserstrom was also a dedicated and skilled *graduate* teacher who participated fully in the life of the University and the College of Arts and Sciences. The award given annually in his honor recognizes each of these qualities. Thus, the recipient of the Wasserstrom Award must exemplify the following qualities: he or she must actively participate in the intellectual and institutional life of the University and the College of Arts and Sciences; must have an outstanding record of graduate teaching and supervision; and must have produced a record of recognized scholarship characterized by its originality.

Our 1998 Wasserstrom Prize Winner clearly meets these criteria: his contributions to the intellectual and institutional life of The College and University are many and strong. He has been a member of the Faculty Council, and has served as Chair of his Department from 1993 to the present. He has been a faculty leader in many initiatives undertaken by The College, and has been active on many all-University Committees over the years, including continuing and long-term service on the University Graduate Fellowships Committee and in the Graduate School's Future Professoriate Project.

The evidence for his outstanding graduate teaching and supervision is abundant: many of his publications have been co-authored with his graduate students, who have gone on to impressive careers both in industry and in the academy. Typical graduate student comments include:

> "He is never too busy to meet with a graduate student to offer advice, serve on a committee, or write a recommendation."
>
> "His support of my career goes far beyond my dissertation."
>
> "He is dedicated to the quality of education of graduate students ... and fosters an environment which stimulates critical thought."

His scholarship has been excellent. He has had virtually uninterrupted funding from the National Science Foundation or the National Institutes of Health since 1963. He has published many articles in the leading journals in his field, and has been an invited lecturer to such institutions as Oxford University and the Johns Hopkins University School of Medicine. He is truly one of Syracuse University's distinguished scientists.

Beyond all these achievements, he is a man of uncommon common sense and unswerving dedication to quality. He is delightful to work with, regardless of the difficulty of the task at hand: a tireless advocate for students and faculty and a strong academic leader. It is my pleasure to invite Richard Levy, Chair and Professor of Biology, to the stage to receive the William Wasserstrom Award for Excellence in Graduate Teaching for 1998.

Chapter 7

[1]References cited in Science is a Human Endeavor

1. Levy, H.R. Glucose 6-phosphate dehydrogenases. Advances in Enzymology and Related Areas of Molecular Biology, **48**, 97 (1979). https://pubmed.ncbi.nlm.nih.gov/367106/

2. Eggleston, L.V. & Krebs, H.A. Regulation of the pentose phosphate cycle. Biochem. J. **138**, 425 (1974). https://doi.org/10.1042/bj1380425

3. Krebs, H.A. *Reminiscences and Reflections*, Oxford University Press (1981). This book contains a very readable account of the author's life. https://www.goodreads.com/book/show/5321887-reminiscences-and-reflections

4. Rodriguez-Segade, S., Freire, M., & Carrion, A. Biochem. J. **170**, 577 (1978), plus two subsequent brief communications in 1979 & 1980. https://pubmed.ncbi.nlm.nih.gov/25652/

5. Levy, H.R., & Daouk, G.H. Simultaneous analysis of NAD- and NADP-linked activities of dual nucleotide-specific dehydrogenases. J. Biol. Chem. **254**, 4843 (1979). Regulation of coenzyme utilization by the dual nucleotide-specific glucose 6-phosphate dehydrogenase from *Leuconosctoc mesenteroides*. Arch. Biochem. Biophys. **198**, 406 (1979). https://pubmed.ncbi.nlm.nih.gov/35541/ https://pubmed.ncbi.nlm.nih.gov/42353/

6. Levy, H.R. & Christoff, M. A critical appraisal of the effect of oxidized glutathione on hepatic glucose 6-phosphate dehydrogenase activity. Biochem. J. **214**, 959 (1983). https://pubmed.ncbi.nlm.nih.gov/6626166/

7. Spector, M., O'Neal, S. & Racker, E. Regulation of the phosphorylation of the beta subunit of the Ehrlich ascites tumor Na^+K^+-ATPase by a protein kinase cascade. J. Biol. Chem **256**, 4219 (1981). (No URL available, presumably because the article was retracted)

8. Vogt, V. M. A scientific breakthrough that turned out to be a fraud. ecommons-new.library.cornell.edu (2013). https://ecommons.cornell.edu/handle/1813/34444

Chapter 10

[1]Excerpts from my letter to Moshe Moskovic, written in circa 2006.

You live in Israel and you have raised your family there. When you and Ora began your life together there, before the State of Israel emerged, you helped to plant the seeds for creating a democratic, just homeland with enormous labor and great hope and spirit. The way seemed so much simpler then, despite the great hardships and struggle. But the way has been lost since then, and the fault, I believe, lies not only with the Palestinians. There is no point in discussing the history of the Israeli-Palestinian dispute with you through correspondence. We come from very different perspectives, each of us having been shaped by our life experiences, and we have become who we are largely because of those experiences. What is right, and just, and essential, and self-evident for you may not be so for me, and vice versa, and it would be impossible, and quite wrong for me to try to persuade you of my opinions. Who knows what my views would have been had I, like you, moved to Palestine instead of England in 1939?

You are Jewish to your deepest core, and a citizen of Israel since the beginning of that country, and I am neither. I am, of course, a Jew, and call myself a Jew, and I feel a strong connection to my ancestors -- as you know from my involvement with my genealogy, and a strong cultural connection with the Jewish people. But that is only a part of who I am. My marriage to a woman who is neither a Jew nor a Caucasian is an essential expression of my identity. In my innermost self, I identify with other persons on the basis of *who* they are, not *what* they are. Those to whom I feel most deeply connected include Jews and Gentiles, white people and persons of color. As the grandson and son of atheists, I spent much of my life without any interest in or yearning for any religion. All my many attempts to connect with Judaism failed to arouse any interest in me. I abhor the exclusiveness with which many religious persons adhere to their own religion while relegating those of other faiths to irrelevance or purgatory. Only in recent years have I come to recognize the need for a spiritual connection, but as in other aspects of my life, I was guided in this quest by my inner identity, and have been drawn to a faith that celebrates diversity and the inherent worth and dignity of every person, irrespective of their religious past, namely the Unitarian/Universalist Church*. It is based on Judeo-Christian principles, has both Christians and Jews (and those of other faiths) as its members, and draws its inspiration not from any one creed, but from a wide variety of spiritual sources. This connection to the wisdom from many religions I find exhilarating

---

*My association with the Unitarian/Universalist Church lasted for several years, but I stopped attending their services in 2009, after my return from Leipzig (see Chapter 11). My reasons are explained in Chapter 10.

and liberating, and for the first time in my life I feel that I have found a spiritual home.

Chapter 12

[1]My Remarks at Betty's Memorial Service. Betty Levy: Seeker of Unity and Truth.

After Betty's suffering for the past months and years I want to share recollections with you from happier times.

When we first met 62 years ago, it seemed highly improbable that a Jewish man who had escaped from the Holocaust in Nazi Germany, and an African-American woman who had grown up on the South side of Chicago would fall in love. Betty was a beautiful, intelligent woman with deep convictions and an original mind. It was extraordinary that two individuals from such different backgrounds had so much in common.

It wasn't long before we began to consider marriage. At that time, inter-racial marriages were rare, and still illegal in 22 states. In 1958, I went to London for a year of post-doctoral research and we agreed that this presented an opportunity to pause and reflect before making a decision. We stayed in touch, and when I returned we resumed dating and within a few months decided to marry.

During our 59 years of marriage we shared many enriching experiences. Our travels included a honeymoon in Mexico, the first half of which was supposed to be a commercial tour, but, instead, for four days we had a Cadillac and chauffeur to ourselves. A year later we went to the Soviet Union, where I attended an international congress of biochemistry, and then we visited several other European countries for five weeks. Three years later we went to Japan, where I attended another international congress of biochemistry, stopping in Hawaii on our return. Other international travels together included several to Canada, one to Trinidad and Tobago, and a year in England, where I spent a sabbatical doing research at Oxford University. By that time, we had our daughter Karen, who went to school in England and returned a year later with a lovely English accent, that she soon lost. At the end of that year we travelled to East Africa, where we went on a safari, visited the Olduvai Gorge and experienced amazing beaches in Dar-es-Salaam.

When we were in East Africa, Betty discovered and became deeply impressed with *Ujamaa*, a uniquely African concept of socialism developed by Julius Nyerere for his economic and social development policies in Tanzania after it had gained independence. She also became captivated by *Makonde* sculptures, carved from a single block of wood, usually ebony or African blackwood. Some of these sculptures are abstract and many reference *Ujamaa* by depicting intricately interlocked human figures as a metaphor for unity, community and continuity. We purchased several of these beautiful art works. Betty was very interested in African-American art and music and attended a one week National Black Arts Festival in Atlanta in 1990.

We also spent many vacations traveling together in the United States, several times at Cape Cod, an Alaska cruise, and a trip to the Four Corners region, including an unforgettable visit to the Grand Canyon.

We shared a deep love of music and we both sang with the Syracuse University Oratorio Society for 30 years, performing at dozens of concerts, most of them with the Syracuse Symphony Orchestra, including a memorable performance at Carnegie Hall in New York. Betty expanded my musical repertoire by introducing me to jazz. We subscribed to Syracuse Stage for many years. For 40 years, we were members of a book group that met monthly for lively discussions about books on many different topics with good friends. We also joined a Havurah, which involved gatherings several times per year with a group of our Jewish friends. We gave talks and engaged in spirited discussions about a variety of Jewish-oriented topics.

Betty was deeply concerned about social justice and human rights. In the early 1960s, when there was world-wide fear about nuclear warfare, we both belonged to SANE, the national committee for a sane nuclear policy, and participated in actions to adopt such policies. When we first moved to Syracuse in 1963, CORE, the Congress of Racial Equality, was engaged in demonstrations against the city's urban renewal projects, involving the destruction of the homes of African-Americans to make way for Route 81 and expansions of

Upstate Medical University. We both participated in these demonstrations, were arrested, and went to jail for civil disobedience.

Betty received her B.A. in Psychology from Roosevelt University, in Chicago, and her M.S. in adult education from Syracuse University. She worked at the Children's Center at Upstate Medical University, Huntington Family Center, the ABC Learning Center, and OCM BOCES in Liverpool. After retirement, she volunteered at the Newland Center for Adult Learning and Literacy, an organization she helped to start in 1990.

Betty was a deeply spiritual person. Something she wrestled with for years was trying to find a religious institution as a home for her spirituality. She repudiated the constraints of institutional religions. In one of her notebooks he wrote, rather whimsically:

> *Love is at the root of spirituality;*
> *Power is at the root of religion;*
> *Spirituality is a do-it-yourself thing;*
> *Religion is a do-what you're-told thing*

The vengeful God of the old testament had no appeal for her and she replaced the Trinity of the New Testament with her own trinity:

> *The supreme god is Truth*
> *Justice is his daughter*
> *and Love is his spirit*

She finally succeeded in finding a church that embodied her beliefs and joined this Unity Church of Syracuse, where she worshipped for many years until her illness prevented her from attending.

Betty was a long-time practitioner of transcendental meditation and learned the TM-Sidhi technique. For a while, she joined a group of meditators who met regularly to practice together. She attended TM courses in Amherst, MA and South Fallsburg, NY, and went with some Syracuse meditators for a week of group meditations at Maharishi University in Fairfield, Iowa.

She was also a feminist, and she and some friends in Syracuse formed a group they called "Perfect Women", who met regularly to share their dreams, aspirations, loves and frustrations, and to nurture, encourage and love each other.

In her extensive reading and thinking she explored many different ideas. Often, she wrote instructions to herself to pursue a topic further, such as this one:

> *Two primary emotions are love and fear, as opposed to love and hate. Indifference is the lack of feeling – to be without the capacity to feel. Analyze this in relation to individual groups; analyze other emotions or feelings in relation to love and fear; analyze love and fear in relation to religion and religious people.*

Her love for learning motivated her, for decades, to take one or two courses every year. Because I was a professor at S.U., she was able to take a certain number of credits for free, and she made good use of that perk. Her curiosity led her to take courses, among many others, on the psychiatrist Jung, The Art of the Pharaohs, Anthropology, with Bill Mangin, the philosopher Plotinus and Neoplatonism, with David Miller and Huston Smith, Black History, and the Science of Creative Intelligence. At Oxford University, she participated in a graduate seminar on Ethnic, Cultural and Racial Studies that included participants from Africa, Asia, Europe and the Americas. She also took courses in expository writing, photography, and pottery making, and she took voice lessons. She also watched many tapes we ordered from the Teaching Company, including those on Einstein's Relativity and the Quantum Revolution; Religion in the Ancient Mediterranean World; Great Ideas in Philosophy; and Ancient Egyptian Civilization.

One of Betty's first jobs was as a psychometrist, in Chicago, which involved giving IQ tests, and there she noticed that over three quarters of the individuals tested did not know that Egypt was in Africa. Later, she wrote in one of her notebooks:

> *I find it very curious that the oldest, the most long-lasting, the most advanced, and the most powerful civilization in the world during its peak, has become a mere footnote in most history books.*

Her fascination with Egypt began in 1971, when she read Sigmund Freud's book *Moses and Monotheism*, which posits that Moses was born into ancient Egyptian nobility and that he was a follower of the black, monotheistic pharaoh Akhenatan. This led Freud to examine Judaism more closely, and led Betty to examine Egypt more closely. The following year, while we were in England, she saw the Tutankhamun exhibit at the British Museum and she was hooked on the study of ancient Egypt. During our year in England, she made frequent trips to London, spending many hours at the British Museum viewing their large collection of ancient Egyptian artifacts. When we returned to Syracuse, she set about to learn all she could about the ancient Egyptian civilization. She also began collecting books, amassing a library that would eventually contain over 150 volumes about this and related subjects, plus dozens more about the African-American experience, spiritualism, healing, and an eclectic assortment of other topics. She spent some of her happiest hours among the many books in her library, contemplating what she read, and setting down her ideas in her many notebooks.

One of the clippings on her office bulletin board, by the black American novelist Anatole Broyard, begins:

A good book is never exhausted. It goes on whispering to you from the wall...

and concludes:

The contents of someone's bookcase are a part of their history, like an ancestral portrait.

She joined the African Heritage Studies Association and visited the Schomburg Center for Research in Black Culture in New York. She became a member of the Association for the Study of Classical African Civilizations, an organization devoted to the rescue, reconstruction, and restoration of African history and culture. She attended their meetings in the United States and went on three excursions with them: to Egypt in 1987, West Africa in 1992, and Brazil in 1995. In W. Africa, she visited the Door of No Return, a museum and memorial to the Atlantic slave trade on Gorée Island off the coast of Senegal, which made a deep impression on her.

So many topics interested her -- Manicheism, Indian civilization, Native American history, the history of racism, cultural evolution, the unity of Black civilizations in Africa, Indochina and China, Astrology -- but the principal theme that she turned to again and again was ancient Egyptian civilization, and the concept that Egypt, not Greece, is the cradle of Western civilization, an idea that others had already explored, but Betty's ambitious goal was to embed her narrative in cultural as well as spiritual themes. It became the focal point of a quest that combined her spirituality, her unquenchable thirst for learning, and the affirmation of her pride and dignity as an African-American woman in a white society

She wrote:

Stepping beyond the hidebound, traditional Judeo-Christian-Greek origin of Western Civilization had an enormously liberating effect on me. There has never been a great civilization in the western world – and perhaps the eastern as well – that was not indebted to Africans. Without Egypt and Ethiopia, Greece and Rome, Christianity and Judaism, could not have occurred.

Her deep spirituality infused her understanding of the ancient wisdom from Africa, and her admiration for Akhenatan, the black pharaoh of Egypt (ca 1400 B.C.) who introduced monotheism hundreds of years before Moses. She wrote:

The ideal of the ancient Egyptians was to live life according to the knowledge of transcendental or cosmic consciousness in unity with the laws of nature. They called it Maat. The divine pharaoh was lord and upholder of Maat, its main attributes were truth and justice. If I had to pick a name for the Egyptian religion it would be "Unity".

She began to formulate a plan for sharing her knowledge with others, perhaps through writing a book. One possible title was "Studies in Africana. An Interdisciplinary Holistic Approach". Topics would include religion, economics, politics, cultural evolution, history, anthropology, geology, philosophy and psychology. She studied all of these subjects and made extensive notes for herself. She wrote:

> *What am I trying to prove? What do I want to become common knowledge? I want to study African history with Egypt as its starting point and Western Civilization as its culmination. I want to make acceptable the concept of Africa as the mother of Western Civilization.*

She even prepared a dedication, that read:

> *To my father, who made the search,*
> *My mother who kept the faith,*
> *My husband who made it possible,*
> *And my child who made it necessary.*

In her notebook, she wrote:

> *I trust this book will unsettle a number of cherished notions, but I hope I'm not being too presumptuous when I say that I believe its ultimate effect will be a step toward organic unity rather than separation.*

She wrote:

> *I'm interested in everything, because anything I come across may be a piece of the giant puzzle. If you ask me to conclude, to summarize, to present my findings, all I can say is: I found unity, and every time I find it, it's like a cosmic smile, and I smile and I know all is right with the world, that the paradoxes are illusions and that all is one. That's why at base I really don't want to communicate my findings as such. I want to communicate the joy of the search, for that is my self-expression. Just as a singer must sing and a painter must paint, I am a seeker of unity. That's me.*

In order to test her ideas, she prepared a series of lectures, presenting them in different venues, including here at Unity. Betty used many pictures in the slides accompanying her lectures, often photos from books that she took herself, showing distinctly African features in many persons one would not think of as black. For example, she showed pictures of people from 7000 yrs. ago in what is now Yugoslavia, comparing them to pictures of contemporary Africans.

She was immersed in this journey of discovery for some twenty-five years. As she lectured about her ideas, she slowly came to realize that she was unable to effectively transfer her enthusiasm to her audiences. An impediment, I believe, was her need to interconnect so many aspects of her search and her difficulty in organizing them in a manner that was easy to follow. Another factor was that she was deeply emotionally involved in what she learned, and did not anticipate that her audience would probably lack such involvement. I think she was disappointed, but not bitter about this. At one of her final lectures she asked for criticism from her audience. She recorded the response in her notebook:

> *I am very grateful to you for listening and giving me your criticisms. I found that my work is too personal to share, so that that which I can share is necessarily incomplete. I cannot shape it to fit the needs of anyone else.*
>
> *What I have gained is a spiritual essence, a broader vision, an illustration of the Science of Creative Intelligence, primarily as a result of the seeking process, rather than the found product. So, if I merely tell you my conclusions, as far as I'm concerned, I've told you nothing of real value, and unless you happen to be on the same wavelength I'm on, the process will be simply boring, confusing and irrelevant. Everyone must discover his own path. You have rendered me a great service by your reaction. I can now get on with my life without feeling that pull of unfinished business. Someday I might write it up, but I no longer labor under the illusion that it might have broad-based appeal, and I can work as a true artist does, with joy and abandon, in the creative process with no one to satisfy but myself.*

Betty was an iconoclast, with a creative mind who was never afraid to challenge what she read and heard, and could express her ideas cogently and forcefully. She instilled in me an understanding of, and appreciation for the Black experience in America, and the history of African-Americans, an extraordinarily enriching experience. She awakened my spirituality, thereby teaching me the true meaning of God. She greatly enhanced the depth and the meaning of my life, and she made me into a much better man. She was a seeker of unity who found her spiritual home here, and so it is fitting that we remember her at this Unity Church. We are deeply grateful to Unity for helping us to celebrate her life.

[2]Message, sent to my relatives and friends in 2000, about Karen's help when I was ill

I appreciate so much your love and concern during these past difficult weeks, they helped to sustain me. Most of you were beneficiaries of Karen's having taken over my correspondence, as even writing a small text exhausted me, and still does. Karen has been the hero in all this, and I want to tell you a little about her that you might not know.

About 26 years ago she moved to California and soon fell in love with the culture, the way of life, and everything else about it. She succeeded in a series of jobs in her field of Human Resources, each one an improvement over the last. Her jobs were with companies in business, finance, real estate and, finally, at the University of Southern California. When we told her, after she graduated from high school and didn't want to go to college, that she would never be able to get a good-paying job, it spurred her on to get one job after another, often two or more simultaneously. It turned out she was good at whatever she did, had a terrific work ethic, and over time she wound up in Human Resources. She was always bold and honest, and never hesitated to tell her bosses what she thought the company was doing wrong. Almost all of them appreciated her criticism and some thanked her profusely and showed their appreciation in various ways. Eventually, in her 40s, she did get her bachelor's degree.

In 2017, she recognized that Betty's long illness was getting worse, and decided to quit her job at the University of Southern California, leave her beloved California, where she had lived for 24 years, and move back to Syracuse to help with Betty's illness and to be nearby. It was a difficult decision for her, but eventually an obvious one, because she values family above all else. She did not look for a job, but her resume was on the web and her reputation in her field was well known. Soon, she was invited by Cornell University for an interview which was quickly followed by a job offer. She took the job, but found commuting every day from Syracuse too stressful, so she moved to an apartment in Ithaca, coming up for visits on weekends.

When Betty had her stroke in May, 2019, Karen took an unpaid leave from Cornell and spent every night with Betty in the hospital, while I was there during the days. She was extraordinarily helpful and resourceful. She helped me find hospice care for Betty's final days, where, again, we were with her for 24 hours every day.

After that, she wanted to return to California and we discussed that, and her insistence that she would not do so until she knew I would be well taken care of. She looked at the Nottingham with me and was as impressed as I, especially by the ability, when necessary, to move from independent care, to assisted living, to a nursing facility. She helped me get the house ready to sell, to make all the arrangements, and to move to the Nottingham. Everything went smoothly and as I was in good health and upbeat about my retirement community, she did decide to move back to L.A., with my complete blessing. She was offered a job in January 2020, by Cedars Sinai Hospital in L.A., to start work in March, 2020. By great luck, she arrived in L.A, the day before they closed the airport.

She started work, under their distancing guidelines, from her apartment, using her own computer. Eventually, they provided her with a Cedars Sinai computer. And then, while doing this, she had another challenge dropped in her lap when I became ill and had to remain isolated in my apartment for weeks before I went to the E.R., and then the hospital, to receive a diagnosis of pneumonia. For Karen, the choice between family and job is a no-brainer: family comes first. She told her boss at Cedars Sinai she needed to take time off to organize taking over my correspondence and bill payments, and to set up aides to come in to help me several hours per day. She spent countless hours negotiating with the Nottingham, with a home health agency here, with my bank, my attorney, talking with my family physician, with my doctor and nurses at the hospital, etc. etc. For her, this is what she loves to do in her chosen role as a beneficiary presence on this earth.

How did Karen get to where she is now, as a truly extraordinary human being (a "Mensch"), from her struggling years as a teenager and young adult? By educating herself relentlessly using multiple resources, to become a deeply committed, spiritual individual with unshakable beliefs and convictions, gathered from multiple sources over many years. It is a process that continues, requires daily practice, and this is her top priority.

I will cite just a few examples. In her early twenties, she was totally out of control with her credit cards, no way our attempts to help succeeded. She found a series of lectures on T.V. by Suze Orman on just this subject. Guided by Suze's program, she overcame the problem. She sought counselling and was fortunate to find an excellent counsellor with whom she developed good rapport, who helped her a lot. She read voraciously and broadly about many spiritual practices, including Native American, Hawaiian, and Eastern Asian. She visited Vietnam, Cambodia, Brazil, Hong Kong, and Thailand to see, first-hand, their spiritual practices. She is a current student of A Course in Miracles and others to deepen her understanding, and to learn and continue to practice forgiveness daily, one key to spiritual well-being.

Some of her convictions were, at first, hard for a father to accept, perhaps none more than her refusal to see a doctor or to take any drugs. But she has been ill several times over the years, and her practice of eating healthy foods, fresh air, no western medicine, and total, unswerving faith, has always seen her through. She is never surprised, she knows it will work, and it always does. Like everything else she believes and practices, this takes daily practice, which she loves.

It is impossible to describe the deepest core of an individual, the principles that guide them, the deep love and spiritual views that shape them. It is so personal and profound, it is almost like invading their soul. But what is clear is how that individual behaves every day, under normal conditions, under stress, in pain. I have been deeply moved how my remarkable daughter, with such a beautiful soul, has achieved her own education, wisdom, principles, and unlimited capacity for love, all through her own relentless efforts, to become a truly beneficial presence on this earth. I consider myself blessed beyond all measure that she is my daughter.

Publications

A. Scientific Articles

1. Koch, A.L., and Levy, H.R. (1955). Protein turnover in growing cultures of *Escherichia coli*. *J. Biol. Chem.* **217**, 947-957.
2. Levy, H.R., Loewus, F.A., and Vennesland, B. (1956). The enzymatic transfer of hydrogen. V. The reaction catalyzed by glucose dehydrogenase. *J. Bio. Chem.* **222**, 685-693.
3. Loewus, F.A., Levy, H.R., and Vennesland, B. (1956). The enzymatic transfer of hydrogen, VI. The reaction catalyzed by D-glyceraldehyde-3-phosphate dehydrogenase. J. Biol. Chem. **223**, 589-587.
4. Levy, H.R., Loewus, F.A., and Vennesland, B. (1957). The optical rotation and configuration of a pure enantiomorph of ethanol-1-d. *J. Amer. Chem. Soc.* **79**, 2949-2953.
5. Levy, H.R., and Vennesland, B. (1957). The stereospecificity of enzymatic hydrogen transfer from diphosphopyridine nucleotide. *J. Biol. Chem.* **228**, 85-96.
6. Levy, H.R., and Talalay, P. (1957). Enzymatic introduction of double bonds into steroid ring A. *J. Amer. Chem. Soc.* **79**, 2658-2659.
7. Levy, H.R., and Talalay, P. (1959). Bacterial oxidation of steroids. I. Ring A dehydrogenation of intact cells. *J. Biol. Chem.* **234**, 2009-2013.

8. Levy, H.R., and Talalay, P. (1959). Bacterial oxidation of steroids. II. Studies on the enzymatic mechanism of Ring A dehydrogenation. *J. Biol. Chem.* **234**, 2014-2021.

9. Talalay, P., and Levy, H.R. (1959). The steric and molecular specificity of steroid dehydrogenases. In *Ciba Foundation Study Group No. 2. Steric Course of Microbiological Reactions* (Wolstenholme, G.E.W., and O'Connor, D.M., eds) pp. 53-75. J. & A. Chuchill, Ltd., London.

10. Levy, H.R. and Popják, G. (1960). Studies on the biosynthesis of cholesterol. 10. Mevalonic kinase and phosphomevalonic kinase from liver. *Biochem. J.* **75**, 417-428.

11. Levy, H.R. (1961). The pyridine nucleotide specificity of glucose 6-phosphate dehydrogenase. *Biochem. Biophys. Res. Commun.* **6**, 49-53.

12. Levy, H.R. (1962). Steroid Ring A Δ-dehydrogenases. In *Methods in Enzymology* (Colowick, S.P., and Kaplan, N.O., eds) Vol. 5, pp. 533-539, Academic Press, New York.

13. Levy, H.R., Talalay, P., and Vennesland, B. (1962). The steric course of enzymatic reactions at meso carbon atoms. Application of hydrogen isotopes. In *Progress in Stereochemistry* (Klyne, W., and de la Mare, P.B.D., eds) Vol. 3, pp. 299-349, Butterworths, London.

14. Levy, H.R. (1963). Fatty acid synthesis and glucose 6-phosphate dehydrogenase in rat mammry glands. In *Biosynthesis of Lipids* (Popják, G., ed), Proc. Fifth Congr. Biochem. Moscow Vol. 7, pp 63-73, Pergamon Press, Oxford.

15. Levy, H.R. (1963). The interaction of mammary glucose 6-phosphate dehydrogenase with pyridine nucleotides and 3-β-hydroxyandrost-5-en-17-one. *J. Biol. Chem.* **238**, 775-784.

16. Levy, H.R. (1963). Inhibition of mammary gland acetyl CoA carboxylase by fatty acids. *Biochem. Biophys. Res. Commun.* **13**, 267-272.

17. Levy, H.R. (1964). The effects of weaning and milk on mammary fatty acid synthesis. *Biochim. Biophys. Acta,* **84**, 229-238.

18. Adams, J.A., Jacobson, H.I., Levy, H.R., and Talalay, P. (1965). The estrogenic activity and enzymatic oxidation of 17β-estradiol-17α-D. *Steroids Suppl.*1, 75-84.

19. Howanitz, P.J., and Levy, H.R. (1965). Acetyl CoA carboxylase and citrate cleavage enzyme in the rat mammary gland. *Biochim. Biohys. Acta* **106**, 430-433.

20. Nevaldine, B.H., and Levy, H.R. (1965). Reversible dissociation and association of mammary glucose 6-phosphate dehydrogenase. *Biochem. Biophys. Res. Commun.* **21**, 28-33.

21. Levy, H.R., Raineri, R.R., and Nevaldine, B.H. (1966). On the structure and catalytic function of mammary glucose 6-phosphate dehydrogenase. *J. Biol. Chem.* **241**, 2181-2187.

22. Olive, C., and Levy, H.R. (1967). The preparation and some properties of crystalline glucose 6-phosphate dehydrogenase from *Leuconostoc mesenteroides*. *Biochemistry* **6**, 730-736.

23. Nevaldine, B.H., and Levy, H.R. (1967). Interaction of mammary glucose 6-phosphate dehydrogenase with o-phenanthroline and its analogues. *Arch. Biochem. Biophys.* **119**, 293-302.

24. Cordaro, J.C., Levy, H.R., and Balbinder, E. (1968). Product inhibition of anthranilate synthetase in *Salmonella typhimurium*. *Biochem. Biophys. Res. Commun.* **33**, 183-189.

25. Miller, A.L., and Levy, H.R. (1969). Rat mammary acetyl coenzyme A carboxylase. I. Isolation and characterization. *J. Biol. Chem.* **244**, 2334-2342.

26. Raineri, R., and Levy, H.R. (1970). On the specificity of steroid interaction with mammary glucose 6-phosphate dehydrogenase. *Biochemistry* **9**, 2233-2342.

27. Miller, A.L., Geroch, M.E., and Levy, H.R. (1970). Rat mammary-gland acetyl-coenzyme A carboxylase. Interaction with milk fatty acids. *Biochem. J.* **118**, 645-657.

28. Olive, C., and Levy, H.R. (1971). Glucose 6-phosphate dehydrogenase from *Leuconostoc mesenteroides*. Physical studies. *J. Biol. Chem.* **246**, 2043-2046.

29. Olive, C., Geroch, M.E., and Levy, H.R. (1971). Glucose 6-phosphate dehydrogenase from *Leuconostoc mesenteroides*. Kinetic studies. *J. Biol. Chem.* **246**, 2047-2057.

30. Nevaldine, B.H., and Levy, H.R. (1974). The effects of ^2H_2O on mammary glucose 6-phosphate dehydrogenase. *Biochim. Biophys. Acta* **358**, 44-48.

31. Ishaque, A., Milhause, M., and Levy, H.R. (1974). On the absence of cysteine in glucose 6-phosphate dehydrogenase from *Leuconostoc mesenteroides*. *Biochem. Biophys. Res. Commun.* **59**, 894-901.

32. Nevaldine, B.H., Hyde, C.M., and Levy, H.R. (1974). Mammary glucose 6-phosphate dehydrogenase. Molecular weight studies. *Arch. Biochem. Biophys.* **165**, 398-406.

33. Dwek, R., Levy, H.R., Radda, G.K., and Seeley, P.G. (1975). Spin label and lanthanide binding sites on glyceraldehyde 3-phosphate dehydrogenase. *Biochim. Biophys. Acta* **377**, 26-33.

34. Milhausen, M., and Levy, H.R. (1975). Evidence for an essential lysine in glucose 6-phosphate dehydrogenase from *Leuconostoc mesenteroides. Eur. J. Biochem.* **50**, 453-461.

35. Miller, A.L., and Levy, H.R. (1975). Acetyl CoA carboxylase from rat mammary gland. In *Methods in Enzymology* (Colowick, S.P., and Kaplan, N.O., eds) Vol. 35B, pp. 11-17, Academic Press, New York.

36. Olice, C., and Levy, H.R. (1975). Glucose 6-phosphate dehydrogense from *Leuconostoc mesenteroides.* In *Methods in Enzymology* (Colowick, S.P., and Kaplan, N.O., eds) Vol. 41B, pp. 196-201, Academic Press, New York.

37. Grove, T.H., and Levy, H.R. (1975). Fluorescent assay of anthranilate synthetase-anthranilate 5-phosphoribosylpyrophosphate phosphoribosyltransferase enzyme complex on polyacrylamide gels. *Anal. Biochem.* **65**, 458-465.

38. Grove, T.H., and Levy, H.R. (1975). Anthranilate synthetase-anthranilate 5-phosphoribosylpyrophosphate phosphoribosyltransferase from *Salmonella typhimurium.* Inactivation of glutamine-dependent anthranilate synthetase by agarose-bound anthranilate. *Biochim. Biophys. Acta* **397**, 80-93.

39. Grove, T.H., and Levy, H.R. (1976). Anthranilate synthetase-anthranilate 5-phosphoribosylpyrophosphate phosphoribosyltransferase from *Salmonella typhimurium.* Purification of the enzyme complex and analysis of mutiple forms. *Biochim. Biophys. Acta* **445**, 464-474.

40. Robison, P.D., and Levy, H.R. (1976). Metal ion requirement and tryptophan inhibition of normal and variant anthranilate synthetase-anthranilate 5-phosphoribosylpyrophosphate phosphoribosyltransferase from *Salmonella typhimurium. Biochim. Biophys. Acta* **445**, 475-485.

41. Grove, T.H., Ishaque, A., and Levy, H.R. (1976). Glucose 6-phosphate dehydrogenase from *Leuconostoc mesenteroides.*

Interaction of the enzyme with coenzyme and coemzyme analogs. *Arch. Biochem. Biophys.* **177**, 307-316.

42. Levy, H.R., Ingulli, J., and Afolayan, A. (1977). Identification of essential arginine residues in glucose 6-phosphate dehydrogenase from *Leuconostoc mesenteroides. J. Biol. Chem.* **252**, 3745-3741.

43. Shreve, D.S., and Levy, H.R. (1977). On the molecular weight of human glucose 6-phosphate dehydrogenase. *Biochem. Biophys. Res. Commun.* **78**, 2369-1375.

44. Levy, H.R. (1979). Glucose 6-phosphate dehydrogenases. *Adv. Enzymol. Relat. Areas Mol. Biol.* **48**, 97-192.

45. Shreve, D.S., and Levy, H.R. (1979). Glucose 6-phosphate dehydrogenase from lactating rat mammary gland and R3230AC adenocarcinoma. *Enzyme* **24**, 48-53.

46. Robison, P.D., and Levy, H.R. (1979). Studies on the subunits of the anthranilate synthetase-anthranilate-phosphoribosyltransferase enzyme complex from *Salmonella typhimurium. Arch. Biochem. Biophys.* **193**, 242-251.

47. Robison, P.D., Nowak, T., and Levy, H.R. (1979). Magnetic resonance studies of the anthranilate synthetase-anthranilate-phosphoribosyltransferase enzyme complex from *Salmonella typhimurium. Arch. Biochem. Biophys.* **193**, 252-263.

48. Grove, T.H., and Levy, H.R. (1979). Evidence for an essential lysine residue on the phosphoribosyltransferase subunit of the anthranilate synthetase-anthranilate-5- phosphoribosylpyrophosphate phosphoribosyltransferase enzyme complex from *Salmonella typhimurium. Biochem. Biophys. Res. Commun.* **86**, 387-394.

49. Levy, H.R., and Daouk, G.H. (1979). Simultaneous analysis of NAD- and NADP-linked activities of dual-nucleotide-specific dehydrogenases: application to *Leuconoytoc mesenteroides* glucose 6-phosphate dehydrogenase. *J. Biol. Chem.* **254**, 4843-4847.

50. Levy, H.R., Daouk, G.H., and Katopes, M.A. (1979). Regulation of coenzyme utilization by the dual-nuclaeotide-specific glucose 6-phosphate dehydrogenase from *Leuconostoc mesenteroides. Arch. Biochem. Biophys.* **198**, 406-413.

51. Shreve, D.S., and Levy, H.R (1980). Kinetic mechanism of glucose 6-phosphate dehydrogenase from the lactating rat mammary gland: implications for regulation. *J. Biol. Chem.* **255**, 2670-2677.

52. Haghighi, B., Flynn, T.G., and Levy, H.R. (1982). Glucose 6-phosphate dehydrogenase from *Leuconostoc mesenteroides*. Isolation and sequence of a peptide containing an essential lysine. *Biochemistry* **21**, 6415-6420.

53. Haghighi, B., and Levy, H.R. (1982). Glucose 6-phosphate dehydrogenase from *Leuconostoc mesenteroides*. Conformational transitions induced by NAD$^+$, NADP$^+$, and glucose 6-phosphate monitored by fluorescent probes. *Biochemistry* **21**, 6421-6428.

54. Haghighi, B., and Levy, H.R. (1982). Glucose 6-phosphate dehydrogenase from *Leuconostoc mesenteroides*. Kinetics of reassociation and reactivation from inactive subunits. *Biochemistry* **21**, 6429-6434.

55. Levy, H.R., Christoph, M., Ingulli, J., and Ho, M.L. (1983). Glucose 6-phosphate dehydrogenase from *Leuconostoc mesenteroides*. Revised kinetic mechanism and kinetics of ATP inhibition. *Arch. Biochem. Biophys.* **222**, 473-488.

56. Adams, M.J., Levy, H.R., and Moffat, K. (1983). Crystallization and preliminary X-ray data for glucose 6-phosphate dehydrogenase from *Leuconostoc mesenteroides*. *J. Biol. Chem.* **258**, 5867-5868.

57. Levy, H.R., Ejchart, A., and Levy, G.C. (1983). Conformations of nicotinamide coenzymes bound to dehydrogenases determined by transferred nuclear Overhauser effects. *Biochemitry* **22**, 2792-2796.

58. Levy, H.R., and Christoff, M. (1983). A critical appraisal of the effect of oxidized glutathione on hepatic glucose 6-phosphate dehydrogenase activity. *Biochem. J.* **214**, 959-965.

59. Schroeder, L., Christoff, M., and Levy, H.R. (1984). Glucose 6-phosphate dehydrogenase from rabbit erythrocytes. *Biochim. Biophys. Acta* **784**, 48-52.

60. Banerjee, A., Levy, H.R., Levy, G.C., and Chan, W.W.-C. (1985). Conformations of bound nucleoside triphosphate effectors in aspartate transcarbamylase. Evidence for the London-Schmidt model by transferred nuclear Overhaus effects. *Biochemistry* **24**, 1593-1598.

61. Levy, H.R. (1985). The effect of oxidized glutathione on NADPH inhibition of glucose 6-phosphate dehydrogenase is indirect. *Biochem. J.* **231**, 806-807.

62. Levy, H.R. (1986). Glucose 6-phosphate dehydrogenase from *Leuconostoc mesenteroides*. In: *Glucose 6-phosphate dehydrogenase* (Yoshida, A., and Beutler, E., eds.) pp. 279-299.

63. White, B.J., and Levy, H.R. (1987). Modification of glucose 6-phosphate dehydrogenase from *Leuconostoc mesenteroides* with 2',3'-dialdehyde derivative of NADP⁺ (oNADP⁺). *J. Biol. Chem.* **262**, 1223-1229.

64. Bhadbhade, M., Adams, M.J., Flynn, T.G., and Levy, H.R. (1987). Sequence identity betweeen a lysine-containg peptide from glucose 6-phosphate dehydrogenase from *Leuconostoc mesenteroides* and an active site peptide from human erythrocyte glucose 6-phosphate dehydrogenase. *FEBS Lett.* **11**, 243-246.

65. Banerjee, A., Levy, H.R., Levy, G.C., LiMuti, C., Goldstein, B.M., and Bell, J.E. (1987). A TRNOE study of coenzyme binding to distinct sites in binary and ternary complexes in glutamate dehydrogenase. *Biochemistry* **26**, 8443-8450.

66. Kurlandsky, S.B., Hilburger, A.C., and Levy, H.R. (1988). Glucose 6-phosphate dehydrogenase from *Leuconostoc mesenteroides*: ligand-induced conformational changes. *Arch. Biochem. Biophys.* **264**, 93-102.

67. Levy, H.R. (1989). Glucose 6-phosphate dehydrogenase from *Leuconostoc mesenteroides*. *Biochem. Soc. Trans.* **17**, 313-315.

68. LaDine, J.R., Carlow, D., Lee, W.T., Cross, R.L., Flynn, T.G., and Levy, H.R. (1991). Interaction of glucose 6-phosphate dehydrogenase from *Leuconostoc mesenteroides* with pyridoxal 5'-diphospho-5'-adenosine. Affinity labeling of Lys-21 and Lys-343. *J. Biol. Chem.* **266**, 5558-5562.

69. Lee, T.W., Flynn, T.G., Lyons, C., and Levy, H.R. (1991). Cloning of the gene and amino acid sequence for glucose 6-phosphate dehydrogenase from *Leuconostoc mesenteroides*. *J. Biol. Chem.* **266**, 13028-13034.

70. Levy, H.R., and Cook, C. (1991). Purification and properties of NADP-linked glucose 6-phosphate dehydrogenase from *Acetobacter hansenii* (*Actobacter xylinum*). *Arch. Biochem. Biophys.* **291**, 161-167.

71. Lee, W.T., and Levy, H.R. (1992). Lysine-21 of glucose 6-phosphate dehydrogenase from *Leuconostoc mesenteroides* participates

in substrate binding through charge-charge interaction. *Protein Science* **1**, 329-334.

72. Adams, M.J., Basak, A.K., Gover, S., Rowland, P., and Levy, H.R. (1993). Site-directed mutagenesis to facilitate X-ray structural studies of glucose 6-phosphate dehydrogenase from *Leuconostoc mesenteroides. Protein Science* **2**, 859-862.

73. Ragunathan, S., and Levy, H.R. (1994). Purification and characterization of the NAD-preferring glucose 6-phosphate dehydrogenase from *Acetobacter hansenii (Actobacter xylinum). Arch. Biochem. Biophys.* **310**, 360-366.

74. Rowland, P., Basak, A.J., Gover, S., Levy, H.R., and Adams, M.J. (1994). The 3-dimensional structure of glucose 6-phosphate dehydrogenase from *Leuconostoc mesenteroides. Structure* **2**, 1073-1087.

75. Gordon, G., Mackow, M.C., and Levy, H.R. (1995). On the mechanism of interaction of steroids with human glucose 6-phosphate dehydrogenase. *Arch. Biochem. Biophys.* **318**, 25-29.

76. Levy, H.R., Vought, V.E., Yin, Y., and Adams, M.J. (1996). Identification of an arginine residue in the dual coenzyme-specific glucose 6-phosphate dehydrogenase from *Leuconostoc mesenteroides* that plays a key role in binding NADP$^+$ but not NAD$^+$. *Arch. Biochem. Biophys.* **326**, 145-151.

77. Cosgrove, M.S., Naylor, C., Paludan, S., Adams, M.J., and Levy, H.R. (2000). On the mechanism of the reaction catalyzed by glucose 6-phosphate dehydrogenase. *Biochemistry* **37**, 2759-2767.

78. Cosgrove, M.S., Gover, S., Naylor, C.E., Vanderputten-Rutten, L., Adams, M.J., and Levy, H.R. (2000). An examination of the role of Asp-177 in the His-Asp catalytic dyad of glucose 6-phosphate dehydrogenase from *Leuconostoc mesenteroides*: X-ray structure and pH dependence of kinetic parameters of the D177N mutant enzyme. *Biochemistry* **39**, 15002-15011.

79. Vought, V., Ciccone, T., Davino, M.H., Faibairn, L., Lin, Y., Cosgrove, M.S., Adams, M.J., and Levy, H.R. (2000). Delineation of the roles of amino acids involved in the catalytic functions of *Leuconostoc mesentroides* glucose 6-phosphate dehydrogenase. *Biochemistry* **39**, 15012-15021.

80. Naylor, C.E., Gover, S., Basak, A.K., Cosgrove, M.S., Levy, H.R., and Adams, M.J. (2001). NADP$^+$ and NAD$^+$ binding to the

dual coenzyme specific enzyme *Leuconostoc mesenteoides* glucose 6-phosphate dehydrogenase: different inter-domain hinge angles are seen in different binary and ternary complexes. *Acta Crystalogr.* **D57**, 635-648.

81. Cosgrove, M.S., Loh, S.N., Ha, J.-H., and Levy, H.R. (2002). The catalytic mechanism of glucose 6-phosphate dehydrogenase: assignment and ^{1}H NMR spectroscopy pH titration of the catalytic histidine residue in the 109 kDa *Leuconostoc mesenteroides* enzyme. *Biochemistry* **41**, 6939-6945.

B. Other articles

1. Levy, H.R. (1988). The impact of science on medicine. In: *Contesting the Boundaries of Liberal and Professional Education; the Syracuse Experiment.* (P. Marsh, ed.), 130-139, Syracuse University Press, Syracuse, NY.
2. Levy, H.R. (2002). The impact of technology and culture on medicine. *The Advisor* **23**, 44-51.
3. Levy, H.R. (2010). Return to Leipzig. *Syracuse University Magazine* **27**, 30-35.
4. Levy, H.R. (2021). *Kindertransport* History. *Kinder-Link* **31**, 1.
5. Levy, H.R. (2021). Science is a human endeavor. *ASBMB Today* **20**, 60-62.

C. Editorials

1. Levy, H.R. (April 2003). Going Nuclear II. *The Voice*, Peace Action CNY.
2. Levy, H.R. (May 2003). Reflections on Iraq. *The Voice*, Peace Action CNY.
3. Levy, H.R., (July/August 2003). Project for the New American Century. *The Voice*, Peace Action CNY.
4. Levy, H.R, (September 2003). Deception: The Basis of U.S. Foreign Policy. *The Voice*, Peace Action CNY.
5. Levy, H.R. (November 2003). Speaking Up - Shocking and Awful. *The Voice*, Peace Action CNY.
6. Levy, H.R. (February 2004). U.S. Nuclear Policy Dilemmas. *The Voice*, Peace Action CNY.

7. Levy, H.R. (April 2004). Afghanistan: The Lessons Not Learned. *The Voice*, Peace Action CNY.

8. Levy, H.R. (May 2005). The Use of Torture by Americans. *Newsletter*, Central New York Chapter New York Civil Liberties Union.

9. Levy, H.R. (August 2006). The National Voting Crisis. *Newsletter*, Central New York Chapter New York Civil Liberties Union.

D. Books

1. Levy, H.R. (2012). Biology at Syracuse University 1872-2020, Syracuse University Press.

2. Levy, H.R. (2012). A Genealogical Survey of Two German, Jewish Families Named Frank, Joined by Marriage in 1898. (self-published).

3. Levy, H.R., and Sotherden, B. (2015). Civic Morning Musicals, 1890-2015, 125 Years. Civic Morning Musicals.

4. Levy, H.R. (2022). Recollections and reflections from my life in Nazi Germany, wartime England, and America. (This book).

www.ingramcontent.com/pod-product-compliance
Lightning Source LLC
Chambersburg PA
CBHW030939150426
42812CB00064B/3068/J